WALDENE

Love in the Shadows

A story of family obligations and affairs of the heart

SUE GUNNINGHAM

First published 2020

Copyright © 2020 Sue Gunningham

978-0-6486646-1-1 (paperback)
978-0-6486646-2-8 (ebook)

This work is copyright. Apart from any use permitted under the *Copyright Act 1968*, no part of this publication may be reproduced, stored in a retrieval system or transmitted in any form or by any means, electronic, mechanical, photocopying, recording or otherwise, without the prior written permission of Sue Gunningham.

Some names and identifying details in this book have been changed to protect the privacy of individuals.

Cover image and design: Busybird Publishing

Layout and typesetting: Busybird Publishing

Busybird Publishing
2/118 Para Road
Montmorency, Victoria
Australia 3094
www.busybird.com.au

DEDICATION

To Mia

A few years after Barry died in the 2009 Black Saturday bushfires, you and I were role-playing Hansel and Gretel. Back then you were my only grandchild - a tiny, four year old girl.

I complained to you. "How come I always have to be Hansel? I'm a girl too. I should get to be Gretel sometimes." You stopped in your tracks, looked me up and down slowly with puzzled eyes.

"Are you a girl?" you asked in obvious disbelief.

I looked down at my shapeless, old t-shirt, exhausted jeans, heavy work-boots and broken, dirty fingernails and tried to see myself through your eyes. So intent had I been on reclaiming the devastated acres of bushland and fighting to gain permission to rebuild a cottage that I hadn't realised what I'd become.

"Yes," I said, tears stinging my eyes. "I'm a girl."

You looked at me in silence, trying to make sense of this revelation.

"Where's your father?" you asked, meaning my 'husband'.

It was then I realised I wanted you to know that long ago, the weary dishevelled 'grandma' you saw that day had been a princess. This story of my time as a princess was written for you, so you'd know I wasn't always so rough and grubby, or such a disappointment as a girl. Perhaps it will help you not to judge people by their appearance and to see me as a woman who was once loved very much by a man.

This manuscript is a recollection of my secret love story from its beginning in 1990 when I first met Barry until we were finally able to be together in 2002. It is dedicated to you my precious Mia, and to my family, in the hope it will help you understand.

Sue Gunningham (Grandma)
January 2020

Contents

THE NOVICE	3
FIRST FORAYS	29
SLOWLY, SLOWLY	61
THE HUNT	95
SWOON	143
LOVE (1)	152
LOVE (2)	189
LOVE (3)	214
STEPPING OUT	243

Christmas Eve 2019

*Life can only be understood backwards,
but must be lived forwards*

Soren Kierkegaard

"Did they take anything precious?" the policewoman asks, glancing around the trashed interior of my tiny cottage in the forest. A large wall poster of Barry headed with the words Vale - Barry Johnston survived the violation.

"There's nothing precious here except my memories ... and I carry those with me wherever I go. No-one can take them from me." At this my voice breaks and tears wash my eyes. I shrug; bite my lip and turn away to regain my composure. The policewoman waits – only the click of the crime scene photographer's camera disrupts the silence.

I step outside into the sunshine and the policewoman follows. "What will you do?" she asks.

Staring at the black fingerprinting powder smeared across the fire-doors I feel a sense of dread. "I can't stay here tonight. It's not safe. The door lock's broken and they've buckled the fire doors. Nothing shuts properly." Clasping my hands prayer-like I rest my lips on my fingertips and look back at the mess inside the cottage. "I'm frightened," I say, more to myself than the policewoman.

"Do you have somewhere else you can stay?" She speaks softly.

"Yeah, I live between here and another house in the suburbs. But it's Christmas Eve. I always sleep here on Christmas Eve." Sensing her confusion I gesture to a picket fence running along a ridge some 20 metres away. "I lost my partner over there ... in the Black Saturday fires. He was in an underground bunker." She inhales and the crime photographer snaps another photo of the scene, this time including the picket fence.

"I've slept here every Christmas Eve for the past ten years - but now I'm frightened."

My mind runs over the site, like one runs a hand over a precious heirloom. The cottage nestles in a valley between rolling hills of native bush where wallabies stand to feel the breeze as lyrebirds sing and dance like whirling dervishes in the undergrowth, scaring the fairy wrens hiding in the bushes. Here lizards and snakes glide across the forest floor and wallabies barrel through the night toward the creek where the wild deer gather and the Pobblebonks spawn tadpoles.

This site has always been a sanctuary, adrift from the world and its troubles. But now, on Christmas Eve someone's forced the doors and broken into the cottage. They've pulled open the drawers and cupboards and thrown the contents about.

"Everyone said I shouldn't rebuild after the fires. But in spite of their well-meant advice I *had* to. There was no choice for me." My voice falters. I turn to face the two police officers. "You see, it was alright for them. They had a life. But I'm sort of ... *anchored* here. I know it's insane." I look away to prevent any response to my words. "But it's my insanity and I'm not asking anyone else to live it with me. So ...." My words trail off.

How can anyone but me ever understand?

THE NOVICE

We hasten with faint but eager steps

BACH

When I graduated as a teacher at 36 years of age my mother gave me a card. Its front cover bore the words: 'What we endure shows our courage.'

On the inside in my mother's best cursive script she'd written:

Feb 1980 – Nov 1989
'Dear Sue you have rewritten the meaning of Courage, Tenacity, and Willpower and most of all <u>no-one</u> of the three generations you take care of, was ever neglected in the nine years it took you to reach this day.
Congratulations on your great achievement. Mum.

In the next decade the cracks would begin to appear.

Day One 1990

I hoped my fear didn't show as I stared into the camera. Off to the side, my sons urged me to smile.

"Say cheese mummy," seven-year old Blake giggled.

Standing nearby, my mother clapped and cheered and called out somewhat ridiculously "Yes, Mrs Gunningham – No Mrs Gunningham – Right away, Mrs Gunningham."

I was to begin my teaching career today. Nine years of study by correspondence and night classes and assignments completed in the still of night had led to this day, to this photo on the back porch of our house - 'My first day as a teacher'.

Now the journey was over and I would move from the safety of this porch out into the world I'd been trying to reach for so long. It was both terrifying and exciting.

My initial placement was to Whittlesea Primary, a small rural school about thirty minutes drive from home. I was to meet the principal at 9 am today, first day back after the mid-year school break.

Just before 8.30 am stepping up the stairs towards the school's front door I was suddenly seized with panic that I'd made a mistake and come to the Catholic school instead of the government school where I was expected. The yard was filled with rowdy students all dressed in the navy school uniforms commonly associated with Catholic schools. As I turned to retrace my steps, the large front door swung open and a man came out.

I froze in my tracks, embarrassed, uncertain how best to explain my presence. The man smiled. "You must be our new teacher. Uhm ... Suzanne, isn't it? Come in we've been expecting you."

I nodded with relief and he stepped back and ushered me inside. We walked down a short corridor before stopping at a door labelled

Principal. "This is Ben's office he said by way of explanation as he knocked on the door.

"Enter!" a loud male voice called from inside and I shrank at the authority inferred in the command.

The man opened the door. "Look who I found out front. It's our new teacher," he grinned at the principal, who rose from behind his desk. The principal was slim and neat. His pale grey suit was complemented by a crisp white shirt and subdued tie. He gave me a thin smile, just enough for me to realise he was a busy man and greeting me was a small but necessary part of his demanding day.

"Suzanne this is Ben Nembis, the principal of this grand establishment." As if suddenly realising his oversight he added, "By the way, I'm John; John Taylor. I'm the Assistant Principal". As he spoke he leaned across and shook my hand. Unaccustomed to shaking hands I responded awkwardly.

"Anyway, I'll be off - almost bell-time. I'll leave you two to chat. See you at morning tea Sue and *Welcome*."

Giving me a warm, easy smile he went out, closing the door behind him. I was sad to see him go. Having rescued me at the front door I felt an affinity with him. He was instantly friendly and likable. Now facing the principal I struggled to think of something worthy to say. Ben waved me toward a chair.

He asked some cursory questions about my educational credentials and experiences. Feeling tiny and vulnerable, I listened to myself saying what was expected, choosing my words carefully, being timid, submissive and grateful.

The principal described the school, its teachers, its policies, its families and his plans for me. "You'll support the three male teachers in the upper school classes by working with small groups of students to deliver a 'specially tailored' curriculum."

A sinking feeling began in the pit of my stomach. There were probably many reasons why some students are selected for a 'specially tailored curriculum,' but something told me most of the reasons were probably not good.

"I'll introduce you to your team later." Ben smiled, obviously pleased with his coverage of the main issues. A moment's silence passed and it seemed he was trying to make his mind up about something. Uncertain of the protocol involved I waited for him to speak again.

"There's one other thing I want to say to you," he finally began, his voice dropping to a murmur. "You'd be well-advised to be careful around one member of your team." He paused, as if considering how best to phrase what he wanted to say.

"You should think carefully and seek advice from the others before being influenced by anything Barry suggests. He's a staunch unionist - rather militant really. He was a draft resistor during the Vietnam War."

The principal paused, no doubt seeking for my reaction. My eyebrows rose in surprise and I nodded slightly, but said nothing.

"He was hidden by the underground movement - eventually went to prison because of it." The words came out almost as a snarl suggesting the principal was somewhat opposed to such goings-on. "He can be a trouble-maker. Be careful of him."

He finished and gave me a fatherly smile, perhaps satisfied his new teacher was obviously 'one of us' rather than 'one of Barry's mob.'

Charged with the task of becoming familiar with the layout of the school, I escaped back out into the long corridor.

"Be in the staffroom at recess in an hour's time and I'll introduce you to the other teachers," Ben said as he waved me off.

I walked softly past the bursar's office, peeped into the empty staff room and visited the female toilets. This main building was old and groaned with the wind. Leaves blew in through the door at the far end of the corridor to tumble along the pale green linoleum and wedge among school bags sagging from hooks along one wall.

The smell of sandwiches and fruit in students' lunches mingled with the smell of paint and craft glue emanating from the art room on the other side of the corridor. I stopped to gaze at some student bark hut exhibits on a table outside the art room. No doubt the breeze bringing the leaves down the corridor in winter, also brought sorely needed fresh air when the summer heat arrived to sweat the plastic lunch boxes and soften the paint and glue of the art display.

After crossing a bleak, asphalted quadrangle and mounting yet another staircase, I turned into a room labelled 'Library.' It was empty and the silence wrapped around me. The colourful spines of the books provided a safe haven at once familiar and calming. Here I could hide for awhile.

Sinking onto a small stool between two aisles of children's books I contemplated the principal's veiled warning. For so long I'd been inching towards this day and now in the first half hour there was already a sense of unease. Why the need to take sides, to be classified as 'with' or 'against' anybody?

Couldn't they just leave me alone to teach? Even working in a team would be okay, but I didn't want to bond with anyone, expand my group of friends. I just wanted to teach.

Perhaps I could ask to be sent to another school?

In his 'welcome speech' the principal had told me many graduates have trouble turning theory into practice in their first teaching post. This insight had filled me with dread. What did I actually know about how children learn or even what they should learn?

This was no longer a university assignment; it was me being held accountable for the education of other people's children.

I wished the wind would blow me out through the gate and into my car. Right now while the yard was empty no-one would notice me leaving. I longed for courage and the sound of my car's engine stirring into life to carry me away from here.

The silence of the library was suddenly broken by the muffled noise in the next aisle. I held my breath. Frightened of being found hiding on my first morning, I reluctantly rose to my feet. Slipping on a half-hearted smile I stepped softly around the book shelf to make my presence known to the first student of my career.

A tall, mountain of a man looked up from a book he was reading. "Hello," he said, his voice both strong and deep. The corners of his clear blue eyes crinkled as he smiled.

"You must be our new teacher. I'm Barry - one of the teachers in your team." I was relieved he hadn't tried to shake hands.

A collage of memories flashed through my mind - the sign on my parents' house declaring 'This is a Labor Party house,' attending 'Save Our Sons' rallies and the 'Moratoriums' demanding the government bring our troops home from Vietnam, of being suspended from high school for repeatedly pinning photos of the Mi Lae massacre on the student notice-board to highlight the human cost of war.

Barry watched me in silence. Laughing nervously, I dipped my head for a second before looking up into his face.

"Hi, I'm Sue. The principal mentioned I'd be working with you." Barry's eyes narrowed slightly and he nodded. The pink of his soft, fleshy mouth widened into a 'knowing' grin between his moustache and clipped beard.

He seemed to sense what the principal had said about him and yet here he was - tall and proud and still apparently unrepentant.

"Would you like to join the Teacher's Union?" he asked and handed me a red bookmark holding down the page of the book in his hand.

The bookmark was an advertisement for the union and provided contact details on one side and some data about what the union had achieved on its reverse.

"I'm the school's union rep, so let me know if you want to sign up. I can get you the forms and organise through the bursar for the subscription to come out of your pay."

"My family are strong union people," I said with some degree of pride. "So I'll be joining."

"Well then, welcome aboard comrade!"

At that we both laughed aloud.

Try teaching

*Come what, come may, time and the hour
runs through the roughest day.*

SHAKESPEARE.

It was decided for a few weeks while I settled in, I'd be a 'support' teacher for the three upper school male teachers. My role was to help out in their classrooms across a range of subjects at various times throughout the week. Eventually I would be given my own teaching space and small groups of 'selected' students would be withdrawn from normal classes to work with me on a 'special curriculum' targeting their particular needs.

An horrendous weekly timetable was drafted to share me equally across the three classrooms. Often I had little or no idea what I would be asked to do. Sometimes I did photocopying and other times supervised students while the teacher photocopied. Sometimes I'd be asked to catch various students up with unfinished work and other times I'd just be in the room supporting the classroom teacher.

"Most of the time I feel like I'm a nuisance to the classroom teacher," I confided to my mother one evening. "They often look surprised when I arrive in their room and they say they'd forgotten I was coming. Usually that means they give me some menial task to keep me occupied as if I'm a parent helper rather than a teacher."

Never good with names, this first teaching post challenged me to learn the names of almost one hundred students across the three classes. It was a nightmare.

Eventually I was given my own space - an archaic classroom in the original heritage-listed building constructed in 1853 when the town first qualified for a one-teacher school. The school now had twelve classrooms and the original building had been used merely as an office storage area for many years now.

My room was dark and musty with the original blackboard and cupboards taking up one wall and the remaining three walls full of shelves of outdated readers and dusty, archived office documents. The thick, double-brick walls blocked all external sounds and kept the room cold all year. The few windows, set high up in the wall, allowed a patterned glimpse of the sky through the security mesh bolted to the outside frames.

'Who'd want to steal these old books and papers?' I mused, watching dust mites slide along shafts of light chequer-boarding across the wall.

Although it was akin to a sensory deprivation chamber it was wonderful to have my own classroom. Here I'd learn to be a teacher, free from the mocking eyes of my male colleagues. I carried tables and chairs from the school shed into the room and on an empty shelf arranged a small allocation of stationary. Hanging a handmade sign on my door: *Mrs Gunningham, Year 5/6*, I was ready at last.

Eight brutish boys were sent to me for one hour each morning from one teacher's class. Through the open door, the only means of getting fresh air into the room, I listened to the boys tearing down the yard to the heritage building.

"Come back here ya' bastard!" The sound of running feet gave way to a scuffle followed by laughter.

"I'll get ya for that ya dickhead!"

"Yeah sure. In ya dreams."

I recognised the last voice as belonging to a tough little boy totally devoid of manners and seemingly indifferent to anyone in authority.

He spent most of his school day on the seat outside the principal's office for one misdemeanour or another.

Get off me, ya poof!" another boy groaned.

"Hey - did ya see Tyson's new shoes?" someone apparently not involved in the wrestle blurted out. "Geez - they musta cost a packet. Reckons they help him run faster."

"We'll see. There's a race at lunch-time - Tyson versus Kelly."

"Kelly'll kill 'im. He's the fastest kid at school."

"Bullshit! I'm faster than Kelly."

'Are not!" The declaration was followed by the sound of more wrestling and grunting.

I despaired of the hour spent with these boys. They continually chided each other and threatened to fight. They barely listened to me and their poor literacy skills made it difficult to keep them interested for long. I lived in fear the principal would visit and see the chaos of the lesson. Surely they'd been sent to me for no other reason than to give their teacher and the rest of the class a break from them.

At the end of the hour the boys would thump and push each other out of the room without waiting to be dismissed. They rarely cast a backward glance at me collapsing into a chair grateful I'd survived another lesson without blood being drawn.

One of the other teachers sent me a mixed gender group of high achieving students and at other times, a group of slow but enthusiastic readers. Both groups were a source of joy compared to the stress of the brutish all-boy group.

Most of my week was spent in isolation in my vintage classroom-come-storage facility working with these small but diverse groups of students. I was teaching, but didn't really feel part of the whole school or its staff.

Barry organised his share of my timetable differently. Initially he asked me to come into his classroom to help during his self-guided mathematics lessons. Barry and I would roam the room helping individual students and correcting work. I watched him joke with the students and saw how he could silence a noisy student by merely raising an eyebrow in their direction.

His teaching style reminded me of the teaching I'd experienced as a child in primary school. Barry was quiet, focused and well-organised. He listened to his students and they listened to him. He expected them to think and to make an effort. He abhorred bad manners and wouldn't tolerate bullying. The students respected him and he made learning seem a wonderful journey able to open up a myriad of possibilities.

"Just a minute," Barry boomed out one day, at the same time grinning at me cheekily from across the room.

"How come there are six kids lined up to get Mrs Gunningham to correct their work and there are only two kids in my line? I think you like Mrs Gunningham more than me."

"We do!" a boy giggled.

Barry laughed, rolled his eyes and shook his head. "Hmph, that's gratitude for you," he lamented, flashing me a smile before bending to resume his conversation with a student.

Two weeks later he wanted me to take responsibility for teaching a specific part of the curriculum to his whole class rather than just helping during maths lessons.

"What would you like to teach?" he asked. My stomach turned in terror at the prospect of having the sole responsibility for an entire class of students. "Do you like reading or writing, poetry, geography, history?"

I hesitated, not confident I'd be good at teaching anything, particularly if it involved the management of a whole class. I thought about the chaos involved with teaching the brutish boys each morning. How would I cope if that experience was multiplied several times over with a whole class? It was too horrible to contemplate.

"I'm happy to do whatever you think I can do," I mumbled, avoiding eye-contact so he wouldn't see my fear. It was wonderful he was trying to give me a fair-go but I hated the idea of failing him. I didn't want to be the cause of him falling further out of favour with the principal.

"What about literacy then? We do a few sessions a week; some creative writing, some reading, some poetry. Would you like that? You could even do some oral stuff like debates or story-telling. What do you think?"

I thought frantically. Being an avid reader and writer there must be something I could come up with to keep the whole class engaged. Then a revelation!

"I saw the bark huts outside the art room. Perhaps building on your 'Early Settlers' theme I could read some classic Australian stories like; *The Drover's Wife, The Loaded Dog?* And we could read some poetry like *The Man From Snowy River*. Maybe we could learn to recite some poetry… *My Country* … or perhaps the lyrics of some Australian songs?" My excitement increased as I spoke. Barry nodded encouragingly.

"That all sounds great" he said, when my ramblings finally petered out.

Having found a nicely illustrated copy of 'The Loaded Dog,' I'd practiced reading it aloud and written some comprehension questions to ask the students.

Still worried about managing a whole class by myself for an hour, I wondered what I'd do if the students became bored or worse still, refused to do what I asked.

When the designated day arrived I mounted the steps to Barry's classroom and knocked at the door. Barry's voice boomed out. "Come in!"

Stepping inside, I hoped my face didn't betray my self-doubt.

"Ah, Mrs Gunningham. Come in, come in," Barry smiled. The students turned quietly in their seats and watched me.

"Now boys and girls," Barry addressed the class, "Mrs Gunningham is going to take you for a literacy lesson. I expect you to behave and do as you're told. I'll be in the back room marking assignments and I don't want to be disturbed by having to come in here and speak to anyone about their manners."

His gaze swept across the sea of upturned faces and he locked eyes with a boy here and there, raising his eyebrows in a silent warning.

I shrank. Barry would be able to hear my lesson through the thin partition separating the classroom from the back room. His threat to the class suggested he doubted my ability to manage the students. I felt embarrassed. His offer for me to take a whole class lesson had seemed kind, but this arrangement now reduced my role to that of a trainee teacher. I'd be mortified if the students played up and he had to assume control mid-lesson.

Barry gathered up his paperwork and moved in behind the partition leaving me to begin my lesson. I held up the picture book and told the students about the author, Henry Lawson. We talked about their social studies theme and what they had learnt already about the early settlers.

The lesson seemed to be going well and I hoped Barry was listening and impressed. I opened the book and began to read. Although I read well, it soon became obvious the students were having difficultly following the story. The text was too old fashioned.

This was made worse by the book being too small for them to view the pictures as a means of clarification.

They began to shuffle in their seats and a few began to whisper. I could sense their frustration. As I read, my mind darted around frantically trying to think how to save the lesson. Barry would be aware of the students' discontent if my reading went on much longer. I began to panic.

"Hmph. I think the words are making it hard for you to follow the story," I said suddenly, closing the book as I spoke.

The whispering students were silenced by this odd outburst from a teacher. Teachers were supposed to champion all books, all reading. And how could words make it hard to understand a story? Without words there was no story. Twenty-six pair of eyes watched me, waiting to see what I'd do next. The room felt heavy with the potential for pandemonium.

"It's a shame, 'cause it's a great story. Henry Lawson was great at writing funny stories about things that can happen to ordinary people." I paused to think. "You know what? This story is so good I'm going to just tell it to you myself. I won't read the book. I'll just tell it in my own words."

I had their attention. They'd probably never had a lesson like this before. No doubt they wondered if I was a real teacher. My behaviour was more like a mother or a teacher helper. Imagine not reading the book to them as part of their English lesson. The 'teacher's-pets' among them no doubt stored the information away, ready to report this misdemeanour to Mr Johnston when he returned.

"Get comfortable," I said. "It's a pretty long story." The students wriggled around in their seats, pleased by my invitation. "Okay? Well, once there were these three blokes; Jim and Andy and Dave. The names were simple back then. They were sort of hobos -

swagmen types." Some girls giggled and mouthed 'blokes' to each other. Imagine a teacher saying 'blokes.' It was too funny. We talked about swagmen and I mimed rolling stuff up in a groundsheet and tying it to a stick. I humped my imaginary swag backwards and forwards across the classroom. I was a swagman on the road in the 1890s. Delighted, the students watched on.

"The three blokes were hoping to find gold out in the middle of nowhere. They'd pretty much run out of money and were down to just eating fish they caught in a waterhole near their campsite. Then they worked out a deal with a shopkeeper in the local town so they could swap some of the fish they caught for stuff like flour and tea and tobacco and matches. Good idea eh?" I said, nodding at the students.

"How many fish for a kilo of flour I wonder? What would you want to swap your fish for if you were them?" The students offered suggestions and we laughed about everyone's different ideas.

The story continued. The students warmed to Tommy, the dog that loved to retrieve things to bring as gifts for the three men. We talked about their dogs and we wondered if Tommy had to eat fish too.

They tried to guess how the swagmen could increase the number of fish caught while at the same time decreasing the amount of fishing required. The students were shocked at the thought of blowing the fish out of the water with a stick of dynamite. They marvelled that men used to make their own sticks of dynamite using calico, gunpowder and beeswax.

In the guise of Andy, I bent over an imaginary campfire to cook potatoes and chops then stood, 'thinking,' with my back to the fire. Suddenly, the silence broke as I acted out Andy's mates yelling 'Run, Andy! Run!' The class watched, enthralled.

"What made them call out to Andy?" I asked the captivated students. They took out their books and scribbled their ideas, during which time I assumed the frozen portrayal of Andy hearing his mates call.

On and on the story went. Slipping in and out of character at different times I role-played each of the three swagmen, I was the retriever and the 'vicious yellow mongrel cattle-dog sulking and nursing his nastiness' under the pub. The students answered my questions, wrote ideas when asked and listened, mesmerized.

Finally the story ended. The hour was over and I breathed a sigh of relief. I'd made it. No pandemonium and the students had heard a classic Australian story, done some comprehension and some writing. They'd speculated, articulated and had fun.

Almost as the last word left my mouth Barry appeared from the back room grinning, confirmation he'd been listening. I was conscious of the students straightening a little in their seats – different expectations for different teachers.

"Well girls and boys I'm glad you were well-behaved for Mrs Gunningham. I flushed slightly with embarrassment. "Brooke, will you thank Mrs Gunningham for us?"

A girl rose to her feet and faced me. "Thank you for telling us the story," she said and resumed her seat.

"My pleasure - thank you for listening." Collecting up my book I nodded to Barry and left the room. Something approaching delight gleamed in his eyes and I was especially pleased this particular lesson had been a success.

As I drove home from school I kept grinning to myself about how well the lesson had gone. It was the first time I'd glimpsed my potential for capturing students' interest. Arriving home at 5 p.m. meant limited time for anything other than helping with homework, cooking and listening to everyone else's day, then reading to the boys when they hopped into bed at 8 p.m.

My husband Alec worked in juvenile justice. His job was never a 'lark' and after work he was ready to disengage from the world. He listened kindly to my lyrical ravings and offered congratulations before turning back to the television. I went out to the kitchen to prepare for the next day's lessons.

The card

*Our dead are never dead to us, until we
have forgotten them.*

GEORGE ELIOT

After the 'Loaded Dog' lesson I craved feedback from Barry. I wanted him to say how well I'd done and discuss other lessons I'd planned for his class. None of my friends were teachers so I had no-one with teaching experience to talk with about my ideas and concerns.

While that's what I told myself, somewhere deep inside me was a niggling suspicion I was really just seeking an excuse to be the sole focus of those hypnotic eyes and Barry's easy grin once again.

At recess and lunch-times I spent as long as I could in the staffroom, hoping to see him. I sat flicking through the newspaper and listening to teacher gossip. No-one spoke to me other than to murmur cheery 'Hellos' and 'How's it going?' without really paying attention to my response, which was invariably the bland "Oh Good. The kids are great."

It was three days after the 'Loaded Dog' lesson before Barry appeared in the staffroom. He nodded to a few teachers before moving almost nervously around the large central table to the corner where the staff mailboxes were situated. No-one spoke to him.

From the corner of my eye I watched his broad shoulders and sturdy neck as he turned away to empty his mailbox. His blue woollen jumper looked hand-knitted. He was slightly balding and his remaining brown hair was beginning to grey. Already his beard and moustache had lost their colour. Rather than age him however, the change gave him a somewhat academic air.

Standing there opening and reading his mail he had an aura of isolation, of aloneness rather than loneliness. I felt inexplicably sad for him.

Having finished what he'd come to do he retraced his steps to leave the staffroom. As he went out through the door his blue-grey eyes met mine for a millisecond and he gave me a tiny nod. I flushed with embarrassment realising he may have sensed me watching him.

I waited a few moments before leaning across to the young female teacher sitting beside me. "How come Barry doesn't have morning tea in the staffroom?" I asked, trying to sound nonchalant.

She gave a derisive snort. "He doesn't drink tea or coffee and he hates small-talk. He's a weird one - just stays in his room most of the time unless he's on yard duty." The teacher returned her attention to a colleague's description of her kitchen renovation.

The school bell rang signalling the end of morning tea. As the teachers poured out of the staffroom the young female teacher fell into step alongside me. She bent towards me and in a hushed voice said, "By the way, just in case you didn't know, Dell is Barry's wife."

Seeing the confusion on my face as I struggled to work out who Dell was, the young teacher gestured furtively to a woman walking a few metres ahead of us who was talking to another teacher.

It was a puzzle. Dell had been sitting in the staffroom when Barry came in to empty his mailbox yet they hadn't spoken to each other. Obviously it would probably have been inappropriate to kiss his wife, but surely a husband and wife would mumble something to each other.

And yet, they hadn't even acknowledged each other. Barry had actually walked behind his wife's chair to get to his mailbox and yet not a word or touch had passed between them. How unusual. Perhaps they were fighting about something. But that didn't ring true with what I'd witnessed. No, they'd behaved as if they were two strangers.

The day before I was next due to deliver a lesson to Barry's class I still hadn't had any feedback from him. It seemed I would have to approach him myself.

At lunch-time I made my way somewhat nervously across the yard to his classroom. Opera music drifted out through the open windows, suggesting someone was inside.

Taking a deep breath, I walked up the steps and tapped gently on the door and opened it. Barry was sitting at his desk correcting work. He smiled up at me. "Hello I was just thinking about you." I felt myself blush.

"I just wondered if you wanted me to do another story with the students this week. Or I could do something else if you'd prefer. I wasn't sure if what I did was okay. The book was too small for them to see very well so I had to tell them the story. But I'd get a bigger book this time. I'm sure I could be better." The words tumbled out in an embarrassing collection of nerves and uncertainty.

As my voice trailed off, I lowered my eyes. Faced with his quiet, steady gaze I felt like a child trying to explain why my test results were so poor.

"The students enjoyed what you did last time." Barry leant back in his chair and chuckled. "As a matter of fact I have to admit I was enormously entertained by the fact you reckoned you could tell a Henry Lawson story better than Henry Lawson himself." He laughed again. "But from what I heard and what the kids said, it seemed you pulled it off. I sat in the back room listening to you and lamenting the partition blocked my view of your character performances. I didn't get any of my work done for the entire hour."

I clapped my hands with glee. "Thanks, that's wonderful feedback. I was so worried I'd made a mess of it all because I hadn't realised the book was too small and the text was so old-fashioned."

"Don't worry. Teaching goes like that. It's what you do to save a lesson when things don't go to plan, that really matters. And you did amazingly well. So as for tomorrow's lesson, you can do whatever you feel comfortable with. Do another book if you like, or read a poem or even get them to write a story if you want."

Barry looked directly at me the whole time he spoke. Manners required I return his look but when meeting his eyes my stomach tightened and my blood quickened. I sensed amusement in his expression, as if he realised how skittish I felt.

I envied his confidence. Did it belong to the man or his position in this context - here in his classroom, sunshine streaming in through the windows to the rise and fall of the taped opera music? The room seemed a galaxy away from the screaming warfare of the schoolyard outside or the droning monotony of the staffroom small-talk.

He was waiting for me to speak. As usual I began with an apology. "Sorry I left it until today to talk with you... thought we'd catch up in the staffroom during the week."

"Ha! Not much chance of that. I prefer to stay in my room and read or listen to music or the radio." He made no apologies nor offered any explanation as to why this might be the case.

"Hm," I nodded, not knowing what I meant to convey. "Well, I'll let you get back to it," Turning to go I glimpsed a bemused look on Barry's face. At the door I glanced back and realised he'd been watching me cross the room.

Later that week the principal told staff Barry would be absent for a few days because his father had passed away. A collection was taken up and someone was given the task of ordering flowers and a card to be delivered to Barry's house.

My father had died eleven years earlier and I still felt his loss greatly. I'd been my father's '*Blossom*' alongside my three brothers. No–one, not even my husband, had ever loved me as much as my father.

I bought a card for Barry and wrote a short note to say losing a father is a most awful thing and I hoped he had a wonderful store of memories of his father to hold onto at this sad time. The words seemed saccharine and unworthy but I couldn't think of what else to say without seeming too personal.

Having written the card I was uncertain how to get it to Barry. I watched his wife guardedly in the staffroom. My own guilt at the effect Barry was having on me made me reluctant to give it to her to pass on. Surely if she looked at me as I explained the card, she'd realise there was something not quite right involved – something I couldn't even put a name to.

No, the card couldn't be merely given to her to convey, and posting it was out of the question, even if I knew the address, because his wife would see it.

The day Barry was due to return to school saw me arrive at the staffroom before anyone else. In a flurry of nervous energy I quickly slipped my card among the other envelopes in his mailbox. Puffing with adrenalin I darted out of the staffroom, back to my tiny cell of a classroom before anyone saw me.

'It's done now!' my inner voice chastised. 'What on earth am I doing? What will he make of it? Why even do it? You are quite out of control.' There was no fully formed explanation for my behaviour. I thought dolefully about the heroine in the book '*Far from the Madding Crowd*' who started a great deal of mischief by sending a misbegotten Valentine's card to a gentleman she hardly knew.

Later in the day Barry's staffroom mailbox was empty. Someone said he was back at school but I didn't see him and felt too embarrassed now to call on him in his room.

I decided to wait until he sought me out or until the next time I was working with his students. It was a mistake sending a personal card rather than just signing the staff card like everyone else. What would Barry think of me? It was a stupid thing to have done. I tried to empty my head of all thought of the card. My nerves were strained at the thought of meeting him in the corridor, yet inevitably there was my next lesson with his students.

Finally the time arrived and embarrassed, I knocked at his classroom door. Barry glanced up from his desk, expressionless, his face closed. He stood up and addressed the students. "Today I'm working in the library while Mrs Gunningham takes your lesson. There is to be no misbehaviour. I'm appointing Merrilyn as my 'deputy.' Merrilyn your job is to keep a record of any misbehaviour and report it to me after Mrs Gunningham's lesson."

This was a surprise. Barry wasn't going to be behind the partition for my lesson. What did that mean? Was he embarrassed by my card or had he merely decided it was time for me to be responsible for the class without his protection? I flushed slightly, reasoning my first idea was probably the correct one. Collecting up a sheaf of papers from his desk, Barry left the room.

The hands dragged around the classroom clock. I suffered through the hour, trying hard not to let my mixed emotions interfere with the lesson. When the bell rang Barry hadn't returned so I dismissed the students and walked forlornly back to my room, there to sit quietly and consider what damage had been done by my foolishness.

I tried to convince myself the card was only sent because the situation had reminded me of the grief attached to the death of my father. Deep inside however I knew perhaps that wasn't my only motivation.

At the end of the day when I was packing up there was a soft knock on the door and Barry stepped into my room. Startled I rested my fingers on the desktop to steady myself.

"Hello," I said. "Hope it was okay for me to dismiss the kids today. You hadn't come back when the bell went and I wasn't sure what to do."

"No that was fine. You did the right thing. I got caught up and didn't get back to the room in time sorry."

"No need to apologise. I just wasn't sure whether to keep the kids in until you came back." Looking down at my fingers on the desk I realised the conversation had become ridiculous.

I glanced up at Barry's face then stared back at my fingers. "Sorry about your dad. My dad mattered enormously to me and when he died it felt like my whole back had been cut off. No-one ever stood up for me like my dad did." My eyes began to sting and I couldn't look up.

Barry moved quietly across to stand in front of me, so close I could smell the eucalyptus soap on his jumper. "I came to thank you for the card. It was kind of you to do that," he murmured.

I looked up. "Just wanted you to know I was thinking of you and that losing your dad is so horrible. I hope you have lots of lovely memories of you and him together. Even though he's gone, you'll always have those memories and they'll help you in the hard times."

"Thanks." Barry's response was simple and earnest. He looked around the room. "It's like a prison cell in here isn't it? Bit like the classroom time forgot."

"Yeah," I shrugged, "... it's small and old and dusty but it's all mine – and beggars can't be choosers."

"Anyway, I'd better let you finish what you're doing before the cleaner arrives to lock up."

I nodded and Barry strode out of the room, leaving me glad he'd come to see me.

FIRST FORAYS

School camp

When a butterfly lands on a rock
For one fleeting moment, The rock knows
what it is to be a flower

ANON

Barry and I taught together at Whittlesea for the last six months of 1990. It was a time full of 'firsts' for me. My first full-time job since resigning a clerical job over a decade earlier to raise my children, my first job as a teacher, first school camp, first curriculum day, first parent-teacher interviews, and eventually my first graduation ceremony as a teacher of year six students. All these firsts occurred in the twenty school-weeks leading up to the December school holidays.

I felt as though I was flying by the seat of my pants most of the time and spent an inordinate amount of time trying to convince myself and everyone else that I'd chosen the right career. My weekly work program was a piece of art, with treble clefs and minims sketched above the *Music* lessons, light bulbs sketched above the *Accelerated Reading* sessions' and cricket bats and footballs depicted above the *Sports* lessons.'

After school I spent hours preparing each one-hour lesson for the following day and so delighted was the principal, he left chocolates and reward stickers in my work program when he inspected it each week.

At home, I tried valiantly not to let my work encroach on my family. My mother was now living in a unit behind our house and she fed my sons afternoon tea each day when they came in from school. Always a champion of a woman's role as 'home-maker' she was happy to help.

On days without staff meetings I could be home within an hour of the boys' arrival and be making dinner by the time Alec came in from work. Most of my school preparation and correction was done after everyone had gone to bed. It was difficult but I'd always anticipated it would be. On the upside the boys and I left at the same time in the mornings, I was home by 5 pm and most importantly, could be with them for school holidays.

Although exhausted and struggling to keep up the pace, my days were happy. I developed a new respect for those teachers who seemed to cope with all the preparation and delivery of their lessons - yet still found time for idle gossip and newspaper reading at morning tea. I hoped no-one would discover how hard I was paddling just to stay afloat.

A month before the senior grades' school camp, our team of four teachers met after school to discuss logistics. The camp was to be held at a purpose built camp on the river at Swan Hill. A 57-seater bus and a 25-seater mini-bus were hired to accommodate all the students wanting to come. As our team comprised three male teachers and me, it was decided to approach two mothers to come with us and help with the girls. Two teachers would travel on each bus and the Principal would drive the mothers in his car.

Standing beside the buses on camp day, the students and teachers watched as the Principal drove away with the mothers. Brian, the team coordinator directed Barry and me to travel in the mini-bus.

Doubting my ability to supervise the over-excited boys who were already pushing and shoving each other to decide who'd sit in the back seat, I was grateful to be with the smaller group of students.

"Who wants to come with me and Mrs Gunningham?" Barry asked and a smattering of hands went up.

"Okay, line-up over here," he said taking a few steps away and throwing down a bag of sports equipment to mark the spot.

"I'll get you to mark them off the roll as they get on the bus if that's alright?" Barry said, handing me a clipboard bearing a list of names. A pen was neatly tied to the clasp at the top of the board.

"Sure," I said enthusiastically, pleased to be given any role other than crowd control. "...only I don't know everybody's name so they'll have to tell me. Is that okay?"

"Of course." He turned to face the students.

"All right everyone." Barry stood tall and addressed the students authoritatively. "Now, as you get on the bus tell Mrs Gunningham your full name so she can mark you off the list. We won't be leaving until everyone's name's marked off correctly so don't be silly. Just say your name clearly and sensibly and then we can pass the list to the other bus."

He paused meaningfully with one eyebrow raised and glared at two boys who were pushing each other in the queue. They instantly stilled and stared down at their feet.

Barry continued, his eyes still fixed on the two. "And in case any of you were wondering, we'll have a rotation for the back seat, so a few people will get to sit there, not just one group."

At this, a collective groan went up from some of the boys. The two in Barry's gaze remained notably silent, lifting their heads only long enough to check if Barry was still watching them. He was.

"Of course some of you might get lucky enough to sit with me for part of the trip." At this the girls tittered and the boys rolled their eyes.

"I'll be able to explain Swan Hill's fascinating history to anyone who's lucky enough to sit with me. So that will be a real treat for some of you."

Another collective groan went up and Barry feigned offense at their reaction.

"No-one wants to hear history," a scruffy boy mumbled without looking up.

"History's boring," said another.

"Yeah, we want to hear music, not you telling us about history."

Everyone began laughing. Barry turned toward me. The students quietened obviously waiting to hear him deliver his 'punch-line.'

"What do you think of that Mrs Gunningham? You'd think they'd be excited at the prospect of learning some history. Children today! It's disappointing isn't it?" He shook his head in mock disbelief.

The rapport between Barry and the students was obvious. They understood his expectations and what the consequences were for poor behaviour, yet he hadn't read them the riot act. He seemed to elicit respect without any outward sign of dominance or aggression. I watched and learnt.

We had eighteen students on the mini bus, meaning there were some empty seats.

"You sit in two seats on the left towards the front of the bus and I'll sit on the right, toward the back," Barry said to me. I was a bit surprised he didn't want to sit with me, but I nodded and when we boarded the bus I sat alone in the seat he directed me into.

Barry moved further along the aisle to plonk down into a pair of seats in front of the back row. A group of five mischievous boys who'd commandeered the back seat immediately complained.

"Aw, do you have to sit there Sir?"

"We're not even playing up."

"Honestly, I thought this was s'posed to be a fun camp."

"Are you gunna sit there the whole trip Sir?"

"Awh ... we should've gone on the other bus."

Ignoring them completely Barry was sitting upright against the window, his eyes fixed on the parents outside the bus who were waiting to wave us goodbye.

"Goodbye Mrs Dylan. Goodbye Mr Brown. Thanks for coming to see us off." Barry waved having a jolly time verbalising his farewells.

The back-seat boys now somewhat deflated, fell silent and stared out at their parents on the footpath.

I realised Barry's seating arrangement for me and him was a 'divide-and-conquer' manoeuvre. Plus he'd taken the additional step of placing himself at the point of most resistance, leaving me to oversee the self-regulating students who were often bullied and jostled towards the front of the bus.

The manoeuvre had not been part of my teacher training and I was grateful to sit in silence and watch it played out. It made perfect sense for teachers not to sit together on the school bus. What had I been thinking?

Most of the students eventually settled and true to his word Barry brought one or two tiresome boys to sit beside him for twenty minutes or so each as we travelled. Their punishment was to have to endure both the snickering of their mates as well as either stony silence or a history lecture from Barry. There were no repeat offenders.

Meanwhile at the front of the mini-bus, which was occupied by most of the girls and a few male isolates, I was free to read a novel, the latest fad-read, *'A Hitchhikers Guide to the Galaxy.'* I found it a difficult read because it was based on a futuristic pile of literary rubbish about a journey through space.

Unfortunately I'd long ago made a pact with myself that once started, I'd always read a book right through – something about honouring the effort of the writer. However this particular book was making it hard to keep up my end of the bargain.

Eventually Barry appeared beside me and broke my concentration. "We're stopping in five minutes for a toilet break and morning tea."

"Okay. What do you want me to do?"

"Can you keep the girls moving along in the toilets? The boys get through pretty quickly and they blow all their spending money in the first milk bar if they're kept waiting too long."

"No worries," I chuckled, closing my book and putting it on the seat beside me.

"*Hitchhikers Guide to the Galaxy*?" Barry's eyebrows were raised, suggesting surprise.

"Yeah - a friend gave it to me." I didn't want to say anything more because I couldn't tell from his tone whether he was impressed or disappointed with my choice.

We navigated the toilet stop successfully and just before we hopped back on the bus Barry presented an icy-pole to one of the girls.

"Well done Cynthia. This is a little reward for achieving the highest cumulative score on the school's final year-six tests."

"Teacher's pet," a boy standing near me whispered to his mates.

"Big deal. Who cares?" one of them replied.

"She's useless at sport," said another.

"Yeah. Too many icy-poles." At this the group of boys erupted into laughter.

"That's enough!" Barry's voice crashed over them like waves in a storm and they fell silent.

Everyone filed back onto the bus. As he passed my seat, Barry presented me with an icy-pole too. "I bought you a present, because your job supervising the girls was harder than mine with the boys."

Blushing, I mumbled an embarrassed, "Thank you."

Swan Hill's pioneering history was reflected in the rustic buildings that greeted us when we finally reached our destination. A number of timber bunkhouses flanked two sides of a large flat, grassed area. A repurposed shearing-shed housed a kitchen and large dining room that doubled as a recreation hall.

Brian allocated the girls to the bunkhouse on the west of the field, while the boys were to sleep in those on the north side. Two large ablutions blocks stood back behind the junction of the bunkhouses allowing easy access for all. The mothers and I shared a small cabin containing three bunk beds in the middle of the girls' wing.

Five hours in the bus had exhausted the students and after dinner and a wander by torchlight around the nearby country-side everyone, including the adults, was ready for bed by 9 p.m.

After setting my alarm in preparation for taking the identified 'bed-wetters' to the toilet during the night, I lay down to sleep. The responsibility of all these little girls in their bunk beds weighed heavy on my mind and I hoped I'd hear any child who knocked at our door during the night. With my eyes closed, a postscript was added that I wouldn't snore and become a laughing stock to the mothers.

The few days at camp unfolded in a flurry of bush walks, creek-wading, games, bush cooking, nature crafts and concerts. On the last night of camp the mothers and I were invited over to the male teachers' cabin for a celebratory nightcap. The Principal was due to arrive after breakfast the next morning to drive the mothers home, leaving the teachers and students to follow in the buses.

The mothers seemed delighted by the invitation. They'd enjoyed themselves immensely, competing with the students in the games and squealing at the chill waters as they paddled the creek. Attending the school camp had also provided them with a previously denied level of intimacy with the teachers.

"I'm not coming. I think I should be here in case one of the girls needs me." My words fell like snow on a spring day. One mother in the process of pulling on a hot pink singlet-top, spun around to face me. The other looked up from her small make-up mirror, mascara wand in hand.

"But you must come. It won't be any fun without you."

I smiled, doubting their words. "No really. You go. I'm not much of a conversationalist and wouldn't want to drink anyway. Besides I should be here just in case. You go. You deserve a night off. You've been great. Really - it's not a problem."

The mothers looked at each other then back at me. "But we don't want to go without you. Can't you come even for a little while? Please?"

I sighed, realising they weren't going to go without a fight. Perhaps I could go for ten minutes? Just sit there like a smiling mute then make an excuse and slip away - probably less trouble than trying to convince the mothers to go without me.

"Alright - but only for a short time. You two can stay on, but when I get up to leave, let me go without any fuss. Okay?" One of the mothers stepped over and gave me a quick hug, relief and happiness in her eyes.

"Sure. Good on you. It's better if we all go." I didn't bother to analyse what she meant.

The men's cabin was as ugly and primitive as ours. Brian was slouched along a lower bunk and Chris was sitting on one of two kitchen chairs brought over from the dining room for the occasion.

Barry was sitting upright, back against the wall on a top bunk. He looked somewhat ridiculous in the narrow wooden bed with the top of his head only centimetres from the rough pine ceiling.

Brian jumped to his feet and ushered us in. The mothers perched beside each other on a lower bunk and I sat on a chair. Glancing up at Barry I nodded and he smiled back. Brian offered the mothers a beer. They declined and with a grin produced two cans of pre-mixed alcohol from a bag one of them had carried over.

"No thanks." I said when Brian held out a can of beer to me.

"Don't you drink?"

"Yeah - but not beer, and not tonight. Thanks anyway." I tried to sound light-hearted. I didn't want to appear a 'wowser.'

"Barry doesn't drink either; only Pepsi." My eyes flickered up to the top bunk again. Barry held up a can of Pepsi and jiggled it for me to see.

"Hm," I said, looking down at my knees, reluctant to re-state that in fact I did drink alcohol, but not beer and not tonight.

The conversation began. Stories about previous camp disasters and mishaps were told, popular films and songs were discussed and various jokes were shared. The room filled with raucous laughter and I soon realised I had almost nothing to contribute; Mona Lisa sitting on a kitchen chair in a rustic cabin watching others have fun.

I stole a glance at Barry. He was watching me. He nodded ever so slightly. Blushing, I looked away hoping my thoughts weren't showing on my face.

How clever to have sat on the top bunk. No expectation you'll contribute to the conversation from up there. I suddenly realised he hadn't said much more than me.

I stood up. "Sorry, I just remembered a promise to one of the girls I'd check on her before she went to sleep. She wasn't feeling well at dinner. Thanks for inviting me over Brian and thanks to the mums for all their help on the camp."

"Here, here," said the men, raising their cans in salute. The mothers grinned at each other.

As I closed the cabin door behind me the conversation inside resumed. I stepped out into the silver shadows cast by the moon shining through the trailing dark clouds. The air was heavy with the smell of rich, damp soil and lush pastures. In the stillness of the night I could hear the rush of the river beyond the camp as it flowed away in search of the ocean many kilometres south.

Curriculum Days

Sophie: Why did you take me?
BFG: Because I hears your lonely heart,
in all the secret whisperings of the world.

Roald Dahl

I'd only been teaching a few months when the school had two curriculum days in quick succession. The first was held at school, but the second day was to take place in the function room of the local golf club. The school was to supply salads and the teachers were asked to bring their own meat for a barbeque.

All the teachers at the school were locals except me, many owning small farms and using their teaching salary to supplement their farming business. In contrast I came from the inner suburbs and my wages went on household expenses. The only 'livestock' I tended was my sons.

"Do you know how to get to the golf course?" Barry asked me as I was leaving his classroom the day before the curriculum day. "I doubt it's in your city street directory because it's beyond the township."

"I have no idea; hadn't even thought about it. I just assumed it must be close by somewhere and I'd follow street signs." I was conscious of sounding like an idiot and wished I'd stop rambling every time Barry asked me something. He tried giving me verbal directions but it soon became obvious I had almost no knowledge of the area around the school or the town.

"I'll draw you a map" he said and moved across to his desk to draw thick, firm lines on a blank page.

I watched him. He was big and strong and uncluttered. His large hands drew so firmly and confidently on the page that his writing made indents on the blotter beneath.

"There you are," he said, handing me the map. "That should get you there without any trouble. The golf course is on the way to my place. I'm about three kilometres further on."

"Thanks. I suppose you play golf then?"

"I can play, but I don't. Prefer to bush walk than walk around a golf course."

"Uhuh," I gave a small chuckle, not understanding why. Every response I made in Barry's presence seemed clumsy and oafish. "Anyway, thanks for the map." I nodded and hurried away, reprimanding myself for being so vapid.

Thanks to Barry's map I managed to find the venue in time for the start of the curriculum day. Sitting in a row of seats facing a small lectern and microphone, Barry nodded across at me from where he was seated beside his wife on the other side of the room. It was unusual to see them seated together.

The morning session was a long lecture and I took copious notes. It was a relief when we finally broke for lunch. Standing in the queue for the barbeque I watched and listened as the other teachers discussed their large slabs of steak and their thick chops. They waxed lyrical about the butcher who'd slaughtered their cow or the one they'd bought the meat from, the marinade they'd soaked it in and how they liked it cooked.

My spirits sank. I'd brought along two sausages. Not specially-spiced, curried, herbed or gourmet sausages - just two thin supermarket sausages from the packet I always bought to feed my family.

I'd been raised in a household where money was forever in short supply and as children when we asked my mother what was for dinner she'd always reply, "Food and be grateful for it. Food's just a source of energy after all, like petrol in a motorcar." No wonder I'd never aspired to be a chef.

When I arrived at the front of the queue Barry was there cooking. His steak was thick and to me, looked large enough to feed a family of four. Surely it cost the equivalent of my family's weekly meat bill.

"I'll cook yours for you if you like," he offered.

Ashamed, I winced slightly and held up my tiny cling-wrapped parcel.

"Sausages?" His eyes smiled.

"Hm ... I love sausages." I said, trying to sound enthusiastic. "They cook quickly and you can make lots of different meals with them."

Immediately the words were out I wanted to retract them. Barry nodded as if he hadn't noticed how idiotic I sounded.

Humiliated, I collected a paper plate from a side table and shuffled around behind Barry to wait for my sausages to be cooked. Perhaps I was hiding – hiding from him, or maybe from the other teachers, but probably primarily from my own shame.

During the afternoon lecture I sat in the back row licking my wounds. At one point Barry left the room. The lecture dragged on and I found myself wondering why he hadn't returned. His wife, fully engrossed in the lecture, seemed unperturbed.

The clock ticked on. When Barry hadn't returned after twenty minutes I went outside to look for him. Being in the back row, closest to the door made it easy for me to slip out unnoticed.

I found him sitting on a bench, leaning against the wall at the far end of the building. His shoulders were drooped and his arms hung loosely across his thighs. He sat very still, his face lifted deliberately towards the breeze that swept up the grassy rise of the golf course to the clubhouse at the top.

Barry didn't notice me and I stood for a moment watching him. He looked the image of loneliness sitting there silently, framed between the indigo sky and the emerald grass. His whole being was sagged back against the unyielding brick wall behind him.

Suddenly Barry must have sensed he wasn't alone and he turned to face me. I hesitated, not sure what to say. After all, it wasn't my responsibility to be checking on him.

"Sorry. I saw you leave and was worried something was wrong. *'Good grief!'* I thought, *'How lame does that sound?'* "Last curriculum day I fainted and no-one even noticed I was missing and I just thought ..." I'd blabbed the words out in a rush and now my voice faltered.

Straightening up, I lifted my face to the breeze as Barry had done, closed my eyes and focussed on the sensation for a moment.

"It's nice here – peaceful." I mumbled, opening my eyes and turning to go. "Sorry I interrupted you."

Barry hadn't spoken as I struggled to explain my presence. Now he threw me a life-line.

"What do you mean you 'fainted'?"

I frowned. "Do you remember the doctor was telling us what to do if a kid gets something stuck in their ear?"

He nodded.

"Yuk - Couldn't stand it!" I grimaced. "Never been any good with stuff about ears. I tried to stay and listen but just couldn't. Had to get up and run outside. Only made it as far as the front door... then fainted."

Barry's eyebrows flew up in surprise. "Fainted? Really? Fainted?"

I looked away. "Yeah – full faint, down for the count. Woke up sprawled down the front steps of the school - pants ripped, knees bleeding. Pretty embarrassing." I gave a short laugh.

"What happened?" Barry asked, now sitting up straight and leaning toward me.

"Well I contemplated suicide of course."

He laughed, obviously taken off guard.

I grinned. "Then I thought of just running away without telling anyone. But I was too groggy to walk to the car park, so just sat there. The Principal found me when he came out to see if the lunch caterer had arrived. I begged him to let me go home and finally he agreed."

"You shouldn't have been allowed to drive yourself home." The thought crossed my mind that this was Barry's 'shop-steward voice' speaking.

I lifted my face to the breeze again to quash any recriminations.

"I was more worried about facing the next day's morning tea inquisition; was preparing to be totally humiliated in the first term of my teaching career!" I paused, tried to calm my voice, focussed on a lone golfer putting on the green. "But no-one mentioned it - seemed I wasn't even missed."

I scoffed, hoping to mask my hurt at this truth.

Barry remained silent.

"Anyway," I said, gesturing to the door behind us, "When you didn't come back to the lecture I wondered if you were okay... thought you might've fainted too."

"Thanks." Barry tilted his head slightly and for a moment we looked directly at each other, which suddenly made me feel awkward.

"It's tinnitus." he said. "I've had it for years - comes and goes."

"Oh, that's no good," I said, having no idea what tinnitus was. My ignorance must have shown.

"... ringing in the ears, sometimes loss of balance - no cure. Just learn to live with it." Barry shrugged.

"Oh," I said again, unable to think of any further response and praying he wouldn't give me too much medical information.

He nodded back towards the lecture room. "Am I missing anything important?"

I made a face. "Hmm... can't say for sure. I don't understand most of it. Lots of education-speak." I chuckled. "Better get back in though," I stared up at the clear sky one last time then moved to go, thought better of it and half turned back to Barry. "Unless of course, tinnitus is contagious... No hope I s'pose?"

We grinned at each other and opening the door I felt Barry's eyes follow me as I stepped inside, leaving him to his breeze and his privacy.

Graduation night

> *So blind was I to see and to foresee,*
> *So dull to mark the budding of my tree*
> *That would not blossom yet for many a May.*

CHRISTINA GEORGINA ROSSETTI

The last week of November that same year Barry stopped me in the school corridor. "Hey, I was thinking about the Year Six graduation ceremony next week. You said you were coming, but the dinner starts at 6 pm. Will you have enough time to go home and then drive back to Whittlesea?"

I winced slightly at yet another reminder I wasn't a 'local'.

"Yeah, no worries."

The earliest I ever left school was 4 pm and I'd reasoned I could do the forty minute drive back to Greensborough, get changed, then brave the peak-hour drive back again – at least another 50 minutes. I'd just make it, as long as I didn't shower, and if no-one at home needed anything of me and if there were no traffic jams going or coming. My mother was going to look after the boys until Alec came home. Dinner was already made and just needed to be heated.

On the other hand, I'd also thought about remaining after the last school bell, changing in the toilets and going to the graduation straight from school. The school buildings would be unlocked until about 6 pm when the cleaner knocked off. Disappointingly neither option allowed the possibility of a shower.

"It's pretty amazing to see the kids arrive. They're almost unrecognisable in their best clothes. Some even come in taxis and limousines like movie-stars." Barry's words implied teachers typically arrive well before 6 pm "What time do you think you'll get to the venue?"

I shuffled the papers in my hand and tried to sound casual. "I've decided to stay at school and get changed here. What time do you reckon would be best for me to arrive?"

Barry hesitated as though turning something over in his mind. "If you want, you can come to my place after school." His voice was low as if he was a little startled to hear his offer aloud.

"No, it's okay. No problem staying at school. The cleaner will be here." I hated anyone thinking I was a problem and needed help. It felt particularly important to me for Barry not to think that.

"It's no problem - honestly. You could have a shower and get changed at my place. It'd be better than staying at school by yourself."

It was as if Barry had heard my thoughts and was now using them to convince me.

I took a breath and aligned the papers in my hand again, buying time to balance his generous offer with my need not to be a problem.

"Okay. Thanks." My voice was soft also. It was if we were whispering a secret.

"Good!" and with that, Barry strode off down the corridor leaving me to ponder this turn of events.

At home I lied saying I was going to get changed at school because I wasn't sure if Barry's wife would be home when I was there. I wasn't sure how my mother and Alec would view me showering at another man's house if his wife wasn't home. It seemed practical to just tell a white lie rather than be put through an inquisition. Barry's invitation had been made out of kindness and I didn't want people questioning his motives.

After school on graduation night I drove the few blocks to where the ceremony was to be held and Barry followed in his car. I parked and hopped in beside him bringing a bag containing my toiletries and change of clothes.

"Thanks for this." Hoping no-one would recognise us and misinterpret the situation, I kept my head lowered and made a major task of settling my bag and fastening my seatbelt. 'For goodness sake,' I silently scolded myself – 'too much Mata Hari and not enough Mother Hubbard!'

The usual sense of awkwardness one feels when hopping into someone else's car surfaced. An invisible line is crossed, putting one in a microcosm of the car-owner's personal life.

The interior of Barry's car was clean and devoid of ornamentation. A one-litre bottle of diet cola lay on top of an assortment of student workbooks, a large pencil case and other classroom equipment in a large plastic tub filled on the back seat. Beside the tub was a battered blue carry-bag containing sports equipment, no doubt ready for Friday school sports.

We drove out of the township and onto a narrow road that wound up through the hills to his cottage, *Waldene*. We didn't pass another house for a few kilometres and the untamed forest seemed to crowd alongside the road to watch our passage. I was relieved when the road cut into a steep hill and a wall of clay became my view from the passenger window.

On the driver's side of the car, the twists and turns of the road showcased the valleys falling away below us. Everywhere was forest - silent and menacing. Eventually a padlocked wire gate suspended between two tall eucalypt trees appeared on Barry's side of the road and he pulled across onto the narrow shoulder in front of it.

"I'll get the gate," he said, opening his door.

Looking through the windscreen I couldn't see a driveway or a house or even any fences for that matter. There was just a gate on the crest of a hill in the forest. Any view beyond the gate was located below the level of the road.

I chewed on my thumbnail and tried not to think.

Barry slid back into his seat and to my horror, swung the car through the opened gate and over the edge of the horizon. Before us appeared a roller-coaster incline; a rough and forbidding driveway running straight down into the forest.

As we dropped beneath the eucalypt canopy, a small wooden cottage appeared at the edge of a tiny cleared spur as if cupped in the palm of the surrounding hills. Beyond it the land continued to fall steeply away into the valley below.

Barry turned the car and reversed onto a small flat parking area a few metres from the front door of the cottage. A flock of startled lorikeets rose up from a garden bed, screeching en masse into the twilight sky - a living rainbow amidst the trees.

I had a sudden rush of nerves and wondered if I should interpret this frightening spectacle as some sort of warning. Noting my expression as he held the door open for me, Barry turned and stared up at the mass of startled birds.

"Sorry - I throw seed out for them. They always arrive about this time." He stood for a moment watching the birds, obviously enjoying the sight. Then he turned back to me. "Don't worry. They'll come back down once we're inside."

Although I was terrified of the mass of flapping, screeching birds, I was grateful Barry had misunderstood the reason for my look of unease. I followed behind as he stepped down onto a rough brick porch that ran the full length of the cottage. A bull-nose verandah shaded both the cottage and the porch. We stood in front of a rough-sawn wooden door bearing a small leadlight window, while Barry fumbled for his keys.

I was reminded of the Hansel and Gretel fairytale and for a fleeting moment had the sensation it would be perfectly appropriate for a wicked witch with a cage and oven to be waiting for us inside.

Unlocking the door, Barry pushed it open, stood back and waved me in. I stepped up into a small foyer. The internal walls and the vaulted ceiling were completely pine-lined and softly yellowed with age. Directly opposite me a door stood ajar exposing a tall window showing the forest behind the house. I took a few steps forward, uncertain where I was supposed to go.

"You can put your bag in there." Barry gestured towards the room with the tall window. He stepped across behind me and went through another doorway on the right. A quick glance suggested he'd gone into the kitchen.

I took a few steps forward. The tall window proved to be one of three set into the far wall of a bedroom. A king-sized bed faced out to the view beyond the windows. Alongside the bed some soft toys sat atop a small chest of drawers. An antique wardrobe and a graceful upright dresser complete with mirror-stand stood along another wall.

Lifting my bag to put it on the bed, I paused then placed it on the mat instead. It felt uncomfortable being in Barry's bedroom; like I should be walking on tip-toes and not looking at his collection of toys or the view from his bed.

Scurrying out of the room, I tried not to notice the romance of the heart carved into the bed head, or the beautiful painting hanging above it - a Grecian lady in emerald robes, her hands tangled in her auburn tresses. She too appeared to stare out at the forest.

Barry was reading his mail at the kitchen bench when I appeared in the doorway. "All okay?" he asked.

"Yes, thanks." I wasn't sure what I was supposed to do now.

"Can I get you a tea or a coffee, some biscuits?" Barry opened a door under the kitchen bench-top and crouched down to fossick inside. "Sit on the couch. There's no rush. We've got a couple of hours before we have to be there."

"Coffee'd be great, thanks." I remained where I was, backed up against another pine panelled wall that soared up behind me.

Squatting like a frog, Barry turned to look at me.

"Sorry I don't know where the couch is." I felt my face flush.

He stood up. "Of course you don't. Sorry. I almost never have visitors and sometimes I forget how to behave."

I followed him past the kitchen bench and beyond the end of the pine wall. The room opened into a large living–dining area. Tall uncurtained windows were fixed into every external wall to provide views of the steep hills flanking the cottage, the valley running away to the south, and the unrelenting forest all around.

An enormous rough-hewn bluestone chimney rose up against the far wall to meet the centre-beam of the vaulted ceiling. The chimney widened at its base to house a massive iron fire-box complete with double doors. The carved lion on each door seeming to dare someone to open them.

Barry gestured me to a worn leather Chesterfield couch. It was positioned to enable a view through one of the tall windows beside the chimney. 'Sit down and I'll get you a coffee - milk, sugar?"

"Black, no sugar." Relieved, I plonked onto the couch while Barry made the coffee.

"You're house is amazing," I called out to him as he busied himself in the kitchen. My eyes scanned the row of etched brass plates lined up above the dining-room doors, the stacked bookcases, the paintings and tapestries. Curios adorned all the shelves and dressers. Every item seemed positioned with deliberate purpose for maximum effect.

"I like nice things. Most of the furniture is from my parent's house." He appeared from the kitchen and placed a mug of coffee and a small plate of biscuits on the coffee table before surveying the room for a minute. "I bought lots of the other stuff overseas. I travel a fair bit."

He looked back at me. "Do you collect anything?"

I laughed. "Yeah - kids and toys. My house is more ... 'lived-in' than yours."

Barry turned a chair from the dining room table and sat down to face me. With a sinking feeling I sensed we were to have a conversation. I doubted we'd find any common ground.

"Aren't you having a coffee?" I took a mouthful from my mug, and reached for a biscuit to save me having to say any more.

"No, I don't drink tea or coffee."

"Ha - just alcohol I s'pose?" I shuffled back on the couch, pleased we could at least discuss alcohol, maybe even pubs we'd been to.

"No, I don't drink - just cola. Remember on camp?"

"Oh yeah, you were drinking cola." I wondered where to go from here. It was exhausting! "So ... no tea, no coffee, no alcohol - just cola?" I shook my head in disbelief.

Barry nodded, offering no further comment.

"Tell me about your house." I hoped this would fill the void for awhile. My experience with men was they find it easier if the conversation is about them.

"Would you like a tour?"

"Sure." I jumped to my feet.

Barry had built the cottage himself, toiling away before and after work. He'd hammered and nailed each piece of timber into place and mortared each stone in the huge chimney. Rainwater collected from the house and shed roofs was held in multiple tanks and then pumped to a large tank up on the roadside to gravity-feed back to the house.

The cottage relied on bottled gas for lighting and refrigeration relied and Barry cooked on a huge wood-fired stove that also heated a water tank built into the roof.

"No TV or stereo?" It seemed unbelievable.

"No – too far down in the valley to pick up a signal."

"Wow, no TV. You must be unique."

Barry shrugged. "Probably - I go to the movies a lot though. At least that way I get to see something interesting instead of the rubbish they put on TV."

I winced, slighted on behalf of the everyman. "So what do you do while the rest of us are watching telly?" Following Barry's lead, I didn't refer to his wife although their living arrangements had me curious.

"I've got a battery-operated transistor and I can usually pick up a couple of stations on the AM band ... and I read. I read lots."

He led me over to two tall bookcases in the lounge room. "This is only some of my books. There are more boxes in the spare room. I'm going to build a library onto the back of the house soon. Then I'll have all my books in bookcases."

It was said so simply, as if single-handedly building an extra room was something people did every day. I had two uncles, three brothers, a husband and two sons, none of whom had ever built more than very unstable billy-carts and perhaps the odd hen-house. I was in awe of Barry.

I leant forward and ran a finger along some of the book-spines as I read the titles. '*Far from the Madding Crowd, Tom Sawyer, Complete Works of Shakespeare, Lord of the Flies, Power Without*

Glory.' While I recognised some titles, I'd never heard of many of them.

I suddenly wished I was my mother. She knew everything about books. When I was about seven, she'd send me every week to the library to borrow books for her, to save her having to take my two younger brothers out for the trip. I'd always to ask the librarian for murder mysteries, but to say if none were available my mum was happy to read anything. I think by the time I was eleven and my brothers were civilised enough to make the journey with her, she must have read every book in the library.

"What sort of books do you read?" Barry asked. I paused, trying to remember some books other than children's stories and teacher reference books that had comprised the majority of my reading for the past decade.

Possibly misunderstanding my silence as an in-depth consideration of the various classics, Barry narrowed his question. "What did you think of the 'Hitchhiker's Guide' you were reading on camp?"

I gulped. "Well … I liked the notion of '42' being the answer to the 'meaning of life'… leaving everyone to wonder what the question must be … and I liked the saying '… so long and thanks for all the fish."

Barry's blue eyes probed my discomfort. He remained silent and I sensed he expected more.

"Well," I said slowly, deciding to bite the bullet, "… other than that I thought it was pretty stupid."

Clapping his hands, Barry said loudly, "Yes! Absolute rubbish! I wondered why you were reading it. I remember you said a friend gave it to you."

"But I always read a book right through - even if it's dreadful. It's only fair to the author."

"That's garbage. The author should write something worth reading, otherwise they let down their end of the bargain." I could see Barry was delighted with the prospect of a debate.

"But it may not be dreadful. I might just not have understood what the author was trying to say. Some writing is difficult to understand - think of Shakespeare."

We bantered on, victories and losses taken on both sides, and shared laughter when some of the points made bordered on the ridiculous.

Suddenly Barry glanced at his watch.

"Geez, it's almost five. We'd better get moving." He jumped to his feet.

"You can shower first. There's plenty of hot water and I put a towel in the bathroom for you." As he spoke Barry beckoned me to follow him.

Stepping back into the entry foyer, I saw two doors I hadn't noticed before. One stood ajar, exposing a navy tiled bathroom.

"The toilet's in here," Barry said, pushing open the other door. His casual reference to the possibility of me needing to use the toilet felt weirdly intimate. I cringed. There was no way he'd hear my urine splashing into his toilet bowl. I'd rather hang on and use the toilet at the graduation venue.

"Thanks. I'll be quick," I said, retrieving my bag from the floor in his bedroom. I stepped into the bathroom, closed the door and slid the flimsy slide-bolt across. Closing my eyes I took a few deep breaths, my ears straining to hear Barry's footsteps retreating. He moved towards the kitchen and somewhat relieved, I heard the door to the foyer close behind him.

Pulling off my t-shirt felt suddenly very risky. 'What was I thinking when I accepted his offer?' I now chastised myself. Here I was, expected to be naked in a shower while Barry sat less than five metres away, albeit behind two closed doors and a flimsy slide-bolt.

Maybe I could just change and re-emerge with no harm done? But no, experience told me hot water pipes always make whining noises to alert the entire household to their use. He'd know I didn't shower! Maybe I could get changed, and let the shower run?

I could feel the clock ticking. I'd said I'd be quick.

I tried to talk some sense into myself in the bathroom mirror. He only made the offer out of kindness. No-one else at school even considered how difficult it would be for you tonight. And now you're making out like he's going to break into the bathroom while you're showering and what? – rape you? We're due at the graduation dinner in an hour. He wouldn't be so stupid! You're being silly – wasting time.

Conceding my reflection was probably correct, I quickly undressed and showered. Barry's soap was a translucent honey colour. It smelt clean and carbolic, like the lumps of laundry soap my mother used to cut for us years ago. I leapt out of the shower and pulled my fresh clothing over hastily towelled skin, all the while on the alert for Barry's footsteps.

I yanked on my underpants. They rolled into a narrow band on my damp skin and my dress sleeves refused to slide down my wet arms. Struggling to dress quickly another possibility floated into my mind.

A girlfriend had once told me about the first night she'd spent with a certain guy at her apartment. She'd asked him to light candles and select music while she showered. When she came out of the bathroom, he greeted her wearing one of her nighties. He'd explained his penchant for wearing women's silky night attire and hoped she didn't mind.

The memory of that conversation frightened me. Although I'd survived the shower and managed to pull on my clothing, I was now scared to open the bathroom door. What would I do if Barry was wearing a nightie? Even worse, what if he was totally naked?

I bundled my clothing and toiletries into my bag, silently slid the slide-bolt back and rested my fingers on the door handle. Taking a deep breath and whispering Shakespeare's words, '... cowards die a thousand times, a brave man dies but once,' I quietly opened the bathroom door.

The foyer was empty and the door to the kitchen was still closed. I returned my bag to the bedroom mat so as to be unencumbered when opening the next door. As I stepped across the foyer the floor boards creaked and I momentarily froze.

Holding my breath I gripped the door handle for a few seconds before deciding to just get it over. I opened the door. There was no sign of Barry in the kitchen.

"Hello, I'm finished." My voice sounded normal in spite of my fears.

"Righto. I'm in here." Following the direction of his voice I found Barry considering a small collection of books he was holding. "Have you read anything by Salman Rushdie?" he asked me.

"No, but I think I've heard of him," I lied.

"I think you might enjoy '*Midnight's Children*' – it won a Booker Prize." Barry handed me a thick paperback book. "Have a look while I shower and change, and if you like, you can borrow it from me."

"Thanks." I looked down at the very thick book and wondered why Barry thought I would want to read a book about children. If I had time to read for pleasure I'd want to escape into fantasy not read about more children.

And so what if it had won whatever a *Book – a - Prize* was? I didn't have time to read it. But with a sinking feeling I knew my manners would mean I'd borrow the book, which meant I'd have to read it and then look after it until I could return it.

An angry glance at Barry's bookcase revealed it contained lots of slim books. Why couldn't he have lent me one of them?

The water pipes signalled Barry was in the shower. I sat on the couch and scanned the back cover of the chosen book – *'a loose allegory of events surrounding India's independence and partition.'* My God I'd need a dictionary just to understand the overview.

Scanning the room I looked for somewhere I could 'accidentally' leave the book when we left the house. Behind the couch was a small table bearing a few scattered books and some pens and paper. I put the book on top of the scattered pile. It was too thick, too evident. I shuffled the pile around and re-positioned the thick book. That might do it.

When Barry came back into the room in a new set of clothes he found me innocently looking out the window. His hair was damp and his cheeks were rosy.

"That feels better. I love a cold burst of water at the end of a shower – sort of invigorating.' He grinned at me as he snapped his watch back onto his wrist. "We've got about 15 minutes to get there, so we'd better leave right now."

I hurried past him to retrieve my bag. "Do you want me to write my name and phone number in the book just in case?" Barry called after me.

'Damn!' I thought. "Good idea," I said and hurried back to the couch. "Hm... I put it down to look out of the window. Um, now where did I put it?" Hoping to make my story convincing I took a few steps back and forth before reaching down to retrieve the book from the table. "Ah ... Here it is."

Barry inscribed it and I dropped it into my bag where it lay like a bloated whale beside my small toiletry purse.

"I think you'll like the book," Barry said as we hopped into his car. "It's about India. Have you been to India?"

"No," I said "... but I've been to Swan Hill." Barry grinned at my pun.

School broke up four days later and Barry's placement at Whittlesea Primary School ended. He was going to Europe with his wife during the holiday break and the following year he would begin teaching at a school about ten kilometres away.

It could have been the last time I ever saw Barry. But in March 1991 a letter appeared in my staff locker.

Waldene Private Lending Library

Dear Mrs Gunningham,
It has come to our attention that the following book:
"Midnight's Children" By S. Rushdie is now overdue.
We would like you to present yourself, your ideas and our book for dinner in the near future.

Yours sincerely,
Chief Librarian.

SLOWLY, SLOWLY

Roadside encounter

> *It was the best of times, it was the worst of times, It was the age of wisdom, it was the age of foolishness....*
>
> CHARLES DICKENS

Although I had every intention of returning Barry's book as soon as possible, the year had different plans for me.

January marked eleven years since my father's death and my mum had finally consented to move in with my family. Alec, mum and I had discussed this change for months and we all agreed she should live with us. She would be less lonely and feel safer under our roof. Also now I was teaching she would be a great back-up if I was running late, or the boys became sick at school and had to be picked up. Mum would live independently upstairs but would be welcome downstairs whenever she wanted to be with us.

I was so grateful Alec consented to my mum moving in. Historically mother-in-laws and son-in-laws are not good in confined spaces. But Alec and my mother had a central ground where they could meet - they both adored my sons, Heath and Blake.

Furniture was repositioned in various rooms of our house and an extension was planned. Part of the roof was removed and work began on the addition of a self-contained upstairs apartment to accommodate my mum.

When the school year commenced I was allocated my own classroom complete with twenty-eight students. It was exciting yet daunting to be totally responsible for this group's discipline and learning. I spent even longer preparing each day's lessons than in the previous year.

My father-in-law passed away in February. Special considerations in his will required my mother-in-law to sell their house. Her extended family took turns consoling her, helping her pack and driving her around to inspect potential rental properties.

When Barry's letter arrived in March requesting the return of his book I had neither the time nor the energy to do anything about it. Had he still been teaching at the same school as me, I could have simply popped the book into his staff locker with a brief note of thanks. But now his being at another school presented a dilemma. I temporarily placed the whole issue in my mental 'too hard basket.'

Second term began with me accompanying a hundred over-excited students on a week-long school camp. On my return, the builders were still disrupting my household and the search continued for a rental property deemed 'suitable' by my mother-in-law.

As I drove to school one day an oncoming car flashed its headlights in the time-honoured tradition of alerting other drivers to the presence of a police-car or speed camera on the road ahead. I slowed and concentrated on obeying all the road rules.

This 'headlight flashing' happened a few times in the next couple of weeks, suggesting there may be a police blitz in operation. Although I'd been looking, I hadn't yet actually seen a police car on the road. So the next time headlights flashed I slowed considerably in order to determine exactly where the speed camera or police car was located.

There was still nothing obvious to see. How annoying if someone was prank-flashing their lights. Perhaps it was just a cheap and easy tactic by police to get everyone to slow down.

The very next morning a car coming toward me flashed its lights. As there were no cars behind me, I slowed to a crawl in order to get a look at the culprit. To my surprise, the car lights flashed again and the car slowed and moved onto the verge of the road.

An unmarked police car – damn!

I pulled over and looking straight ahead, wound down the driver-side window and waited for the policeman to cross the road and walk back to me. Behind my car I heard the gravel crunch beneath footsteps.

"Hello, fancy meeting you here." Barry's grinning face appeared at my car window.

"Hi ... did you just flash your lights at me? Is there a speed camera up ahead?" I glanced back to confirm a policeman wasn't walking behind him.

Barry chuckled and straightened up. "Yes and no; yes I flashed my lights at you, and no, there's no speed camera as far as I know."

I relaxed, now knowing I wasn't going to be fined. I looked up at Barry. "It's funny because lots of cars have been flashing their lights on this stretch of road lately. Have you noticed? There must be a police speeding blitz around here somewhere."

"Mmm ... No, there's no police blitz." Barry shook his head, looked down at his shoes, tapped his fingers on the roof of my car and stared off down the road.

"Why would you say that?" My forehead wrinkled as I struggled to understand.

Barry turned his face toward me. "It was me. I've been sort of saying '*Hello*' whenever we drive past each other on the road in the morning. Didn't you recognise my car?"

I looked back at his car in my side-view mirror. "No. Why would I? It's just a car, a white car."

It was perhaps the first lesson Barry learnt about me. Raised in a family with little money and many mouths to feed, I'd learnt not to notice 'stuff'. I noticed people and emotions and words and actions – but objects, 'stuff,' didn't feature much on my Richter-scale.

My mum had silenced her family's requests for 'things' by repeatedly quoting 'I thought I was hard done by because I had no shoes until I met a man who had no feet.' The message had been absorbed into my psyche.

"It's a Holden Commodore and it's got a huge bull-bar on the front. How could you not have noticed the bull-bar at least?" Barry seemed slightly taken aback.

"What's a bull-bar?" I screwed up my face puzzled at the term. "You don't even own any bulls do you? Why would you have a bull-bar?"

Barry shook his head and scoffed in disbelief. "Anyway, I wondered if you'd finished reading the book yet."

Running my hand across my face, I pinched the skin into a wrinkled mess at my mouth. "Sorry. It's been a very busy few months. I meant to return it sooner but it's a bit hard now you've moved schools. But now I understand about the flashing lights I could give it to you on the way to school. You could just pull over."

My words tumbled out. I was embarrassed about not returning the book or even apologising before this. How awful Barry had been forced to attract my attention on the road in order to get his book back. It's pathetic to borrow things and not return them. Now here was me guilty of that very crime.

"Good idea. I don't have my diary with me, but some mornings I have to be at school early for meetings or yard duty so can't stop. Can you phone me at school tomorrow a bit before nine? I'll check my diary and let you know a day that suits. Okay?"

"Sure," I said, immediately worrying at the thought of phoning his school and asking for him. Surely they'd want to know who I was... and what would I say? Barry returned to his car and drove away. Starting my car, I turned the radio up and tried to ignore my concerns; tomorrow would come soon enough.

By next morning I had a solution. "Hello," I said into the phone, "I'd like to speak to my brother please - Mr Barry Johnston." I spoke quietly even though alone in the staffroom.

"Yes, I'll page him for you. His car's in the car park so he must be around somewhere - won't be a minute." A school announcement echoed down the phone-line requesting Mr Johnston come to the office.

"Hello Judith." Barry sounded surprised his sister would phone him at school.

"It's me, Sue. I wasn't sure who to say I was."

"You could have just said it was you." I sensed him holding back a chuckle.

"Yeah, sorry, I should have." Again I felt like an idiot.

"Anyway, I've checked my diary and I can be beside the road at the same place again tomorrow, but after school. I could be there about 4.15 pm. Will that work for you?"

"Sure... and I promise to bring the book."

"Good. I'm interested to hear what you thought about it."

His answer made me frown. Although I'd read the book, most of it had gone over my head. Hopefully Barry wasn't going to turn this into a 'book club discussion,' because it would be very one-sided and he'd soon realise he was dealing with a 'dill'.

"Okay, see you then. I'd better go - bell's about to ring." Hanging up the phone I took a deep breath. Oh well, all that remained was to return the book, have a brief chat, show my stupidity and then drive home and never see him again.

Barry's car was parked under a tree on my side of the road when I arrived to meet him after school the next day. He got out and went around and opened his passenger-side door.

"Hop in; may as well be out of the sun."

Sliding into the seat I was conscious of what people might think seeing two cars parked beside the road with a couple sitting together in one car. As teachers, we were both fairly recognisable to most of the locals, so hopefully our meeting would be short.

I passed the book across. "I can't stay long. My son starts secondary college next year and we're trying to decide where to enrol him. There's an information session tonight."

"How many children have you got?" My spirits sank at his question. The 'meeting' would not be short.

"Two - Two boys - Boys are best." It came out automatically. It was something I always said and I knew its truth.

Barry scoffed. "Why do you say that?"

I shrank a bit. "I only had uncles and brothers and now have sons. My mum and I were the only girls for three generations. But my mum was so proud to be a 'mother of sons.' Boys are best. She's right of course – boys aren't bitchy like girls. They're not deep and they laugh easily. They don't fuss and they get over things quickly - don't hold grudges. Yep, boys are best."

"Hmph," Barry looked through the windscreen considering my words. "Funny, I think it's a shame girls only get to choose a boy for a mate. Girls are so different to boys. Their pretty and studious, they try harder and keep their desks and books tidy. Boys are like puppies; rough and tumbling, not much committed to schoolwork. If I ever had a child I always thought I'd prefer to have a daughter than a son."

He looked down at the Rushdie book. "Did you like it?"

Here was the much dreaded conversation.

"Yeah it was interesting. I think you need to know a bit of history to understand it fully. It had some great phrases in it though. I copied some into my scrapbook."

"What scrapbook?" I hoped his question signalled the end of any further discussion of Mr Rushdie's prize-winning book.

I flushed. "Lots of people collect objects. I collect phrases... been doing it for years. If I read something wonderful it gets written in my scrapbook. Then at any time, I've got pages of amazing phrases to read. It's better than reading any one book really. Some things are so beautifully written you just want to read them over and over. They stand alone."

Barry tilted his head, watching me intently as I spoke and I wondered if he thought me ridiculous.

"One of the teachers at Whittlesea told me you used to be a journalist. I suppose that's why words fascinate you."

I shook my head. "No. I studied journalism at Uni for two years and worked casually on some newspapers for awhile. But I wasn't a *real* journalist."

"Still, you'd know how to write."

"Probably – a bit anyway."

"I'm hoping to write a history book. I've got a filing cabinet filled with research notes and documents, but can't work out where to begin, or how to set it out. Maybe you could give me some ideas?"

"I wouldn't be much help. I'm no good at history."

"You wouldn't have to be good at history. I just need some ideas about how to organise it all and where to begin."

Barry waited for me to answer.

"Mm, maybe." The conversation was now becoming awkward.

I reached for the door-handle. "... Better go; can't be late for the info night."

"Just a sec." Barry stretched into the back seat of his car. "I brought along this other book you might like to borrow. Herman Hesse – he's an amazing author. Have you heard of him?"

"No." This time I answered unenthusiastically, hoping to derail the book-borrowing practice.

Disregarding my effort completely Barry continued. "His books changed my life." I took the book from him, noting with some consolation that at least it was slimmer than the last one.

"Thanks. This one will be returned much quicker than the last." I hurried back to my car hoping all the while we hadn't been recognised together beside the road. Yet another borrowed book that would eventually need to be returned - Good grief! It reminded me of the Disney story 'The Sorcerer's Apprentice', where a misplaced spell produces an army of continually dividing mops that march on the errant apprentice, threatening to overwhelm him.

A few weeks later my lunch was interrupted when the bursar said there was a call for me on the staff-room phone.

"Hello, this is Sue Gunningham." A wave of panic swept through me - had one of my boys been in an accident?

"Hello. Can you just hang on a minute?" It was a male voice I didn't recognise.

There was shuffling and movement at the other end of the line. Then another male voice, "Hello, is that Sue?"

"Yes. Who's this? Is everything alright?"

"It's Barry." I spun around and stared at the noticeboard on the wall behind the phone. Over my shoulder I could hear the teachers mumbling as they read the paper and talked about their day so far. My ears strained to determine if Barry's wife, sitting at the far end of the staffroom table had somehow heard his voice on the phone.

"Oh." I felt the blood surge into my cheeks - guilt for again not having returned his book, now combined with the guilt implied by such a covert phone call.

Half covering the receiver with my hand, I tried to calm myself, already aware I was puffing with adrenalin in a 'flight or fight' response.

"I was wondering if you'd finished reading the Hermann Hesse book," - just a librarian querying an overdue book apparently.

"Yes. Thanks. Sorry. Bit slow returning again." Clipped sentences, whispered like a spy.

"I wondered if you'd come for dinner at Waldene. I'd like to talk to you about your writing and you could return the book then."

"Okay. When?" I replied, at the same time knowing it was impossible. I just wanted the call to end before anyone in the staff room guessed I was talking to Barry. There would be time later to work out how to get out of the dinner invitation.

"I'll send you some dates and you can let me know."

"Okay. Have to go now." I hung up the phone and left the staffroom immediately.

Back in the empty classroom my breathing finally calmed. I clasped my hands on the desk and studied my fingers, tried to empty my mind. But without warning, I grinned and a small shiver ran across my shoulders.

Lifting my clasped hands to my chin I chewed on my thumbnails and replayed the phone conversation in my head.

'He likes me.' Though whispered, the words seemed to reverberate around the room.

It had been a long time since a man had noticed me. I was a home-maker, a mum, a wife, a daughter and a teacher. I cooked, I cleaned, I shopped, I paid bills, I washed, and I taught. This routine was broken occasionally when I escaped for a few hours on a Sunday to wander around the art gallery while my husband and the boys played football or watched it on television. I saw myself more as a 'coat stand holding everyone's coats' so my family could live their lives unencumbered. I didn't think of myself as a person of interest.

'No,' my inner self said, 'he just wants his book back and some writing tips. Besides, we're both married, even if his marriage is weird. Anyway stop analysing everything. It was just a phone call asking for the return of his book. Pretty risky to phone me at school though - and who was the other guy who spoke on the phone first? What was he told to convince him to phone on Barry's behalf?' My mind ran on asking questions and examining this latest phone call from every angle. Mercifully the school bell rang leaving me no further time for reflection.

Over the next two weeks Barry flashed his headlights several times on my way to and from work. I started scanning the road ahead looking for his car with the now distinctive bull-bar.

Occasionally I even managed to return-flash my headlights or at least offered a timid wave as our cars drew level before passing each other. School broke up for the holidays and with a peculiar mixture of relief and something akin to disappointment, I realised Barry must've had second thoughts about his dinner invitation.

My holidays were filled with taking my sons to sports clinics and craft sessions. We went to the movies and had picnics in the back yard. It was my mother's first school holiday living in our house and she accompanied us with delight everywhere we went.

When school resumed in August an envelope appeared in my staffroom locker. It contained a hand-drawn map and a card.

The Lending Library will be available for the return of overdue books on the following evenings by appointment.

Tues 13 August
Monday 19 August
Tuesday 20 August
Thursday 22 August

I hope that you will avail yourself of these opportunities to make good your past sins. Your penalty will not be too severe if you act soon.

Your impatient
Chief Librarian

Breaking bread 1991

*A Jug of wine, a Loaf of bread – and Thou
Beside me singing in the Wilderness*

OMAR KHAYYAM

13 August 1991

Dear Sir,

I have received your memo and respond herewith. The borrower of the said book shall appear at the pre-determined location on Monday 19th to answer the charges referred to in your correspondence.

However, it is to be understood from the outset that the appearance of the borrower will render void any fine or penalty hereto intended by the borrowee.

The borrower will expect a repast between 5 and 6 pm and will be obliged to furnish beverages (alcoholic and non-alcoholic).

Respectfully,

Patron - Waldene Lending Library

Why did I have dinner with Barry at Waldene that night?

- *I owed him for being so kind to me when I started teaching*
- *I probably did know something about writing – small gift of thanks*

- *He was a gentleman and intelligent and interesting*
- *I don't know how to say 'No' (without offending)*
- *It was just dinner, three hours maximum (5 – 8 pm) then we could go back to 'Before'.*
- *It would be nice to just be fed without having to cook or clean-up*

Thinking it through, there were risks and I hoped it wasn't a ruse to lure me into trouble. But Barry seemed genuine – a gentleman and he'd only ever been kind to me. It seemed unfair to measure him against some ill-fitting stereotype of a 'bloke on the prowl'.

In any case, I was a little thrilled to think he valued my writing skills – even if they were in reality, fairly minimal.

I told Alec I'd been asked to help one of the teachers with some writing and he and his wife had asked me for an early dinner at their house after school. Alec accepted the story without question.

Recently Alec had started guest speaking at night to various charity groups to raise funds to for sporting equipment for the juveniles he worked with. Guilt caused by his easy acceptance of my lie caused me to ask, "Will you be home for dinner that night, because I can get mum to feed the boys if you're going to be out."

"What night? Did you say Tuesday?"

"Yeah."

He thought for a minute then said, "No, that's fine. I'll be home. I'll cook dinner for the boys and me.... might buy some fish. I'll cook some for your mum too." I flinched. Whenever he cooked fish the house smelt for days afterwards. I'm not a fish eater, so rather than my absence being an issue, it instead provided menu possibilities.

On Tuesday night, following the hand-drawn map I drove up through the hills to Waldene. I opted to park on the roadside and walk down the steep driveway. Fighting a rising sense of fear I stumbled and staggered down the rocky surface in search of Barry and his fairy-tale cottage.

A soft orange glow issued from the kitchen window indicating life inside. I walked past Barry's car parked on the small landing near the front door and stepped down onto the paved porch. Given the isolated location of the cottage, it was surprising Barry hadn't heard me parking. I pulled the Hesse book from my carry-bag to be sure to return it.

After knocking softly at the door, I stepped back. From inside the house came a sudden flurry of sound and soon Barry's face peered out through the small leadlight panel set into the door.

"Who's there?" he called out playfully, his face blurry behind the bevelled glass.

"It's me – Sue."

The door flung open. "I'm glad you could come." Barry's voice was softer now, almost shy, as if the door between us had been his shield.

"Here's your book. It was a good read. Thanks," I pushed the book toward him, hoping this might negate the need for a further book–club chat.

He ushered me into the kitchen where the smell of curry filled the air. Over in the lounge area the doors to the firebox stood open and a fire blazed in the grate. The room was warm, the glow of gas-lighting adding to its cosiness.

Again I wondered if Barry's wife was somewhere in the house. Perhaps they no longer lived together but maybe she'd also be here tonight. Being too shy to ask directly I decided to wait and see if she appeared from somewhere.

"You said you like curry, so that's what we're having. Hope that's alright with you."

"Great! I love curried sausages." I was amazed he'd remembered me saying anything about curry.

"Umh ... well... actually." Barry hesitated. "It's not curried sausages. It's beef curry – diced beef. Is that okay?" he asked, a hint of worry flashing across his face.

Inside I shrank, ashamed because my family's meat budget rarely stretched beyond ground mince and sausages. "Sure." I tried to sound unfussed.

"I grind my own mix of spices and herbs for the curry. Learned how to in India. What do you use to make your curry?" It was obvious Barry had asked the question to start a conversation, establish a common ground between us.

Good grief, I thought, a cooking conversation - best to just get it over quickly by telling the truth.

"Clive of India curry powder – you just open the lid and shake it on. Too easy."

"Really?" Barry paused for a moment as if waiting for me to laugh. When he realised I was serious, he laughed instead. "Fair enough," he shrugged and directed me towards the couch.

"Wait a minute. I brought some stuff for you, well for the dinner really."

I swung a plastic supermarket bag onto the kitchen counter and began to unload its contents.

"There's some lemon mineral water – I know you don't drink alcohol ... and some pate ... do you like pate? ... And some dry biscuits." Foraging in the large carry bag on my shoulder, I extracted a bottle and plonked it beside the groceries. "... And some champagne."

My eyes ran over my little pile of offerings on Barry's neat, navy-tiled servery bench. They'd seemed a good idea when bought. But now, in the mellow light cast by the fire and the gas lamps and surrounded by the stunning smell of beef curry made with hand-ground spices, my gifts seemed drab and wretched.

I glanced at Barry - wished I could grab the items back from his view.

He looked at my offerings then his eyes swept up to mine where he no doubt sensed my shame. "Thanks. I didn't know you liked pate or I'd have brought some. Will I open these for us to have now?" He picked up the pate and the biscuits.

"That'd be great" I said turning toward the couch.

"I've got a very chilled bottle of champagne in the fridge. It's colder than yours. Would you like a glass of that or will I open your bottle?" I was grateful to Barry for handling my pathetic offering so tactfully.

"A cold champagne would be great. Thanks."

From my position on the couch I faced the dining room table. It was set for two, so his wife wouldn't be joining us after all. Polished steel cutlery flanked the two thick white dinner plates. A bowl lined with a white linen napkin held some crispy dinner rolls. Alongside the rolls, a clay pot was filled with butter, its burst of yellow so bright compared to the insipid colour of the margarine at my house. In the centre of the table, two tall candles flanked a glass vase containing a tiny bunch of native violets.

Holding a cut-crystal goblet up to the light, Barry inspected it, before producing a bottle of champagne costing double the price of the bottle I'd brought. I watched the wine splash into the goblet. It sparkled as the fire-light bounced off wafer-thin shards of ice floating within. He came across to the couch, a platter bearing the pate and biscuits in one hand, and the wine in the other.

"Here you are m'lady." He handed me the glass and put the platter on a large, solid coffee table. The goblet was freezing in my hand. I took a sip and was startled when the cold, cold wine seared across my tongue and down my throat, leaving the ice-shards in its wake. Barry turned a chair from the dining room table and sat down to face me. I took another gulp of wine to steady my nerves.

"Beautiful fire.." I gazed into the flames and wondered how the lion-sentries on the firebox doors felt about this invasion of their territory.

Barry nodded. "So - you were a journalist?"

"No… I didn't finish the degree. I worked on local newspapers a bit, but I was a mum with a toddler and then I got pregnant again. I had to leave the course. It operated like an apprenticeship. No industry job, no study."

"But you've been published?"

Hm," I nodded, feeling a bit uncomfortable. It was like a job interview and I made me wish I hadn't come.

Barry stared into the fire - the weight of his silence on my shoulders. I could at least make an effort. "… Just local paper stuff – local government bungles, the biggest cabbage in the annual cabbage festival, innovations at playgroup, hat parades at primary school – just rubbish. My shining hour as a writer was having my poetry published in my dad's army magazine. At least that mattered. It made my dad proud."

"Do you write poetry as well?" His question took me by surprise, as if I was a rarity.

"Badly," I sighed. "Everyone writes tragic, black poetry in their teenage years. It's like a rite of passage isn't it?

But once when watching the ANZAC Day parade on TV my boyfriend, who's now my husband, said something disparaging about the men marching. What he said made me angry so I wrote a poem about my feelings for my dad and all the men who'd marched. You see in my house it was a family tradition to watch the march on TV every year. Mum'd get us kids together in the lounge and we'd wait and wait for my Dad's battalion flag to come into view, then we'd all search the faces on the screen looking for him. Sure enough – he'd appear. He was always smiling. Mum said the cameras picked him out because he was so handsome."

I looked down at the glass in my hand so Barry wouldn't see the sheen of tears in my eyes.

"Probably sounds crazy but, I knew he'd won the war," I continued. "And secretly, as a little girl, I believed he'd done it single-handedly. I thought he was wonderful. There was no doubt in my mind why the cameras always filmed him." I rubbed one eye quickly to prevent a tear escaping.

"Anyway I wrote a poem to put my boyfriend in his place - poured out all my pride and gratitude for the ANZACS. Later when my dad read it, he cried. Then unbeknown to me he took it and read it to all the men at his next battalion meeting. They asked my dad if they could print it in their magazine. The next year they asked me for another one. I was so glad to be able to do that for my dad."

I stopped talking and stared at the fire, unable to go on. The silence grew louder.

"It's a nice memory," Barry said quietly and I could tell he was moved by my story. But whether it was about my dad, or the poetry, or a little girl's belief in her dad's ability, or the teenage girl who wrote in her dad's defence, I wasn't sure. He jumped up and went into the kitchen and began banging saucepans around.

"Do you need any help?" I asked, hoping he'd say no, because I wasn't much of a cook.

"No. But I'll pour you another wine and you can sit to the table if you like. Dinner's ready." He appeared around the corner of the servery holding the bottle of champagne.

Over dinner Barry explained he'd been the secretary of the Draft Resistor Union when the Australian government was conscripting boys to fight in Vietnam.

"They gaoled me for a week in 1971 for failing to register for national service, and again in 1972 for refusing to attend an army medical. I spent ten months in hiding before Whitlam won the 1972 election and abolished conscription."

"A gaol-bird-eh?" I was a bit shocked to find Barry had been this much involved in the conscription battle.

"Yeah – only two weeks inside though, thanks to the election outcome." Barry scoffed and sat back in his chair. "I've got all the meeting minutes and papers from the Draft Resistors Union. That's the history book I want to write and hope you can give me some tips on where to start."

His request embarrassed me. My writing experience was limited, but he still seemed to believe I knew something that could help him. I tried to think of lessons from my Journalism course. Perhaps there was something there to share with him that would be useful. I couldn't remember learning anything about compiling historical accounts, but I didn't want to sound like a complete moron.

"Well, it seems like it will unfold chronologically, so really you just need to start writing. Pick one key date in the history and write all that happened that day. Keep doing that for key days and eventually you'll have written everything you need to say. The writing's the hardest part. Then you lay the pages/days on the floor and study them and themes/chapters will start to emerge. The main thing is to start writing."

I lifted a cube of beef to my mouth, hoping to signify the end of the lesson.

"Perhaps." Barry didn't sound convinced, but by now my 'river' of writing tips had run dry.

"Tell me about Herman Hesse and his books," I said in an effort to shift the topic.

We discussed Hesse and other authors we each enjoyed. Barry described reading Biggles adventures as a young boy and I spoke about the sadness I always felt when imagining (the Great) Gatsby watching the green light on his lover's jetty across the bay.

I mentioned '*The Seven Minutes*,' a book I'd just finished reading. "It was full of arguments and counter-arguments about what constitutes pornographic writing and whether it should be banned and lots of stuff about censorship in general. It really made me think."

Barry felt adults should be free to read whatever they wanted, while I was adamant that pornographic text should be banned. We debated the issue back and forth. It was wonderful to engage in a substantial conversation and I learnt a lot about Barry's attitudes and beliefs. We even found laughter in each other's arguments.

"It's impossible to have a proper debate with you." Barry said at one stage, his arms uplifted in mock frustration. "You don't follow the rules of debating. You go off on tangents."

"Rules of debating? That's teacher-talk! You've just invented debating rules 'cause you're losing the argument." I took a sip of champagne, my eyes laughing at him over the edge of the glass.

"You're supposed to challenge the facts presented, not bring up some crazy, vaguely-related idea that's just popped into your head. That's not a debate."

"Who made you the 'debating boss'? I can say new stuff if I suddenly think of it." I didn't have a clue about the rules of debating but was enjoying the banter immensely.

When Barry left the table to prepare dessert I could see myself in the reflection of the window behind his empty chair. Caught in the candle-light my face was glowing and my eyes were large and shining with excitement. The pine panelling behind me was suffused with the warm red glow from the fire. I looked like an enchanted character in a fairy-story.

"Anyway," Barry asked as he spooned ice-cream into bowls, "... why the book is called *The Seven Minutes*?"

"Mm ... well ...," I paused trying to gauge the direction the conversation might take following my answer.

Seeing my hesitation, Barry stopped mid-serving and stared across at me waiting for a response.

"Well ... the core of the story is a woman's description of what she felt both emotionally and physically during sex and orgasm. That's the seven minutes. Then a publisher prints the book and a bookseller sells it. And a legal battle ensues about pornography and who in the chain can, or should be charged."

I was shocked I'd said the word 'orgasm' aloud. I'd never said it before.

Barry nodded, said nothing and resumed spooning ice-cream.

"It's fiction of course - but interesting all the same." I looked across to the fire and lapsed into an awkward silence.

"Seven minutes?" Barry posed the question without looking up.

"Mm." I glanced across at him.

He nodded slowly as if pondering something, nodded again almost imperceptibly and said nothing more. I could sense an unspoken question hanging in the air. I looked back at the fire and Barry returned to spooning ice-cream.

He carried the dessert across to the table. "I hope you like apple crumble."

I breathed a sigh of relief and asked about the ingredients, knowing I was unlikely to remember them or ever attempt to replicate his dessert.

After dinner Barry told me about his life in the forest. He described the local wildlife and how peaceful it was to sit on the banks of a creek in the valley below his cottage. His description was beautiful – almost whimsical. It was hard to believe there could be such a wondrous place.

He took me around the cottage to show me some of the souvenirs he'd bought overseas and to describe the heritage of his antique furniture. In his bedroom he picked up a small wire birdcage on top of the dresser. Placing it on the opened palm of one hand, he held it toward me. Inside the cage a tiny metal bird was perched on a swing.

"I bought it in India from a street-stall. The stall-holder told me it was a puzzle."

Shrugging I stared at the cage harder trying to work out what the puzzle might be.

"He said" - Barry assumed an old Indian man's accent.

'You see, the bird he is so small.
He can fit through the bars on the cage.
He knows.'

At this Barry looked up at me and smiled. He held the little cage closer for me to see it better. Then he continued in the old man's voice.

'He knows.
He knows he can be free if he wants.
But he doesn't want to.
He wants to stay in the cage.
Funny yes?

Barry looked at the cage as if remembering the old man. "Then," Barry continued, "...the old man said" –

'He can be free,
But he chooses to stay.
... Like love maybe?'

"It's a beautiful story," I said, staring in at the tiny bird.

Placing the cage back on the dresser Barry grinned. "Yeah, well he probably just made it up to help him sell a poorly-made tourist souvenir. But I bought it anyway, for the story more than the cage itself.

We wandered out to the front porch to see the spectacle of the stars in the ink-black sky and hear the creek rushing along the valley. We stood perfectly still at one end of the brick porch listening.

Standing behind me, Barry reached across my shoulder to point out the direction of the creek. I could smell the wool of his jumper and feel the brush of his arm against my back. His large hand and strong fingers stretched out in front of me.

"The sound comes up through there, where the creek bends around a curve in the hill." Barry's voice sounded deep and haunting in the darkness.

It was a struggle to refocus my senses; to listen for the creek. Almost too scared to breathe, I could hear my heart beating, hear Barry listening, and sense him behind me, watching.

"Can you hear it?"

"Yes. And I can see all the stars and taste the air. It's amazing here."

We stood for a few minutes of silence until I shivered slightly.

"We'd better go back in," Barry said, "It's getting cool out here now."

Stepping back into the kitchen I glanced at the large wall clock. "My God, it's seven-thirty! I'm due home by eight; have to go. Sorry." Grabbing my carry-bag, I thanked him for dinner, apologised for not doing the dishes and headed for the door.

Barry followed me. "Where's your car?" he said looking around outside.

"Up on the road... didn't think I'd be able to drive down the driveway or back up again for that matter."

'Wait. I'll get my keys and drive you up." Without waiting for my answer, he disappeared back into the house, only to emerge a few seconds later carrying his keys and a book.

"Another Herman Hesse," he said, handing the book across to me as he unlocked the car. "Seeing you liked the last one I thought you might like to read another."

"Great - thanks." And this time I meant it.

At the end of the week another card arrived in my staff mailbox.

25 August 1991

Even Cinderella didn't run away until the clock struck twelve...and she left a glass slipper – not a plastic container of cracked pepper pate. It <u>was</u> good to see you again.

Your Librarian

Technology

> *The least of things with a meaning,*
> *is worth more in life than the greatest*
> *of things without it*
>
> CARL JUNG

A few weeks later six teachers from Barry's small school came to attend a teacher professional development morning at Whittlesea Primary. I wasn't looking forward to being in the same room with Barry and his wife and hoped he wouldn't mention my recent visit to Waldene. It was impossible for me to gauge what his wife knew of our harmless dinner meeting.

The facilitator of the program divided all the teachers into two teams and we moved to the large open space of the Art room. On the floor in the centre of the room was heaped a mountain of Lego blocks and tiny plastic toys. We were to learn team-building and use team-work to create a model structure to engage primary school children.

When I looked up from examining the pile of plastic on the floor, Barry winked at me from his position in the opposing team. Embarrassed, I turned to listen to what the self-appointed leader of my group had decided we would build. There was a time limit on the activity and one could sense the typical pressure 'to win' as our male leader spoke.

Across the room the other team were all talking over each other, interspersed every now and then by the easily recognisable deep timbre of Barry's voice. He spoke slowly and calmly and the other voices quietened as he spoke.

Meanwhile our team leader was still trying to come up with a winning idea. The rest of us stood around waiting for his decision and his instructions.

I glanced at the other team. Barry was on the floor sorting Lego into coloured piles. Others had formed into pairs and were discussing and negotiating the different heights of some sort of repeated structure they intended building as part of their overall design.

"A zoo!" our team leader finally announced with great excitement. "All kids love a zoo. And look there are some animals in the pile." He gestured to the mountain of plastic material.

"Sue and Leigh, you grab all the animals you can get. Think zoo!" Pleased not to have been paired with Barry's wife for this task, I crouched down and Leigh and I frantically plucked plastic animals from the pile. On the other side Barry calmly collected building blocks and put them into colour co-ordinated piles.

I sensed his smile, sensed him somehow a victor already.

The timekeeper soon announced both teams should by now have started building. As directed by our team leader my team had collected animals, building blocks, and some plastic swings, slides and fences. Now we waited for him to explain our next step.

"An outside wall - make a square enclosure!" The team did their best but our walls were too high, too low. They didn't match. The sides of the square were irregular. They didn't meet up. We built and trialled and corrected and re-corrected. We hung monkeys precariously from thin plastic straws and propped ladders against irregular walls. We erected fences between three lions and a hippopotamus and added a stunted, somewhat broken plastic tree for 'authenticity'. The time-keeper sounded the alarm and each team stood beside their structure.

Our 'zoo' was incomplete; more caged than free-range, more like a box than something kids would gravitate towards. Our team leader was asked to describe the concept behind our design. He explained how good it could have been if we'd had more time, more animals, more props. He sounded pathetic, just like our zoo.

But he was probably right. It was almost impossible to construct anything much with so many people in the team, so little equipment and such a small amount of imagination or time.

Meanwhile Barry's team stood beside a small castle complete with turrets, each one a different colour. A narrow walking platform ran around the top of the turrets, and here and there a small soldier stood on alert. A huge opening in one wall of the structure housed a gangplank made of blocks and held by string.

Barry volunteered to explain his team's structure. "It's the castle of a fair princess ... perhaps Cinderella," he said, and I blushed. The innuendo of his team's creation under his instructions was not lost on me.

"She walks daily around the turrets to speak to the guards on watch. She tells them fairy stories she's read and she sometimes brings them treats to eat. The guards in this palace are partial to cracked pepper pate and champagne." Everyone laughed. Barry smiled and his eyes swept over my team. I bit my lip and stared down at my feet.

He continued. "The draw-bridge to the castle is always open to welcome villagers into the palace but it can also be lifted to protect the princess from the outside world if needed." One of the teachers pulled on a string and the drawbridge lifted to block entry to the castle.

It was a beautiful story and the castle would be attractive to all the little girls at the primary school, while the functioning drawbridge and the turrets, from which the guards could shoot, would delight the boys. It was a perfect solution to the challenge set by the curriculum coordinator.

I glanced at the other team who were all flushed with pride at their creation. My eyes were drawn to Barry and he nodded ever so slightly.

At the end of the day I joined the teachers traipsing out to the car park and was surprised to see Barry walking alongside his wife. He was carrying her basket of books and papers and they were talking to each other as they walked. I slowed my pace to keep a distance between us. They stopped at her car and she unlocked the doors. Barry lent in and placed the basket on the front passenger seat as his wife slid into the driver's seat. They mumbled something to each other and Barry stood up, his fingers resting on the car roof.

Noticing me walking across the car park Barry grinned at me. His wife spoke and he bent down to answer her. I took the opportunity to get into my car and drive away. Here was proof he and his wife were still in a relationship.

A feeling of sadness settled over me. Driving home I chastised myself for feeling that way when I should be grateful the pressure was now off. Barry's actions towards me were obviously motivated by his general kindness. There was no need for me to keep analysing every conversation we had. I could rid myself of any further guilt and go back to what I was 'before'. 'Before what'? I wondered. Shrugging, I opened the car windows fully hoping the breeze would blow some sense into my head.

No room at the inn

You never can tell whether bad luck may not after all turn out to be good luck.

WINSTON CHURCHILL

Only two weeks remained of the school term. My family was booked to go to Hawaii for part of the holidays and my time after school was filled with getting our clothes, passports and travel arrangements organised. There was no time to even read the last book Barry had lent me, so I was free of any angst in relation to engineering its return.

In the staffroom his wife told other teachers about the travel plans she and Barry were making for the Christmas break. I'd discerned they lived in separate houses - she with teenage children from a previous marriage and Barry alone at Waldene, but couldn't understand their relationship. Barry continued to flash his car-lights at me on the way to or from work and I would wave as we passed.

In late October, my son Heath went on his final primary school camp and preparations began in earnest for his primary school graduation ceremony and his secondary school orientation days. My diary overflowed with the details of concerts, parent information nights, twilight events, Christmas functions, presentations and award ceremonies. While some of diary entries were mine, other handwriting showed where my mother and Alec organised their life through me and my availability.

The Whittlesea students' graduation evening was scheduled for Monday 16th December and as the date drew closer I was once again confronted with the dilemma of whether to drive home after school and risk making it back to Whittlesea by 6 pm, or stay at school and get changed there.

I contemplated phoning Barry to ask if there was a possibility of me coming to Waldene like last year's graduation night. But given we hadn't spoken since August and I hadn't returned his last book, I was reluctant to phone him.

However a few days before the graduation date, I left home half an hour earlier on the pretext of having some urgent paperwork to complete before school. My plan was to phone Barry from the staffroom in the hopes he would be at work by then.

There were only a couple of cars in my school car park when I arrived and the staffroom was empty. Closing the door, and with my heart in my throat I dialled Barry's school. A male answered.

"Hello, I wonder if I might speak to Mr Johnston. It's Sue Gunningham from Whittlesea Primary school." I tried to sound as if my time was limited, with barely enough for this inter-school conversation. I held my breath, hoping not to be asked the purpose of my call.

"Sure. No worries Sue. I'll get him for you." The phone clicked and I was put on 'hold'.

The clock on the staffroom wall showed 8.15 am. Teachers would begin drifting in any minute now. A nervous tremor ran through me and I turned to face the wall behind the phone, silently urging the go-between to be fast in his search for Barry. Another click on the phone.

"Hello. This is a lovely surprise." Barry's voice was warm and sunny.

"Hi. Sorry to bother you."

I felt my face flush. It was one thing to wave from the safety of my car, but quite another to actually be speaking to him again.

"No bother. What can I do for you?"

My courage began to ebb. Better make my request quickly while still brave enough.

"It's the Year 6 graduation next Monday and I wondered if there was any chance I could just lob at your place after school like last year? No problem if it's inconvenient. Just thought I'd ask in case it's a possibility. I could return your book."

'Lob?' Why did I say that? I never say 'lob'. Why would someone ever say 'lob'?

Then in an apologetic voice I added, "Sorry I've still got your book. Everything's been such a rush lately I just haven't had a chance."

Nerves had caused me to speak too quickly and I felt myself panting when I'd finished talking. I regretted mentioning the book. It sounded like a plot, as if using the potential of its return as a lever to obtain a 'Yes' to my request.

"Is that the 16th of December?" Thankfully Barry didn't appear to have misinterpreted my request as some sort of ploy.

"Yes - next Monday the 16th." I gripped the phone a bit harder, closed my eyes. 'You shouldn't have phoned him,' my inner voice whispered.

There was an intake of air at Barry's end of the line and his voice sounded a little louder, as if he was holding the receiver closer to his mouth.

"Sorry. I'm not home that night. I promised to go to a mate's daughter's end-of-year dance concert. I go every year. Wish you'd phoned earlier; I wouldn't have gone to the concert if I'd known you wanted to come to my place."

This seemed an overly generous response and I opened my eyes and hunched my shoulders in embarrassment. "It's okay. No problem. Just thought I'd ask. I've got other options."

Now, I just wanted to end the conversation.

Obviously he was only being polite. I didn't figure anywhere in his life and there was no reason he would have been thinking about the dilemma I faced at this time last year. Clearly he hadn't given me another thought since the 'Cinderella' castle-building activity.

Voices sounded out in the corridor. I was terrified Barry's wife would come into the staffroom and find me on the phone to him.

"Anyway, better go. The mob's just arrived." I tried to sound unfazed.

'The mob? Who says 'the mob'? Farmers! Good grief, I was bordering on ridiculous.'

There was a brief silence before Barry spoke. 'Sure. Sorry I couldn't help. And don't worry about the book. I know you'll return it." His voice was quiet, soft.

"No problem. Have a good day." I cringed, recognising my sign-off words as those used by vacuous attendants at fast food outlets.

I hung up the phone and wriggled to loosen the tension in my shoulders and neck. Standing perfectly still for a few moments, I stared at the three blood-red zeroes on the emergency services pamphlet pinned on the wall behind the phone. The lettering was solid and serious.

'Zero - zero - zero' - they seemed to yell at me. I felt emotionally exhausted yet the day had hardly begun.

After school on graduation night I changed in the staff toilets and sat alone in the empty staffroom until it was time to leave for the dinner. While waiting, my thoughts returned to the nervous time spent at Barry's this night the previous year and I convinced myself how very fortunate it was to have been saved the distress of having to go through all 'that' again. In fact, I told myself, the events had unfolded in a way to achieve the most sensible outcome.

The morning after the graduation an envelope was waiting in my staff mailbox. The handwriting on the Christmas card inside was firm and flowing. The words brought a smile to my lips.

17 Dec 1991

Dear Cinderella,
Imagine my excitement and then my utter depression after your telephone call. Still I must struggle on... the possibility of another meeting exists.
I will probably last until February (March, April, etc, etc.) ... or will I?

Best wishes,
Your personal Librarian

I didn't see Barry again that year.

THE HUNT

Flying blind

> *The eye sees all,*
> *But the mind shows us what we want to see.*
>
> WILLIAM SHAKESPEARE

The school year began with all the excitement and worry that besets every teacher confronted with a roomful of children entrusted to their care. We hope in the months ahead we will nurture them, teach them and make a difference to them. Every year of my teaching career I have felt equally humbled and overwhelmed by the parents' faith in me.

I thought of myself more as a mum than a teacher; albeit an easy-going mum with curiosity, an enthusiasm for learning, a bias for laughter and an enormous dollop of whimsy.

The drive from my home to Whittlesea allowed me the joy of travelling from built-up suburbs to seemingly endless fields, where lazy cows stood chewing their cud and sheep slept in pools of shade beneath scrappy, eucalypt trees. I often stopped along the roadside for a few minutes to soak in the view and take in the peace of the rural landscape. Although on the map my school was only about 20 kilometres from my home, in reality it may as well have been on another planet. Everything out here seemed calmer and offered more space – to think, to be, to just breathe.

Driving different routes to work every day, allowed me to sometimes drive between the 'dancing' trees flanking Plenty Road and at other times around the back roads, past the huge, frightening expanse of the Yan Yean Reservoir.

Here on summer mornings a thousand crystal eyes sparkled across the water's surface.

One morning a large billboard had been nailed to a lamp-post along the main road. Bold black letters declared:

Cinderella –
the book?

It was no doubt the 'teaser' advertisement for the upcoming drama production to be staged by the private school a few kilometres further along the road.

One of my past Year Six students had played the role of 'Oliver' in 'Oliver Twist' in his first year at a private secondary school. He'd sent me a ticket and on the night of the performance I'd sat enthralled throughout. Although the boy had been a student in my class for twelve months I hadn't realised he could sing like an angel.

When the performance ended I was both so proud of him and so ashamed of myself. Pushing a bunch of flowers into his hands I told him through tear-glazed eyes how amazing he was, then hurried away into the darkness of the car park to conceal my embarrassment.

Now here was an advertisement for this year's performance. Hopefully I wouldn't receive another ticket from an ex-student as it might mean seeing yet another hidden talent I'd failed to unmask during their time with me. I made a mental note to include more drama in my curriculum, maybe some music and dance as well. Probably best to cover all bases.

Just before the end of term not only did Barry flash his lights at me on the way to school, but he put his indicator on and pulled over to the side of the road. Puzzled, I pulled over too. Barry did a u-turn and parked behind me. He walked around to my passenger side door and bent down to grin at me through the window before hopping in beside me. It was the first time he'd been in my car and immediately I felt awkward and worried about us being seen together.

"Hi," I said, trying to sound casual.

"Hello." His tone seemed a bit formal, with a hint of anger. "I left you a sign. Did you get it?"

"Hmm ... a sign? When? No... I didn't get a sign. What did it say?" I felt like an idiot. Surely I would have noticed a sign if he'd sent one to me. My habit was to clear my inbox in the staffroom every day. There had been no sign. My heart froze momentarily. Maybe his sign had been put in someone else's inbox. Damn him! He had no right to send me a sign.

"On the lamp-post - it said 'Cinderella - the book?' Didn't you notice it?" Barry watched as I tried to grasp his meaning.

"Oh my God - sorry. I thought it was the name of a play. Didn't realise it was meant for me."

While speaking, my thoughts split into two threads: How could I not have realised the huge sign with its salient message was directed at me and the last unreturned book? Yet at the same time, why would I think the sign related to me, when in my entire life, no-one had ever gone to such trouble to attract my attention?

Seeing my anguish, Barry offered a solution. "Come for dinner again. You can return the book then."

It was embarrassing to be late returning yet another book. Now the situation had become even more complicated. The fields stretched out beyond the car window and the cows chewed on unperturbed. Inside the car I tried to calm down, think sensibly. The passing traffic seemed full of prying eyes that could bear witness to the two of us sitting next to each other in my tiny car.

Then before I could stop myself I said, "Thanks. I'd like that." My God, what a stupid thing to say! How can that even happen?

"What about next Thursday?" Barry suggested. "You could come straight from school and we could have an early dinner. I'd still like to talk to you about my 'Draft Resisters' book and you could bring the Hesse book back."

Feeling somewhat like a drowning woman I scribbled the date Barry had suggested into my notebook. "Sorry it's taken me so long to return your book. It's just that ..." I mumbled.

Barry spoke over me. "No problem. It'll be great to have you and the book back at Waldene again." He opened the car door and hopped out. "See you next Thursday," he said, drumming lightly on my car's roof before returning to his car.

The days passed too quickly and on the allotted Thursday I drove to Waldene, this time determined to refuse any further attempts by Barry to lend me another book. My plan was to return the current book, have a meal and leave as soon as manners would allow. That would be the end of it.

The end of what? I pondered. 'Well certainly the end of the guilt and the fear we'll be discovered. 'We?' We're not a *we* - merely two colleagues sharing a meal and a conversation. What is there to be *discovered*? Why do I feel so guilty? If Barry was a woman this would be a lovely intellectual friendship... but he's a man, and men are always a bit suspect.' My mind rambled on.

It was a relief when Barry's driveway came into view on the side of the road. My inner voice fell silent to be replaced by a rising sense of happiness. Barry's car was parked down near the front door. As I approached the cottage, the door flew open and Barry stood there grinning. "Right on time," he called out. It was obvious he'd been waiting and was delighted to see me.

Once again he treated me to an amazing meal and wine, and our conversation roamed from books, to writing, travel, history and music. We both seemed to have been storing an ocean of thoughts and images, reflections and information within us, waiting to find someone to talk with. Our conversation went on and on without pause.

After three hours I stood up to go. "Please don't lend me any more books. I'm an unreliable borrower and the pressure of not returning them to you is too stressful for me."

Barry jumped to his feet. "But I don't mind waiting. I know you'll look after them and eventually return them."

"No, please. It's just too stressful and I feel guilty for taking so long to get them back to you. Please don't lend me anymore."

Barry looked disappointed, but accepted my request.

"Thanks, it was a wonderful evening," I said. "I hope I didn't talk too much." It was difficult to know what to say now our time together was over.

"Not at all; it was wonderful to be able to talk with someone who's interested in something outside of schoolwork. I had a great night too."

Barry walked me up the long driveway to my car and stood watching me drive away. On the way home I convinced myself this was the best outcome for everyone. It was good no-one had been hurt by the brief friendship between Barry and me and now everything could go back to how it was before.

Each morning when Barry flashed his lights at me on the road I felt a little sad our friendship was reduced to a small wave as we passed each other. But it was for the best.

The day after the May Day Rally there was a letter waiting for me in my staff inbox.

Inside the envelope was a bright red May Day ribbon bearing the words:

A Socialist World – Yes
U.S New World Order - No

An accompanying single page computer-printed letter conveyed the following message.

Sorry I missed you at the march on Sunday.
I looked all around for you, but the crowd was too large.

Your librarian.

I sent Barry a short thank you note, pleased he'd remembered my family's political bent toward socialism.

A few days later I saw Barry walking along the road side after school. When I pulled over he explained his car was being serviced in Whittlesea and he'd walked the five kilometres from the service station to his school that morning and was now walking back.

I insisted on driving him to his car and he happily swung into my passenger seat. "Read any good books lately?" he asked cheekily by way of a conversation starter.

"No time," I said shooting him a sideway glance. "What about you?"

"Yeah a few. I've been looking at books similar to the one I want to write about the Draft Resistor's Union. Still can't work out how it should be set out." He paused as if waiting for me to suggest something. "I never did show you my collection of photos and documents about that time did I?"

"No. On my last time we talked non-stop but we didn't get to those. Anyway, you know I wasn't a real journalist so I'm not much use to you."

"Still, I'd appreciate your help. Perhaps you could come for a couple of hours and have a look at the collection and make some suggestions? Wouldn't have to be for dinner if you didn't want; but it'd be great to get your opinion."

"Sounds like a 'Come up to my room and look at my etchings' type of offer," I laughed, immediately regretting my words.

"No - seriously. I really want to write the history but haven't got a clue where to start."

We'd arrived at the service station and Barry lingered in the car for a moment. "What do you think? Can you help me?"

"Let me think on it," I said in an effort to end the conversation.

Next day when I was patrolling the school front fence doing lunch-time yard duty, a passing car honked its horn. Startled I spun around to see Barry driving slowly past the school. He smiled and waved to me.

For the rest of the week, Barry honked to me as I patrolled the fence at lunch-time. It was becoming embarrassing so I was glad when the roster ended and my area changed to a different part of the yard away from the road.

Another envelope in my inbox - my name and school address typed in the same Apple computer font Barry always used. This envelope contained one typed page and one hand illustrated and coloured piece of thick parchment paper. The illustration depicted a burning candle, and some tangled ivy draped across the text '*10 long weeks!*' Cobwebs had been drawn hanging from the text' and across the bottom of the page was drawn a golden chain. In the lower right hand corner of the parchment were two small kisses.

The typed page had been printed using a mediaeval font.

Dearest Princess,
The days have become weeks and now are becoming months, since you last graced my humble residence. That night lives on in my unworthy heart yet I greedily seek further communion....
I beseech thee to grant my request at thy convenience, but prior to Christmas this year please.

Yours respectfully
The Librarian.

Soon after, the bursar summoned me to a phone-call in the staff room. The mysterious stranger from before asked again, "Is that Sue?" before passing the phone to Barry.

"Hello, I wondered if you've thought anymore about helping me with writing the history book."

A mix of fear and delight went through me. Was he genuinely wanting my help or was this a ruse? He didn't seem like a predator and the few times I'd been to Waldene he'd always behaved with the utmost decorum. Maybe like me, he'd enjoyed our conversations so much and just wanted someone he could talk with. There was no doubt he lived an almost hermit-like existence in the forest.

It was also true the conversation we'd shared last visit was more exciting than my usual family conversations at home, where talk focussed on what happened today and what needed to be done in preparation for tomorrow.

Giving Barry the benefit of the doubt, I made arrangements to visit Waldene on reporting day. "My last interview should end by 3.30 pm so I can probably get to your place about four."

Barry was silent for a moment, perhaps stunned by the ease with which my decision had been made. "That's wonderful – a bit over a week away. Will you stay for dinner?"

"No, thanks anyway. Just a couple of hours, alright?"

"Sure - thanks. See you then."

After hanging up the phone, I quickly left the staff room to avoid any inquisitive looks from the other teachers.

Hesitation

Life itself is the most wonderful fairytale

HANS CHRISTIAN ANDERSON

There was a large thick envelope pushed into my inbox when I arrived at school a couple of days later. Inside were 28 photocopied pages from a theoretical book about 'The Meaning and Importance of Fairy Tales.' The pages were devoted to the discussion of 'Cinderella'.

A stark white index card accompanied the photocopied pages. On the card in a clear basic font was typed;

> *'Does this interesting theory tell us anything about our relationship? I like the part about Cinderella's third visit to the palace (...I do not count the time you came to fill in time and have a shower). It's a pity I am simply the librarian and not the handsome prince. xx*

I tried to skim-read the 28 pages. They were full of long unfamiliar academic words, psychologists' theories and psychoanalysts' findings that I could barely understand. Most of it seemed to be horrid speculation about darker meanings that could be attributed to Cinderella's actions. For goodness sake, I thought, it's just a fairy story!

Barry had folded down the corners of the two pages relevant to Cinderella's 'third' visit. Given that after school in a few days I was to make what Barry regarded as my 'third visit' to Waldene, I was interested to discern what he might be thinking.

One page explained Cinderella had actually been to two preceding balls at the palace but on the third visit failed to watch the clock and was forced to hurry away. In the hurry she lost her slipper. At midnight she reverts to her former self and the guards at the gate report no-one leaving the palace except a 'badly dressed country wench'.

Hmm – 'a country wench'? My forehead wrinkled as I pondered the attributes of a stereotypical country wench.

The other page proposed by evading the prince, Cinderella shows she wants to be chosen for the person she really is, and not merely for her appearance. Theorists suggested that on a deeper level, repeating the visits to the ball symbolises a woman who wants to commit personally and sexually, but at the same time is afraid to do so.

Hmm – a country wench masquerading as a princess, or someone afraid to commit both personally and sexually? It seemed a no-win choice. Both options frightened me regardless of which Barry was musing on. But he was probably only teasing me, probably using these weird speculations solely as a topic of conversation.

In any case, I'd only be there two hours, hardly enough time to look at the document collection for his proposed Draft Resistor's book, let alone any other conversation.

When I arrived at the cottage the front door was open and there was no sign of Barry.

"Hello," my voice echoed along the hallway. No answer. "Hello, anybody home?" Speaking a bit louder this time elicited some movement in the back rooms of the house. Standing on the porch I felt slightly uneasy, and was hoping Barry hadn't turned into a creep who would appear around the corner naked. Just when I'd decided to leave, he stepped into the hallway.

"There you are," I laughed, relieved to find him fully dressed. "Wondered where you were. Thought it was the wrong date - was just about to leave." I laughed again and wondered why I was behaving like such a twit.

"Sorry, only just got home. I was in the study getting my files out of the filing cabinet." Barry stepped back and ushered me inside. "Come in, I'll get you a coffee."

"That'd be great - haven't had a coffee all day. Parent-teacher interviews don't allow much time for breaks with a class of thirty students to get through."

Uninvited I sat on the couch while Barry busied himself in the kitchen. On the coffee table in front of the couch lay six large hanging files bulging with photos, official documents, newspaper cuttings and letters. Barry sat down on a dining chair and faced me from the other side of the coffee table.

"So," I said, waving my hand over the files, "This is a quite a collection."

"Yeah - I kept everything I was involved in and my first wife and my mother kept all the relevant newspaper cuttings for me too. There's so much information it's hard to know where to start and what matters most. I won't be able to include everything in the book."

He looked up from the files to me as if I'd have a solution for him. "Well," I said, taking a sip of my coffee to buy time, "... why don't you start by telling me the story from start to finish?"

"Really? Are you interested?"

For the next hour Barry described his involvement in the Draft Resistors Union during the 1970s. Back then, aged twenty-one (and a member of the Australian Labor Party since his 16th birthday), he was legally directed to register for National Service.

"No government has a right to conscript people into a war." He said it firmly like a call to arms.

"So you were a Conscientious Objector?" I asked, not really understanding what a Draft Resistor was.

"No!" Barry said emphatically. "I'm not against war per se. I'd fight if I thought Australia was under threat. But people should have the right to volunteer to fight or not, depending on the circumstances of the particular war.

"But that wouldn't work. No-one would volunteer to fight surely? The government decides who we're at war with and they have to raise an army from somewhere."

"That's where you're wrong. There'll always be people who'll volunteer to fight. That's why there's always an army on the Australian payroll. Then there's another group of Australians who would volunteer to fight if they believed in the circumstances of a particular war."

"Hmm," I felt a bit out of my depth and was trying to think about why his idea wouldn't work.

"Besides," he continued to drive the point home, "Imagine how hard it is to train people to fight a war if they don't believe in the cause? Compare that scenario with a regiment of soldiers who volunteered to be in that particular war. Which regiment will have the most devoted, enthusiastic soldiers?"

"Yeah, that seems to make sense." I bit my thumbnail and considered his words.

"Anyway, the Draft Resistors Union set about sabotaging the conscription of Australia's young men for the Vietnam War. We staged a sit-in at Melbourne University and held lots of rallies." He scoffed at a memory. "I registered my dad's two ferrets to fight and they actually received letters from the government calling them up for national service. What a joke!"

"Is that why you went to gaol?"

"Yeah; - one week in Pentridge in 1970 for failing to register, then another week for failing to attend a medical examination. Then in 1972 they sent me a summons for refusing a call-up notice and I was threatened with 18 months gaol."

"God, what did you do?"

"I went into hiding. Different trade union members hid me. I lived in lots of different houses... was even stowed away on a ship by the Seaman's Union for awhile."

"My brother was in the call-up ballot," I said. "But he was one of the lucky ones. His number didn't come out so he wasn't conscripted. I bet your mum was devastated when your birth-date was drawn from the barrel. I'd hate for my sons to have to go to war."

"No you don't understand." Barry lent forward in his chair. "The Draft Resistors didn't register for national service. We had no intention of being conscripted regardless of whether our birth-date was drawn out or not. That meant that we automatically went on the conscription list; our punishment for failing to register."

"God," I said yet again. "Wouldn't it have been easier to just register and take your chances? Did your birth-date come out?" I was amazed to hear the government had taken this strong stance against people protesting about conscription.

Barry sighed. "I was a Draft Resistor for a reason - a cause. It wasn't about me, it was about conscription."

Watching him, I could see how genuine he was. Here was someone who personified those things I'd been raised to respect. Here was someone who stood up to be counted, even when it might mean he would sometimes stand alone. I felt humbled.

"So what happened to bring you out of hiding?"

"The left wing of the Labor Party endorsed me as a candidate for Hotham electorate. I stood against Liberal Minister Don Chipp. There was no chance I'd win of course. I couldn't come out of hiding to attend political rallies because the federal police were hunting me. It was more about getting press coverage for Labor's intention to end conscription if they were elected."

I listened enthralled. "Wow! What a story! No wonder you want to write a book about it."

"Gough was true to his word and conscription ended after Labor's election in 1972. My police record was cleared and I was allowed back to teach."

Barry grinned suddenly. "Funny thing though – I met Gough for lunch in Paris in the mid 80s. When he saw me, he lifted me off the ground in a bear hug and shouted, "Johnston you bastard. You'd have made a hell of a soldier!"

I chuckled at the irony. "It's a wonderful story and you must write it." Somewhat nervously I ran my hand across the pile of documents on the coffee table. The task of helping Barry write such a story seemed overwhelming. I really wasn't much of a journalist and anything I could suggest would be pathetic.

But Barry insisted I give him some tips, so once again we talked about him beginning by writing a description of one key day at a time until eventually the whole story would be told.

"Just begin writing. Tell it chronologically. Maybe even use dates as chapter headings? I should've taped what you just told me. You could've started by writing that, then come back and fill in the finer details. What you said flowed perfectly. It's an amazing story, even to listen too. You don't need my advice. The task seems huge, but all you need do is begin writing. One step at a time – the way you lived it."

It was after 5.30 pm and I needed to leave soon. It was possible my visit had disappointed Barry but it was the best I could do given my limited knowledge. Worried the conversation might now turn to a discussion of the Cinderella paper, I prattled on about my day, about a newspaper article I'd read, about the flowers in my garden, even the weather.

Barry made me another coffee and after handing it to me he sat at the far end of the couch. "Look at the sunset," he said, gesturing towards the floor-to-ceiling window at the other end of the couch. Beyond the window the valley laboured restlessly as it prepared for nightfall. The sun was slowly being dragged beyond the hills, its fingertips streaking a blood red trail across the violet sky. A heavy cloak of humidity pressed down on the forest and the air was pregnant with the threat of thunder and lightning.

I could feel the sun's glow reflected on my face as I watched its golden death. I sat perfectly still. Somewhere in the room a clock ticked. Moments before, we'd been talking. But now the lavish display of the dying sun beyond the window demanded our attention and we sat on the couch in silence save for the sound of us breathing.

Barry was sitting an arm's length behind me on the couch and I was very conscious of him; knew as I looked at the view, he instead studied me. I could feel his eyes studying my profile. My nerves were alert to him. I continued to stare out the window, now seeing nothing. I tried to remain perfectly still, as if in so doing, I might slip from his notice. But my senses strained to perceive him.

Then gently, like the faint brush of a breeze on a hot day, I felt his fingertips fleetingly toy with a stray curl of hair at the nape of my neck. I struggled to conceal the delicious shock that tore through me. My skin, where he had made contact, felt electrified, yet I remained motionless. I wondered if it was an imagined touch. No words were spoken, only the clock ticking to mark the passage of time.

Barry's fingers returned to softly trace then retrace a line from my hair to the top of my spine. I looked out at the world and heard his silence - felt poised on the edge of something. Instinctively I knew if I turned to face him, everything would change. A door would open and a threshold would be crossed - if I turned my face toward him. My answer to his unspoken question lay in the turning of my head.

As his fingers caressed my neck, the sky bled and the sun dropped below the horizon to drown in the landscape. Slowly, almost despairingly, I turned to face Barry.

We lent towards each other and my heart leapt in my chest. His blue eyes, the merging of our breath, mouth-on-mouth – I closed my eyes and abandoned myself wholly to the kiss. His lips were soft and gentle and his arms around me felt strong and secure.

We parted and ever so slowly I opened my eyes. Barry scanned my face as if trying to read my thoughts. I dipped my head shyly and he hugged me to him, burying his face in my hair.

"I'd better go," I said gently pushing myself away from him. Barry reached out and placed his hand over my hand where it rested on the couch between us.

"Don't go." He said the words quietly without emphasis, as if he knew already it was an impossible request.

"S'posed to be home by seven. Promised I'd make dinner. I have to go." It wasn't actually a reply to his plea but rather a direction to myself to leave now. We walked up the driveway neither of us mentioning what had just happened. I hopped into my car quickly; hoping to signify the kiss was a mistake and could not be repeated.

"You must start writing. Your story is wonderful and no-one but you can tell it."

On the way home I kept running my fingertips along my lips, trying to resurrect the memory of Barry's mouth on mine. Nothing

I could do felt as wonderful as that moment, that forbidden kiss. A line from a partly remembered poem by Robert Browning came into my head: 'How sad, and mad, and bad it was – but then again, how sweet.'

When I arrived home the boys were watching television. My mother sat in the kitchen with me while I made dinner. Guilt prompted me to talk more than usual, as if filling the room with my voice would reassure everyone I was home at last. I talked about how long it had taken to do all the parent-teacher interviews and how hard it was to summaries every child's progress in detail.

Dinner was ready when Alec came in. My mother went upstairs and Alec began complaining about his day. I asked questions and listened sympathetically. No-one had noticed any change in me.

A day later an envelope appeared in my staff inbox. Barry had written to me immediately upon my leaving Waldene using the same mediaeval font of his earlier letter.

Dear Princess,
Thank you for honouring me with your presence tonight. I of course was very appreciative of your fond attentions...
Now begins the long wait and the hope that you might be induced to make the journey up to my mountain retreat once again.

Your loyal servant,
The Librarian xx

A second page advised 'a fellow monk' had asked 'the librarian' to request advice from me '...in your capacity as Princess' about a problem he had. I was told the letter from the 'fellow monk' would follow shortly.

It seemed we were playing out a beautiful fairy story. My love of whimsy was aroused. I re-read the letter and wondered if the term 'fond attentions' was Barry's polite way of reminding me of our kiss. But then again, he may have been referring to my interest in his book idea. My conscience decided to settle on the second possibility to appease my guilt.

The next mail brought a single page typed in mediaeval font from 'the Librarian' explaining an attached handwritten letter was from the young novice monk.

> *'...You may find it both ardent and pompous but please treat the young fellow kindly. Older souls such as myself simply look for trust and beauty.'*

Four small pages of parchment paper were filled with handwritten cursive script. The lettering was thick, and here and there little blotches of ink suggested the whole letter had been written using a quill of sorts.

Barry had gone to a great deal of trouble to continue the fantasy. It was so charming, like nothing I'd ever experienced since being a little girl making up stories and playing dress-ups to amuse myself.

The 'young novice' asked me (as 'Princess') to '*render unto (him) such goodly advice as thou might deem worthy.*' He then went on to describe his 'problem.'

> *Lately I have been troubled by a new and frightening experience. I have, to state it boldly, met a most comely wench and have felt the stings of sweet Cupid's arrows...*
> *I know that Lust is a sin, but can the warmth I feel be bad? When I think of the fate of Abelard, I quiver with fear...*
> *I promise you that my intentions are pure and that my romantic aspirations are to engage our souls, rather than our body and soul.*
> *What shouldest I do?*

1. *Be content to wait for her to call?*
2. *Meet her occasionally at a secret rendezvous for lunch?*
3. *Would she be offended if I offered to share the purifying steam of a Turkish Bath with her?*
4. *Would it be appropriate to invite her to enjoy the fabulous pleasures of Hindustan with me?*

> *I invite your comment Dear Princess.*
> *Your devoted subject,*
> *Apollodorus*

School broke up for the two-week winter break the next day and my family and I went to holiday in the Victorian snow fields.

There I stole time to write a response to Apollodorus. I explained sometimes lonely people find someone they connect with and they might misinterpret this 'connection' for love. But although love is wonderful, it's often short-lived, whereas connecting with a kindred spirit platonically can be deeply satisfying and often long-term.

Making mention of Apollodorus' vow of celibacy I highlighted the impossibility of him attempting a dual life with both a lover and the institution of the Church and all its expectations.

> *'Imagine the stress – surely akin to the stress on Cinderella to return to the carriage by midnight prior to its reincarnation as a pumpkin."*

I begged Apollodorus to consider the broader consequences of his current path and the potential harm of a short-term love affair, to both him and the lady in question.

The letter was posted to arrive at Barry's school at the start of the new school term.

Apollodorus

Platonic love is like an inactive volcano.

Andre Pevost

A week later a thick envelope appeared in my staff inbox containing two pages typed in medieval font from 'The Librarian.' He described the downfall of Apollodorus following receipt of a letter from 'The Princess.'

> *(He) locked himself in his cell ... to sob and moan until the early hours of the morning. Upon awakening, his fellow monks discovered he was missing ... I searched and searched the villages and forests and mountains. Finally I came upon a small cottage hidden in the trees and there I found the young scoundrel! ...he was not alone! The maiden was maiden no more! He claimed to never have been so happy.*
> *I thank goodness that I am beyond such temptations. It is a joy to be able to share the intimacies of the mind, immune from the pernicious lusts of the physical world.*
> *I remain your loyal and faithful servant,*
> *The Librarian xx*
> *PS I read in the ashes of Apollodorus' fire the charred remains of your letter... a strange line about pumpkins at midnight. Alas the words before it, had been destroyed. Was it a secret potion?*

I elected not to respond to this letter. While the make-believe tale was playful, the messages between the lines scared me.

The following week no letters were delivered to my staff inbox and although I daily drove past the pole that had once held the 'Cinderella sign,' it remained mute. Barry had apparently interpreted my silence correctly as an 'end' of such correspondence. It was all for the best I told myself a hundred times over.

But without the letters, the magic had gone from my days. I conceded life was not normally supposed to be magical. Now I could focus my attention more fully on making sure my sons did their homework, attended their swimming, football and tennis lessons on time, and that food was bought and cooked, washing was done and torn jeans were repaired.

No-one in my household seemed to notice any difference in my demeanour. Sometimes I wondered if they noticed me at all unless there was an upset in their life.

Ten days after Barry's last letter to me, I weakened and posted him a short poem. It mused on the downfall of Apollodorus and lamented his rejection of a platonic friendship, which '... *although celibate may include an innocent chase of a hunter for the fox.*' A swift response arrived.

My dearest, dearest Princess,
... It seems to me there is a lot to be said for a love which stops short of a sexual act.
... Your analogy of the fox and the hunter is interesting... Are you suggesting the vixen enjoys the chase? It seems to me the pleasure of the pursuit could be enhanced by the fox allowing the hunter to come teasingly close... I miss you."

Your Librarian xx

Then two days later a single page of medieval font framed by a hand-sketched chain of hearts asked:

MAY A LIBRARIAN PURSUE A PRINCESS?

Shrinking at his question, I retreated and began varying both the time I left for school each morning and the route I drove; anything to avoid seeing Barry along the road. Even when I failed and he flashed his lights, my wave was curt. I berated myself for sending the poem rather than letting things be.

There was no future in this charade for either of us. My life belonged to my children and my family. The choice had been made with the birth of my first child and I had no right to put their happiness at risk just because I'd found a kindred spirit in Barry.

A week later another decorated page arrived.

NOW IT'S ME WHO IS DESPERATE FOR A LETTER.

My heart sank when I saw Barry's car parked on my side of the road when driving to work a few mornings later. He was parked in the stretch of road where all my varying routes to school converged for the last two kilometres.

Although embarrassing and difficult, it seemed best for me to explain face-to-face we could never be more than friends. I would apologise for unwittingly leading him on and explain my inappropriate behaviour as the result of me getting caught up in the enchantment of our fairy-tale letters.

Barry remained facing out through the windscreen of his car even though he must have seem me pull in behind him on the roadside. It seemed he was not going to make this easy for me.

The fact he didn't turn around to greet me suggested he was feeling either angry or foolish. I bent down and knocked on the passenger-side door. Barry looked across and gave a slight nod. I opened the door and slid in beside him.

"Hello," he said.

"Sorry I haven't replied to your last letters. It's just ..." It was difficult to find the right words now we were together in his car.

Barry turned to face me, his blue eyes once again seeming to look deep inside me. "It's just what?" He crossed him arms, sighed and leaned back against the door.

I clasped my hands and rested my mouth on my thumbs, desperately seeking words to explain my stupidity. Whatever I said mustn't hurt him or make him feel he'd been taken for a fool.

"I don't have anything to give you except friendship. I'm married; two children, a husband and a mother all rely on me. I can't ruin my sons' childhood or do anything to hurt them. I should never have gone to Waldene or written to you. It's just I didn't think..."

"Didn't think what?"

My gaze swept out across the fields that usually gave me such joy to look upon. "It's just I hadn't thought you'd like me much." My explanation wasn't explaining the depth of what I wanted to say. Drawing breath I began again. "You see... I'm an onion. There isn't anything inside me. There's no 'me' really; just layers of other people's stuff piled on top of me. If you peel it at all off, there's nothing underneath. I'm nobody, with nothing to offer you. I'm sorry. It's my fault. I got caught up in the fairy-tale and shouldn't have. I'm so sorry."

"Do you like talking to me?" The question took me by surprise.

"Yes, but that's got nothing to do with it."

"You seem to forget I'm married too."

"It's not the same. You don't have children and you don't even live with your wife." As soon as the words were out I regretted saying them. They sounded hurtful, painted Barry as if he was all alone.

Seemingly unfazed Barry continued, "Well I like talking to you too. I don't think you're an onion at all. You're interesting and intelligent and you make me laugh. It seems a shame for us not to be friends at least. Can't we just continue as friends? I won't put any pressures on you or interfere with your family or your life. But I'd love to be able to talk sometimes. What do you think?"

This time it was me who sighed. "I don't think it would work."

"Why not? I promise I won't put any pressure on you. You'll be in total control of what happens between us. I won't do anything to hurt you or upset your life. I'd just like for us to talk together every so often."

How could I tell him my times at Waldene, his letters and our conversations together had become the high point of my life? That it was not him I was frightened of but me.

I bit my lip. "But what if this is dangerous for my family? You understand I want my family to stay a family don't you?"

Barry sighed. "I know that and I've promised not to do anything to hurt your family. But I want us to be friends, want to be able to talk with you."

"We're just going to be friends and that's all - right?"

"I promise," Barry said. "Nothing else will happen unless you say so."

"Okay, as long as we both know we're just friends and nothing else can come of it, then I s'pose it'll be okay." My inner voices murmured a warning.

Thereafter Barry parked often beside the road and I'd park behind him and sit in his car to chat for a few minutes before we each continued on our way. On Fridays a small group of teachers, including me sometimes went for a drink after school. Barry asked if now and then I could meet with him instead. "It'd be great to be able to sit and talk for an hour instead of the few minutes by the roadside," he said. "Maybe we could even go for a walk?"

It seemed a nice idea. My mother didn't expect me home until a little later on Fridays so spending some time with Barry or going for a walk wouldn't present a problem. We made arrangements to meet at a park the following Friday afternoon.

Barry's was the only car in the car park when I arrived. He was sitting on a rug under a huge spreading ghost gum.

"I should've brought a picnic" I laughed as I flopped down beside him.

Barry reached behind and brought out the crystal goblet from Waldene and a small bottle of champagne. "No need, m'lady, I kept this in the school fridge so it would be chilled for you." He poured me a drink and I laughed again, thrilled with the gaiety of the experience.

"This is a wonderful picnic. Thank you." We talked and talked, then went for a stroll around the gardens before waving goodbye to each other. It had been a lovely end to the week.

Our roadside meetings continued and I was kept alert never knowing where or when Barry would be parked waiting for me. We frequently met for an hour or so after school, sometimes for a glass of champagne on a picnic rug, sometimes to crunch ice-creams in the car and sometimes just to walk and talk about school and people and the world in general. Barry had been teaching for years longer than me and he became my sounding board for lessons I was considering for my students.

We were getting more and more familiar with each other and sometimes I'd take his arm as we walked. Sometimes our shoulders would brush against each other as we laughed or leaned in to examine a newspaper article or school document. True to his word Barry never put any pressure on me to do anything more than be his friend.

Our frequent meetings meant that four weeks went by without any letters being sent between us. Then on the last Wednesday of term a familiar-looking envelope appeared in my pigeon-hole. I smiled wondering what surprise it contained. It was another single page framed by hearts.

TURN LEFT AT ***** STREET ON FRIDAY MORNING IF YOU WOULD LIKE AN END OF TERM KISS.
THE LIBRARIAN xxx

Friday morning in spite of all my best intentions, I turned into the designated street on my way to school. Barry was waiting for me and I slid in beside him angry.

"Really? – an end of term kiss? I thought this was a no-pressure friendship?"

Barry tuned his face away and looked out at the landscape. "I said … 'If'. You didn't have to come. I actually didn't think you would." His words hung hard and cold in the air around me.

I shook my head. He was right of course – why had I come?

"But you came here anyway? How long have you been waiting?"

"It doesn't matter." Barry turned his ice blue eyes on me. "You came. That's what matters to me." He said it quietly, not like a victor, more like a 'believer.' I was overwhelmed. He was so quiet and solitary, like someone existing outside life - watching, but never expecting anything wonderful for himself.

"You shouldn't have written the note. It's wasn't fair to do that." How could I explain my lack of trust in myself?

"The holidays last for 16 days. I won't be able to contact you. I thought…"

"Thought what?" I snapped at him and even as I spoke I was reminded of an earlier time when Barry had challenged me to answer the impossible.

"Nothing... except if I could just know where you'd be on the holidays I'd be able to think of you there and somehow it'd be easier for me."

Looking at his gentle face almost broke my heart. I offered him nothing, yet he wanted to wait; to dream of me, of us – his amazing fairy-story. Taking his hands in mine, I kissed his palms, then lent across and kissed his mouth. He was so perfect for me. It was sad we'd met so late, when our lives were complicated by other people and their needs.

I was taking my mother and sons to Canberra for the first week of the holidays. Alec only had one week off so we'd all be at Phillip Island for the second week, returning home the day before school re-commenced.

Toward the end of the holidays I began writing a personal journal. Much of my writing centred on missing Barry, remembering sensations and experiences we'd shared, how fragile our relationship was, how constrained our time together was, and how much I loved talking with him, sharing stories and laughing.

My journal entry for Barry's 43rd birthday said:

I stood by the phone this morning and thought of you. I toyed with the idea of phoning you, even resting my fingertips on the handpiece for a few moments. But no, it wouldn't have been acceptable behaviour. But now the eventual outcome is known to you. I finally surrendered and as if you understood my need, I sensed you smile at the sound of my voice. Is it possible you also have stood with hand upon the phone dreaming?

Later, after the holidays I let Barry read my journal and he added a note to my entry.

> *... I would love to be interrupted by you at any time (even 3 am). Your telephone call in the afternoon was the nicest thing that happened to me on my birthday. Yes, I often look at the phone and wish I could use it to reach out to you.*

Guilty

*They whose guilt within their bosoms lie,
imagine every eye beholds their blame.*

SHAKESPEARE.

Guilty! When I die they may as well write the word on my headstone. Even before meeting Barry I spent an overwhelming part of my life feeling guilty and apologising. Since becoming a mother it seems as if the only time I have to myself is snatched furtively from the bits of my life no-one else needs or wants. I seem to run here and there at everyone's beck and call, dashing to arrive on time, apologising for being late, forgetting something or getting things muddled. Guilty!

Even Barry had unsuspectingly made me feel guilty. One afternoon during a roadside encounter, he presented me with a large package wrapped in pretty floral paper. "I wanted to give you a present and this seemed perfect. I hope it's okay."

Panic-stricken, I snapped at him. "You mustn't give me presents! Where will I put this? I'll have to hide it." Then softer, "Please don't give me presents."

Barry remained calm though he must have been disappointed at my reaction. "Just open it. It's a book," he shrugged. "Just say you bought it yourself."

I unwrapped the package without enthusiasm. Inside was a large hard-covered book full of magnificent photos of the Eiffel Tower. I gasped. "I'd never spend so much money on a book like this for myself." It was a fact as well as an apology of sorts.

The money coming into my house went on the mortgage and essentials first. It was a habit learned from my parents who were quick to tell their offspring "...the most important thing is to own your home. Then whatever happens, 'they' can't put you out on the street."

The lesson so ingrained in my psyche sometimes riled Alec and my sons. Alec was more a 'spender' than a 'saver' and we walked a fine line when negotiating our finances. My sons were prone to peer pressure and although they weren't demanding about most things they each had their particular 'needs' in order to save face with their friends.

Heath ruined many pairs of cheap running shoes in quick succession until I realised the false economy of not buying him one pair of the expensive brand runners he needed to be like everyone else. When I finally bought him some, he loved them with a passion. Blake had other needs; mostly to do with Disney characters with merchandise generally beyond the reach of our weekly budget.

Barry's offhand suggestion I explain the gorgeous Eiffel Tower book as something I'd bought for myself was so ridiculous it was laughable. Any new books in my bookcase had a library return-date stamped inside the back cover.

Yet I couldn't help but be moved by Barry's gift to me. During one of our earlier conversations I'd described my excitement as a twenty year old, travelling overseas for the first time; my prime purpose being to see the Eiffel Tower. The thought of the iconic monument in Paris, 'the city of romance,' had captivated me from the moment I'd first heard of it as a little girl.

The night I arrived at the Eiffel Tower it was raining and no-one on the tour but me wanted to get off the bus. The rain had mingled with my tears as I stood alone, having travelled half way round the world, to stare up at the magical structure towering up into the black sky amid a field of golden lights. My heart almost broke with joy at the miracle of me being there.

Barry had remembered my story and gone to the trouble of buying this wonderful gift for me. No-one else had ever really connected with what it had meant for me to achieve my childhood dream. It was as if he could see inside me, read my soul, knew what mattered to me. I was overwhelmed, unsure what to say, how to return a sense of calm to the moment.

"Is it okay? Do you like it?" Barry asked nervously.

"It's beautiful," I said, turning the pages slowly, almost frightened to look at him, so moved was I by his perfect offering. "But you mustn't buy me things. I'd have to hide them and I'd be frightened they'd be discovered or broken and that would be awful. Besides, I don't need presents and I'm not really good at receiving them. I like the idea of them but get embarrassed when opening them. And then I'd have to buy you presents - and it would all become too hard. So don't buy me presents. It will just make me feel even more guilty."

Throughout my ramblings Barry had watched me turning the pages of the book, running my hands over the images, almost 'feeling' the memories as much as looking at the photos. When I finally stopped talking and stole a look at Barry, his face seemed rather stern.

"Have you finished?" His voice matched his expression. I nodded. "I like buying presents for people. And I don't expect you to buy presents for me in return. I won't buy you anything that will get you into trouble, but you should let me buy you presents. It'd make me happy and there's no need for you to feel guilty about receiving them."

I nodded again, realising this was not an argument I was going to win.

Weeks turned into months and Barry and I saw each other regularly before or after school. Often I'd phone him at Waldene when returning from my early morning swim session. Sometimes he'd phone me at school via his phone-accomplice, to speak for a few terrifying moments on the staffroom phone.

Then one day I received a letter written perhaps deliberately in bright red ink. At last the words appeared on the page, so there could be no further doubt.

> *...so I suppose I have come to the stage where I should say what we have both avoided saying. But how can I say 'I love you' without having it sound, well, you know?*
> *So there it is – love! What can be done for us? Am I right in concluding that you have been affected too?*
> *I know what we are doing is probably not very sensible, especially for you. However ... you make me feel wonderful and even missing you is a sincere joy.*
>
> *Barry xx*

I wrote to Barry the same day to describe my burden of guilt with regard to our friendship. Perhaps my hope was he'd retract his declaration of love. Although the loss of him from my life would be awful, there seemed no way we could continue on this path without dreadful consequences.

> *'...A married woman, who wishes to remain married can <u>never</u> really 'love' anyone other than her family. It is unacceptable to all the rules of 'together forever-ness'... the alternative is to develop an emotion called 'caring for'. It probably means the woman loves many other people, but always to a lesser degree than would jeopardise her family. It's all so complicated and fragile.*

I've nothing to offer you. I'm me – married, mother and willingly tied to both occupations for the duration.
Truly what is to become of us?'

A hand-written note arrived the next day:

Dear one,
I hated your letter... to see there in print, that blatant, horrible reality was so depressing.
I apologise if my previous letter made you feel awkward. You once said you feared I might 'offer love.'
I'm not 'offering' love. I've already given it to you. You had received it long before my words were written. You don't have to reciprocate, but it will keep flowing over you all the same. At present it is out of my control too.
I don't know 'what is to become of us?'

Your loving Librarian xx

That night in my sleep I walked a wonderland of dreams involving Barry and throughout the next day my mind kept wandering back to recall cameo times we'd spent together. Next day on yard duty I found myself staring up into treetops contemplating our relationship, Barry's marriage and my marriage from every angle.

Pondering the analogy of the 'hunter and the fox,' momentarily I considered the terrible possibility that perhaps it was me who was the 'hunter' after all. Maybe I was in this impossible situation for somehow allowing Barry to open a door on my life and dazzling me with the light beyond.

There had been no roadside encounters, phone-calls or letters since Barry's last letter to me and I assumed he, like me, was coming to terms with the fact that there was not, nor could there ever be, any 'future' for us. He was a pragmatist and would not waste his energies on a hopeless case. If he needed a woman in his life, and I was not convinced of that, there were countless available females in the education field.

When a week later Barry's car was parked beside the road in the morning I pulled in behind him and steeled myself for an unpleasant conversation. Barry stepped out of his car and walked back toward me.

"Can I hop in?" he asked standing beside my car.

'Sure." I said, gripping the steering wheel as he hopped in and not trusting myself to look into his face. An escape from the upcoming conversation seemed impossible. Yet as horrible as the situation was, it needed to be faced - to end everything, to break free.

"So … the letter you sent me. I've been reading it and re-reading it and now I have something to say to you." Barry's tone frightened me but I needed him to be angry and fed up with me – to tell me he'd decided not to see me or contact me again.

Stiffening in my seat I waited.

"What?" My eyes swept his face momentarily before returning to study my hands on the steering wheel.

"Look at me." His words, quietly spoken, hung in the air, a plea rather than a command.

"I'm afraid to. You're angry at me and I'm sorry I let everything go this far."

Reaching across, Barry lifted my left hand from the steering wheel and held it like a trapped bird between his palms. Shifting in my seat until my back was pressed against the door, I turned to face him.

"I can't be angry at you, he said. "I don't have the right. I can be angry at myself, and I probably should be for allowing me to get into this situation…but I don't want to be anywhere else." At this his lips brushed my hand and he looked up at me.

"Please don't," I murmured, shaking my head and pulling my hand away from his clasp.

"I think we're special and I want to share things with you – ideas, music, art, novels – and 'caring' if that's all you can offer me. I know you have other responsibilities and I respect that. Obviously I want much more than I can hope to gain, but you'd expect that."

"But the piper always has to be paid. It's inevitable." My voice sounded thin and tortured. As I spoke my stomach muscles flexed in anguish and my chest tightened.

Barry flinched slightly as if I had hit him. "If by 'inevitable' you mean 'sex', then you're wrong! I wasn't looking for sex from you. I wanted to inhabit a small part of your mind, a part not shared with anyone else."

With his hand on the car door handle he delivered his final words, "There's nothing more I can say. You'll do what you'll do, and I'll be happy or sad. But I'd feel cheated if we couldn't be together for one more proper conversation."

He glanced down at his watch. If we didn't leave now we'd both be late for work. "Can I phone you later?" he asked.

It all felt so overwhelming. It had started so innocently and been so playful but now it was so frightening. I doubted Barry would get out of my car if my response was 'No.'

"Yeah, okay," I lowered my head as a spoke. At least this conversation would now end, leaving me free to drive away.

That day the lunch-room talk was full of everyone's plans for the end of year holidays. There were only a few weeks of standard curriculum and final testing to get through before the whole school would go into 'Christmas mode.' Then classroom attentions would turn to the lighter tasks of making Christmas decorations, writing letters to Santa and singing carols.

Listening to the conversations around the table I overheard Barry's wife describing the four week trip to Morocco she and him were going to take over the Christmas break. I listened with envy as she painted a word picture of where they would go, what they would see, and the plans and disagreements they'd had in organising their itinerary.

When I could stand it no longer, I left the staffroom and wandered out into the schoolyard to listen to the breeze blow through the trees. That night I wrote a Bon Voyage card to Barry.

I walked in the yard today while your wife described your upcoming Moroccan trip to the lunch-crew in the staffroom. Outside the wind was blowing… The wind is lucky. It can go wherever it wants. The air from here in Whittlesea can blow and blow until it playfully whips the sands of Morocco around the feet of the tourists. On the other hand, the trees rooted here can only stand and watch with straining eyes until the wind disappears around the first bend in the road. You're like the playful wind and me - well I must assume the role of the tree.
Bon Voyage!

The next day a handwritten note was lodged under my classroom door when I arrived at school.

You're probably not going to believe me, but I could say this while looking deeply into your lovely eyes; I would willingly give up the whole trip to Morocco if I could be with you. Let me take you to India – I want to be with you in Venice too. I

will <u>hate</u> being away from you.
P.S. The wind is not always playful and trees may be transplanted (with great care and loving patience).

At lunch-time I was summoned to a call in the staffroom. Barry's secret ally was on the phone again. "That you Sue?"

"Yes."

"Just a sec and I'll put the big fella on." He chuckled and then Barry spoke.

"I've rung to say goodbye."

My body sagged slightly – the words I'd been seeking, now spoken, took my breath away. There was a momentary silence on the phone and I sensed Barry listening for my reaction.

"I'm off to school camp for the next three days. Thought I'd ring to let you know. Did you get my note this morning?"

"Yes, but you're being ridiculous. Please don't say that again." Relief flooded through me. I was uncertain if it was because his 'goodbye' statement was a joke or merely because he'd phoned me.

Barry's voice softened. "I have enough money to take us anywhere in the world you want to go. Just say and I'll arrange it."

"Stop!" I broke in over his words. There was a stunned silence at the other end of the line. I softened my tone. "I hope you have a nice time on camp - hopefully no bed-wetters or homesick kids. See you when you get back. I'm going to hang up now, okay?"

Not waiting for his answer I placed the phone back in its cradle and left the staffroom. Walking along the corridor I was conscious of the sunshine streaming in the windows and the sounds of children laughing out in the yard. It was a happy day.

A final word

*Every heart sings a song incomplete until
another heart whispers back.*

PLATO

Two days later when tidying my classroom after school, the bursar's voice sounded over the school intercom, "Phone call for Mrs Gunningham in the library."

The cavernous library with its row upon row of books, and now devoid of children was silent and cold. The librarian was nowhere to be seen as I stepped into her small office.

"Hello?" I said into the phone, unsure whether the caller had been put through or if the bursar just wanted to speak to me.

"Hi Sue, putting the call through now." The bursar gave no indication of who was phoning me.

After a brief burst of static came Barry's voice. "There you are. Thought you might have gone home already."

"What are you doing?" I was instantly worried the bursar would now be alerted to the 'situation'. "Aren't you on camp?" I looked over my shoulder scanning the room for eavesdroppers.

"Yes - but I wanted to hear your voice." Barry seemed oblivious of the stress he caused me each time he phoned me at school.

"That's so stupid," I said, yet smiled at the simplicity of his explanation.

"Probably ... but I organised a roster so each teacher gets half an hour free a day and I wanted to spend my half hour talking to you. Don't waste the time being angry at me."

I sighed. "I'm not angry, just a bit surprised."

"Last time we met you promised me at least one more long discussion so I want to ask you to dinner at the cottage again - next Wednesday. You could come straight from school and we could eat early."

I bit my lip and leant against the desk. "But…" The single word hung limp in the air, going nowhere, saying both everything and nothing at the same time.

"You promised you'd at least hear me out."

Closing my eyes, I sighed. "Okay… but not for dinner. I'll come for a couple of hours and then you have to agree to stop all this."

"Just hear me out then I promise to agree to whatever you decide."

Hence a few days later I was knocking at the door of his fairytale cottage and sitting on his couch while he fussed around creating an offering of torn pita bread, hummus and the now familiar crystal glass of ice-splintered champagne. The afternoon sun pressed against the windows and the forest beyond rustled in anticipation.

We talked about the weather and told each other 'school camp' stories. All the while Barry sat in a hardback chair opposite me on the couch. When I glanced at the clock he moved to sit at the other end of the couch from me.

"I've been trying to work out a way to convince you how wonderful it would be if we could be together for a serious amount of hours," he suddenly said. "We could get to know each other so well in that amount of time. I have a fear you'll end this 'relationship' before it's ready to be ended."

Dragging my hand across my forehead I turned away to stare out the windows, down toward the valley.

Undeterred Barry continued to speak, his voice gentle, swirling out like honey to mingle with the glorious gold of the sunset. "I'm jealous of time. I wish we could spend an afternoon, a day, a night, or a weekend together. We could do something extravagant or something quiet and private."

When I made no response he leapt up and went over to the sideboard to retrieve a small package. "I've bought you a present. I know you don't like presents but this is only a small diary; a diary to mark a new beginning - a beginning of which you are totally in charge. Nothing in our future needs to be what you refer to as 'inevitable.' The prospect of sex isn't why I'm attracted to you. In this diary you can write what you organise to happen. It will include me or it won't. I will do whatever the diary asks of me."

He placed the package on my lap before returning to his position on the couch. It was hopeless. I felt as though I was fighting the sunset and love and family and expectations and protocol all in one battle. And there at the end of the couch sat Barry, silent, perfect and waiting. The silence lengthened between us as outside twilight began to filter across the sky.

"What a crock!" I finally blurted out. I'd never used the phrase before but had a feeling it meant '*a crock of sh...t*!'

Surprised, Barry shuffled in his seat. "What?"

"It's rubbish to say you're not after sex. Don't treat me like an idiot!" I was angry but not sure who my anger was directed at – the possibilities seemed endless and even included me.

Barry shook his head and sat quietly as if contemplating an answer, thought better of it and said nothing. I wanted to scream, to throw things, to abandon myself to him. But instead I pulled at my hair, covered my face in my hands and began to weep.

The couch creaked and Barry's arms enfolded me. 'Shhhh..." he stroked my back like the parent of a distraught child. I relaxed into his hold. "It's not inevitable" he murmured into my hair.

"Yes it is. I know ... and then a bridge will have been crossed."

"Come lie on the bed with me and I'll prove it's not inevitable."

And I let myself be led along the corridor to the bedroom, there to lie crying softly beside him in gentle embrace.

"In the old movies, the actors doing bedroom scenes had to keep one foot on the floor," he said into the silence.

I was grateful he'd introduced this quirky fact into an otherwise risky situation. "Surely it's impossible?" I murmured, conscious he was trying to lighten the mood and stem my crying.

"No it's true," he said with a schoolboy grin. "Let's try it and see?"

We spent a very funny few minutes trying to embrace while one or both of us kept one foot on the floor. We were like children stretching and tumbling and giggling on the bed. It certainly wasn't sex but it was somehow more intimate than we had ever been and full of laughter rather than shame.

When I left the cottage the new diary was in my bag and we hadn't resolved anything. Barry walked me out. It was difficult to leave him – this man living alone almost silently here in his secret place in the forest. I took a step back toward him and buried my face in his chest. His soft woollen jumper smelt faintly of smoke from the wood-stove. We stood without speaking and Barry's arms tightened around me. His lips brushed the top of my head and I closed my eyes luxuriating in the strength of his love.

"Don't worry Princess. It'll all work out. I can wait. Just be happy and try your best to make time for me somewhere in your life. I love you and there's nothing I can do about it."

The next morning I phoned Barry at 5.30 am before going swimming. "Yes?" he answered somewhat aggressively, having been startled from his sleep.

"Sorry, it's me – Sue. Were you awake?"

"I am now," he laughed. "Are you okay?"

"Sort of …" Now we were actually speaking I felt shy. "I wanted to thank you for last night and for the diary." I paused unsure what else to say. "I don't think the story about movie stars is true. Did you make it up?"

"No. It's a well-known fact. Ask your mum." It was difficult to tell if he was making fun of me.

"Anyway," he said lowering his voice, "after you left last night I missed you so badly. I tried to write a poem about pressing my lips to the crystal glass where your lips had been. I tried to describe the incredible experience of lying beside you on the bed. But too much was happening in my mind to write well. So I just wrote one sentence on a blank page. Will I read it to you?"

"Hmm, maybe." It seemed we had made no progress in our attempt to discontinue this relationship. Down the phone I could hear Barry walking around the cottage.

"Here it is," he said. "I left it on the table when I finally went to bed. Are you ready?"

"Okay." Standing perfectly still in the phone booth I closed my eyes and held my breath.

"It says, *Oh what a nice evening!!* It's underlined and has two exclamation marks at the end. What do you think?"

"I think it's beautiful," I whispered.

"Can I meet you today after school in XXX Lane? Even for half an hour? Four o'clock?"

"Okay," I said again. 'But now I'd better get to the pool. Sorry to wake you."

"Don't apologise. You can phone me anytime day or night. I'm always waiting to hear from you. All I do is think about the next time we can be together. You've taken over my life."

We met after school and talked for half an hour about everything except what had happened the night before or what it might mean for the two of us going forward. Once again Barry started waiting for me beside the road before or after school on most days.

During one of those talks the conversation wound back to my accusations of 'the inevitable' happening if we continued to see each other. Barry was adamant. "If it's to happen then you'll instigate it, not me. It'll be your decision, not mine."

"It's all such a nuisance: such a complication. I sometimes wish I was a boy."

Glancing sidelong at me Barry laughed. "I'm glad you're not. I love all your girly curves and bumps. If you were a bloke I wouldn't like you half as much."

"Probably should just 'do it' - get it over with." I mused aloud, ignoring Barry's comments. "Perhaps the experience would be so dreadful it'd bring this relationship to a sudden end anyway. Maybe it'd be easier than this constant battle."

The idea almost seemed to make sense. Perhaps it might be better to just get it over with and then we could both go back to our previous lives. No-one would know except us. No-one would be hurt. In a way having sex with Barry once would be a small price to pay to safeguard my family's happiness. But then my conscience reeled in horror at this loose organisation of the facts.

On the phone a few days later Barry asked if we could meet during our lunch break for a change. He described a grass verge on the bend in an unmade country lane that ran between open fields equal distance from his school and mine.

"It'll be like having a picnic," he said enthusiastically. "I'll bring the rug and we can sit on the grass and talk while we eat lunch."

It was a wonderful idea. The days were warm and sunny now as Spring drew to a close. Although unfamiliar with the lane he'd described, I knew fields stretched out along that part of the main road; fields full of contented cows chewing slowly and methodically far from houses or traffic.

At lunchtime, leaning back against his car bonnet, arms folded across his chest, Barry watched me drive towards him down the lane. A trail of dust rose up behind my car momentarily marking my detour off the main road. A rug lay on the grass in the shade of two straggly eucalypt growing beside a wire fence. Torch-like, the midday sun probed the branches to seek out interlopers in fractured shards.

I turned my car off and smiled timidly at Barry through the windscreen. As he walked toward my car I drew breath. This rendezvous felt 'different' from our other meetings. This was not an unexpected roadside encounter on the way to or from work. Nor was it a dinner organised for the discussion of writing or exchanging books. This was a deliberately organised clandestine meeting – a secret tryst between could-be-lovers.

"Hello," Barry said opening my door.

"Hi." I fussed about getting my lunch and drink bottle from the back seat. I wondered if this was my way of slowing the momentum to the point where there would be only minutes left before it would be time to leave again. Sitting on the rug we made stilted conversation about the weather, the flies and the stillness all around. We ran out of inconsequential topics, fell silent and focussed our attention on eating lunch.

It felt as though we were in a poorly contrived painting - the scenery was beautiful yet the characters in the foreground were unreal and remote. I struggled for something to say to break the awkward tension. Although we'd done nothing immoral the situation seemed heavy with deceit.

"I've got a surprise for you," Barry said suddenly jumping to his feet and holding out his hand to help me up. "It's in my car." Walking ahead of me he opened wide the rear door of his car and stepped back so I could look inside.

The back seat, normally home to a tub of school books and Barry's gym bag, was today devoid of all school paraphernalia. Instead a crisp pale blue sheet had been neatly stretched across the seat and a matching pillow placed at one end. In the centre of the pillow lay a small bunch of lavender tied with a pale blue ribbon. A soft lilac throw rug was folded at the other end of the seat.

My senses recoiled. "What's this about?" I asked in horror.

Barry gave a short laugh. "Well, you said it might be best to just get it over with so I thought I'd help."

Stepping back in horror I almost tripped in my rush to negate what he'd said. "You must be kidding! You said you weren't after sex, said I was in charge of the decision." Hurrying back to the picnic rug I gathered up the remains of my lunch.

Barry shut his car door and called after me, "So that was a complete waste of time wasn't it?'"

"Absolutely!" I snarled

He came over and stood in front of me as I wrestled the remains of my lunch into my bag. I didn't look at him and after a few moments he held my arms by my sides forcing me to stand still.

"You're such a funny little poppet. Sometimes you talk so worldly, and then at other times you're like a little girl. I thought I was helping you, but now I realise I misunderstood. I promised you nothing will happen unless you want it to and I meant it. So there's no need to be cross at me." He released his hold on my arms and I looked up into his face.

"I'm sorry. I got a fright. I thought ..."

"You know me better than that. I'd never hurt you. Now give me a smile and I'll know everything's alright between us again. Then we'd better go or we'll be late back to school."

I smiled shyly and we folded up the rug. I kissed Barry goodbye and thanked him for his misguided but well-meant intentions.

As we both hopped into our cars I called out a parting comment. "... And by the way, thirty minutes to eat lunch and make out was never going to be long enough. What *were* you thinking?" Now free of my earlier shock I threw back my head and laughed mischievously.

Barry's car window wound down. "You really are a little witch," he yelled before blowing me a kiss and driving away.

SWOON

Swoon

> *Ask me no more: thy fate and mine are sealed, I strove against the stream and all in vain; Let the great river take me to the main: No more, dear love, for at a touch I yield; Ask me no more.*
>
> ALFRED TENNYSON

The time of my third Year 6 graduation night was fast approaching so I phoned Barry to ask if it would be possible for me to come to Waldene for the few hours between the end of school and the start of the ceremony. He was delighted at the prospect.

The enormous clock above his kitchen door showed 4 pm. Barry must have hurried home in record time to be at Waldene by the time I arrived. The windows beside the fireplace captured our reflection as Barry ushered me into the living area. I plopped into my usual position on the couch while he opened a bottle of champagne.

"I have to be back at the graduation ceremony by 6 pm so I'd probably better not have anything to drink," I said, my words more a question than a statement.

"One won't hurt," Barry said as always, and I smiled to myself, remembering the time he'd told me he liked the faint taste of champagne on my lips when we kissed. It was a funny comment from a non-drinker.

I watched him pour the wine. The gas lighting behind him outlined his beautifully familiar profile in hues of soft orange and yellow. Once again I marvelled at how perfect he was. It had been over two years now and although we now exchanged kisses and occasionally lay fully clothed on his bed, talking and staring out at the forest, Barry had respected my edict that we couldn't ever be more intimate.

And yet, as I watched him tonight I wanted that intimacy more than anything. I sometimes wished he would force himself on me and absolve me from any guilt in the outcome. But it was not his way, and while I loved him for his integrity and felt safer with him than anyone else in my life, my level of frustration was these days almost at fever pitch.

At home Alec was receiving another round of treatment for a knee injury sustained at work. He was often irritable with the pain and because of limitations placed on what he was allowed to do. The boys and I tried not to upset him. Even the rub of clothing on his knee caused him pain and for some time I had been sleeping on the couch or a single-bed mattress on the bedroom floor, so he could sleep undisturbed. Seeing this unusual sleeping arrangement, my mother had once chastised me. "Your father wouldn't have stood for that!" she scolded.

I had no answer for her. How could I explain there was no comparison between her marriage and mine? I was no longer in love with my husband and I doubted he loved me. We were just two people role-playing 'happy family' for our children's sake. Thereafter I kept the bedroom door closed to hide our shame.

Barry handed me the wine glass and flopped down beside me. He stretched his left arm almost protectively along the back of the couch behind me. When the conversation ebbed, he slid his arm off the couch and wrapped both arms around me in an embrace.

I took a sip of the wine, Barry's trademark ice-shards stinging my tongue. Closing my eyes I focussed on the biting cold in my mouth.

"Is everything okay?" Barry asked nervously, his body suddenly alert.

Opening my eyes it was obvious he was worried I was about to say something important, perhaps try once again to end the relationship. I put down my glass and looked directly into his eyes. His fear was almost palpable and he sat upright, silent and still.

Lifting his left hand, I cradled my cheek in his large, strong palm. Barry's skin was warm and soft. I imprisoned his hands, palms together within mine before speaking.

"I can't do this anymore." My eyes swept his face before falling to study our hands. Barry stiffened slightly but said nothing. "I just can't keep doing this. It's too hard. I can't anymore." The clock ticked on and our silence widened. He was not going to offer any help.

"What time is it?" I asked.

Barry glanced at the clock. "Four thirty-five." Then as though refusing to acknowledge my previous anguished statement he said, "You'd better think about having a shower if you're going to have one. I put a towel in the bathroom for you. It's a bath-sheet actually - yellow. I know you like yellow and I like the idea of you wrapped in a fluffy yellow bath-sheet. Like a duckling." He smiled, obviously pleased with the image.

His words were simple, their sentiment almost child-like but they went straight to my heart. It was time. I stood up. Barry watched me, now forced to consider what I'd just said. Sorrow and hurt showed in his face.

Standing silently beside the couch I looked down at him. He was everything I needed, everything I wanted. I took his hand and he stood up slowly. In silence I led him along the hallway to the bedroom and we sat on the edge of the bed. Leaning toward him I claimed a kiss - a long exploratory kiss. I could feel Barry's confusion. He was unsure what I was implying. He obviously didn't want to break his promise not to pressure me into anything I'd later regret.

Part way through unbuttoning his shirt, I stopped and pulled off my t-shirt. Barry watched as I pulled back the blankets on the bed and slipped between the sheets. The cool cotton against my heated flesh made me shiver involuntarily.

Standing beside the bed with his shirt unbuttoned Barry asked "Are you sure?" His voice was thick with emotion.

"No – but I need to do this ... or I think I'll die." I fell silent, exhausted by what I was feeling. There were no words, no explanations. My body was operating independent of whatever my sensibilities might be. I was beyond – beyond everything outside of this man, this room, this consuming need, this moment.

I listened from deep beneath the blankets as Barry undressed and slid in beside me. We lay rigid, timid beside each other for a few minutes. I could hear myself breathing; felt every hair on my arms electrified in anticipation.

Gently, stealthily, Barry's hands moved; fingers walking across the pale cotton sheet between us. He found my ribs and moved closer. I felt the warmth of his hand lying on my naked stomach, felt him lift his head to look at my face. Our lips met – gentle then intense, soft then strong, calm then passionate.

I wasn't thinking so simply as 'having sex' or 'making love' with Barry. I just wanted to press myself so hard against him I'd be absorbed into his being; wanted him to mould into me and me into him. I wanted to kiss him so softly, so tenderly we'd breathe each other's breath, breathe until our breath became one breath. I wanted to feel myself inside him, feel him inside me.

'Swoon'- it is the closest word created to describe the sensation. I neither cared nor was conscious of what our bodies were doing.

I was locked into the melding of our minds and our souls and our hearts. No doubt the body parts fell into place like a jigsaw - mouth against mouth, breasts against chest, belly against belly and thigh against thigh.

The French notion of the little death, 'le petit mort'- may be correct, but for me this moment was the exquisite death of 'me' in order to reincarnate as 'we'. And so the time arrived and I was no longer conscious of the ticking clock.

Later, when we fell apart, we lay in silence, each feeling both the victor and the conquered. Silence - floating, no thoughts, bliss - swoon.

Finally I spoke, my eyes still closed. "Hello." It was a whispered secret.

Barry rolled over to hold me in his arms. "I love you," he murmured.

"I know." I could think of no other words worthy of the moment. Entangled in each other we drifted again in a state of wondrous euphoria.

Then I spoke into the silence, "I'd better shower." My voice sounded languid, sleepy. I wished I could stay in this moment forever.

"Mm," Barry replied.

Dragging myself up, I slipped away to the bathroom, all the while trying to conceal my nakedness. It was silly, but Barry had never seen me naked before and my shyness returned when leaving the cover of the sheets.

I'd bought a special dress for the school graduation dinner. It was a princess-line with a bodice of crushed velvet the colour of which alternated between ice-blue and silver with every movement. Beneath my breasts the dress fell away in soft folds of embroidered blue satin down to my calves. Wide gathered sleeves of the embroidered satin were caught in slim bands at my wrists.

Hanging around my neck on a fine silver chain was a purple-blue paua shell cut into the shape of a small heart. The iridescent gem glinted against my skin and hinted of faraway oceans and magic and romance. The blue dress highlighted my eyes and Barry said I'd never looked so lovely. He insisted on taking photos of me in the forest before I left.

Later, seeing myself in his photos I was easily recognisable as a 'woman in love' - a woman who was staring back at her lover behind the camera, a woman who was only a few breaths away from their last shared kiss.

It took an enormous effort for me to focus on the students and their graduation ceremony after leaving Waldene that night. Without provocation, like a torch probing the darkness, my mind kept wandering back to re-examine this moment or that of the few hours I'd just spent with Barry - hours that had changed our relationship forever.

Just before midnight, I waved goodbye to the Principal and the few remaining teachers to drive back to Greensborough. At last, hidden safely inside my car I gave myself up to total reminisce of Barry and me and this night of nights. I overflowed with love for him and was grateful we'd finally consummated our relationship. Then just as quickly I worried about what might happen now and what tonight might mean for my family.

One part of me berated myself for letting it get to this, while another internal voice soothed me with the knowledge nothing further need happen if I didn't want it to. I reassured myself by thinking Barry might break off our relationship now I'd given myself to him. Although this last thought filled me with sadness, it would probably be the best outcome for everyone. My mind lurched backwards and forwards considering all the options and their consequences. But nothing could detract from the euphoria I felt thinking about of Barry and me together earlier that night. I looked at my eyes in the rear view mirror. Lit by the soft glow of the dashboard lights the swollen black pupils sparkled with the secret they now held.

Half way home amidst the pastures there was a country petrol station alongside a small bluestone hall. A couple of feeble street lights lit the buildings in the dark sleeping landscape. I slowed to navigate the intersection I knew was beyond the hall.

Barry's car was parked on the narrow gravel forecourt in front of the hall. Surprised yet worried, I pulled in behind him. Before I'd turned off the engine Barry loomed up beside my car, opened the passenger door and slipped into the seat beside me.

"Is everything all right?" I asked, my throat dry with the thought he was about to tell me it was over.

Instead he took my hands and kissed my fingertips. "After you left me tonight, it was as if the house died. I wrote you a long letter. I wanted to tell you how much I love you and how wonderful tonight was. But there was so much to say and I wanted to give you the letter myself, wanted to catch you on your way home and put the letter into your hands. There wasn't time to write everything I wanted to say because I wanted to be here, to see you on your way home."

He'd spoken in a rush, yet his words were beautiful. Barry wasn't here to break it off. He loved me. I'd thought it might be true before, but here, in the darkness, halfway between Waldene and Greensborough - halfway between two worlds, I could see it really was true. He loved me.

I took the pure white envelope Barry held out to me and started to open it. But he put his hands over mine to stop me.

"No - read it when you get home. Don't read it now while I'm with you. Just let me look at you for a few minutes and then I'll go. It's already late. You need to get home." We held hands and stared into each other eyes. We smiled at words unspoken and Barry lent across and kissed me. "You're so beautiful," he murmured and I blushed. He opened the car door. "You drive away first. I'll ring you at school in the morning." And with that he returned to his car.

I started the ignition and reluctantly, sadly pulled out onto the road again. Barry flashed his headlights as I drove away. In my rear-view mirror I watched him pull out, circle around and drive back toward Whittlesea.

The warmth of my car's interior seemed to have left with Barry. Driving home I kept glancing at the white envelope lying on the passenger seat. Close to Greensborough I pulled over to the kerb to read it by torchlight.

Dearest, dearest Princess,
So here we are at a new stage – and I am wondering where we will go next. Tonight was a surprise to me – a most lovely surprise…
Don't be afraid, I'm not about to start pressuring you…
I think you know what I would like and I'm sure it frightens you. It frightens me a little too…
So how are you feeling? I hope you feel as wonderful as I do; except I am missing you. Are you missing me? I really, really hope so!
I love you,

Barry xxxxxx
Your personal Librarian

LOVE (1)

Falls Creek

*In a choice between love and fear,
choose love.*

MARIANNE WILLIAMSON

"You're not going though, are you?"

Barry was walking ahead of me on the track around the small lake where we often met after work. His question puzzled me. A girlfriend had asked me to go away with her for a weekend. She was rostered to do two half-days' maintenance and cleaning at a ski-chalet during summer in order to maintain her winter access rights.

"I don't have to do any of the work. I'm free to go for walks, read - whatever. It'll be great."

Barry kept walking, said nothing.

"Diane said she only has to work for a few hours each morning, so she and I will get to hang out together in the afternoons."

Barry stopped abruptly and turned to glare at me in anger. "That's not fair! Why would you go away with Diane and not with me?"

"Don't be ridiculous! How can I go away with you for a weekend?" My words had come without hesitation and I immediately felt the guilt rise inside me again. Lowering my eyes to avoid Barry's gaze I dropped my voice. "I'm married. I've got children. My mother lives with me. You know that! You've always known that! How could I possibly go away with you for a weekend?"

I stole a glance at Barry. His clear grey eyes looked at me full of reproach and misery. It was written in his face, in the disappointed slump of his shoulders and arms, and in the silent plea of his upturned palms. The air was heavy with his unspoken dreams for us.

But I wasn't free to love him - maybe never would be. I was a mother, a wife, a daughter. It came with a swathe of obligations and expectations, all aimed at maintaining a 'happy family'.

Ever since Barry and I had first met I'd wrestled with my emotions, struggled not to fall, not to lose myself to him. Now this - it was impossible! How could he think there'd ever be a time when we could go away together for a weekend?

"Why do you have to push me? I don't have anything to give you. I have nothing. I belong to everyone else. You knew that from the start, I'm an onion – just layers of other people's 'stuff.' I'm no-one." Hearing myself I felt ashamed, ashamed of how small I'd become as an individual.

"I don't ask you to leave your family. I only ask you to try and spend as much time with me as you can." Barry's tone reflected his disappointment in me.

I struggled to think of something to say; an excuse, an apology, something to appease him.

Then so softly I had to strain to hear his words, he simply said, "I'll be there. I'll drive to the main car park of the ski resort on Saturday and I'll wait there all day."

"No, no, please don't," I begged, grasping his elbow. "It's too dangerous. I can't come. It's silly." I gathered his hands in mine and held them tightly, terrified by his words. I shook my head and tears welled in my eyes. "Please don't, please don't. I won't be able to come to you. Diane will get suspicious. It's a long drive and we won't be able to meet up anyway. Please don't come. I'll ring you on Saturday. I promise."

Throughout my ranting Barry stood silently staring into my face, his eyes seeming to bore through to my soul. But suddenly he stepped back, pulling his hands from my grip.

"You'll come to me or you won't. But at least I'll be close to you, and that will be something." He said it humbly. His face clouded and he looked away. The muscle in his jaw clenched and he took a deep breath.

At that moment I wanted to reach out and hold his face in my hands, wanted to gently kiss his eyelids and his neck and be enfolded in his arms and held against his chest. I wished he could lift the yoke from my shoulders and spirit us away to a secret place of our own making.

Instead I looked down at the path and shook my head, realising no words could alter his decision. The prospect of a quiet weekend away from everyone drained away, to be replaced by an overwhelming sense of guilt and foreboding.

Diane and I were to set off at 4 pm on Friday in the hope of arriving at the chalet five hours later. I hadn't seen or heard from Barry since Tuesday when we'd met at the lake. Friday morning a letter arrived for me at work. It was a postcard with a picture of a little girl standing alongside the open gate of small stone cottage. The message in Barry's handwriting was brief:

Halley's Comet
Chairlift -
12 Noon
Saturday
XX

Nervous from the moment I woke at the ski-lodge on Saturday, I stayed in bed listening to the minutes ticking by on a large wall-clock. Diane and I were sharing a bunk room with three other women who were also there to do maintenance and cleaning tasks.

After breakfast I summoned up enough courage to tell the group I'd decided to go for a walk for a few hours to get some air and check out the views. "Besides, if I stay here I might have to help with the cleaning." I laughed, trying to sound casual.

"Good thinking," Diane nodded. "But don't get lost. Turn right at the bottom of the path outside the chalet and a walking trail takes you to the reservoir in about thirty minutes. It's pretty there."

"I'll probably do that, so don't expect me back before 3 pm. It was awful to lie but if I didn't walk to the car park, and if I didn't meet up with Barry, then it wouldn't really be lying anyway.

I set off from the lodge, unsure where I'd walk. I was angry at the pressure Barry had put me under. Arriving at the fork in the path I hesitated then turned left and started along the pathway leading to the car park.

Below me the mountains rolled away, the dense forest in the lower regions a swaying carpet of green. But here near the top of the mountain were stunted snow gums and scrubby shrubs tortured by blistering heat in summer and suffocated by thick layers of snow in winter. The ground was rough and unusable for anything but snow skiing and summer rambles.

The whole area was a national park with strict building regulations applying to the series of chalets comprising 'the alpine village'. It was early autumn now and the village was totally deserted save for the chalet where Diane was a member.

As I walked, my mind grappled with the whole situation. My steps became shorter and my pace slowed. I stopped and the wind buffeted on all sides as if it too felt the need to push and pull at me. Birds screeched overhead and the gnarled snow gums bent to witness my struggle, perched on the edge of 'I will' or 'I won't.'

I clasped my hands, sighed and rocked gently back and forth. Probably from a distance I could be mistaken for a lonely soul praying on a mountain. Yet the image belied the turmoil of my thoughts.

After a few moments, I roused and turned back on the path in the direction of the reservoir, silently cursing Barry and banishing all possibility of an 'us'. I hurried along, anxious to be far from the car park. The walk to the reservoir and back to the chalet would swallow up the few hours available. There would be no time left to meet Barry.

The further away from the car park I walked, the more upset I became. He would be sitting there in silence and alone - just waiting. Imagines of him waiting filled my mind.

But perhaps he hadn't come after all, I reasoned to myself. Maybe he didn't care as much as me about any of this. Perhaps this was just some sort of cruel game he was playing– or a test of some sort.

As each new thought filled my head I discounted it, knowing he'd be there, that he'd wait all day, just as he'd said he would. My pace slowed. I wondered what I was proving, who was being hurt and how.

Alone and bereft I stopped, somewhere between a reservoir and a car park, somewhere between what was and what might be, pushed my hands deep into my coat pockets and stared at the ground. I wished the decision could be made by someone else, wished happiness didn't have to be weighed against guilt and duty. I wished…

Turning, I stared back down the path. No-one was coming. No-one would arrive to rescue me. I'd have to make the choice myself.

Deciding to at least see if Barry had come to the car park as he'd threatened, I once again retraced my steps, walking quickly, yet nervously. I thought about whether Barry being in the car park would be a good thing or a bad thing; tried to prepare myself emotionally for what I'd find.

It would be good if he wasn't there because then I'd know where I stood with him and we could end the affair and my life could go back to what it was before we met. But at the same time there would be some hurt if he wasn't there, because I loved him and wanted him to love me back, wanted him to prove true to his word, wanted him to fight for me.

On the other hand if Barry was there, it would be proof he really did loved me. But that would also mean I'd have to choose; to do or say something to end our relationship, or allow it to continue, thereby accepting the possibility of it becoming the deeper bond already haunting our every meeting.

As the car park came into view I crouched in the scrub. The huge expanse was empty save for Barry's car parked at the far corner from where I hid. My heart surged at the sight of the familiar vehicle, but I was uncertain what to do next.

Barry wouldn't know of my presence unless he saw me in his rear view mirror. Standing up slowly, I stepped into the car park, my shoulders hunched as if to shrink me from view. Lowering my head, I buried my hands deep inside my coat pockets, there to clench and re-clench my fingers. I had no idea what to say to him. Although I walked the shortest route - a straight line, it seemed to take an eternity. Now and then I looked up at the silent car before me.

Barry's outline was evident in the front seat. He made no movement, gave no indication he'd seen me. I tried to ignore what this might mean, instead just concentrated on breathing and trying to stay calm. My hope was when I arrived at the car Barry would initiate the talking, leaving me to take my lead from his words.

Somewhere deep inside me perhaps the right words would form subconsciously and come out when needed. But for the moment I could think of nothing, nothing but to walk to his car.

Nervous and embarrassed I approached the driver's side door. Barry sat perfectly still, seemingly oblivious of my presence. Instead his gaze remained fixed on the valley rolling away beyond his car. Uncertain, I stood and stared at the view too, as if that was what had drawn me across the car park. Only the whispering wind disturbed the awkward silence.

I bent down to look through the car window. Barry turned his head very deliberately to look up at me and a rush of emotion surged across his face. Yet still he remained stoically silent. We looked at each other and I felt myself drowning in the crystal blue of his eyes - his beautiful, sad eyes. He pushed a button and the window opened.

"So," I began shyly, "... you came."

"I said I would." Barry turned away toward the valley again, as though frightened of what he might read in my eyes.

Straightening up I scanned the horizon feeling confused and exhausted. *'Lost, lost, lost'* – My mind shrieked as the wind tossed my hair and flicked my legs with its icy fingers.

"It's cold," Barry said into the silence, his eyes locked on the valley. "You should get into the car." His voice was low and gentle.

Inside my coat pockets my nails dug into my palms and I bit my lip and tried to think. Barry bent forward to look up at me. The love in his expression was fringed with fear. He watched me struggling, searching in vain for the words I'd thought would come of their own volition.

He leaned over and unlocked the passenger door. "Come on. It's too cold out there." He smiled at me, a youthful joy spreading across his whole being.

Shrugging, to signify that which I couldn't explain, I stepped around the car and slid into the passenger seat and Barry pulled the seatbelt across my chest. His woollen jumper brushed my cheek and the click of the seatbelt sounded like a key in a padlock.

He relaxed back into his seat and we sat in companionable silence - contemplating the inferences attached to the situation.

"So, we could drive to the reservoir," Barry finally said.

I smiled at the irony. "Good idea. Diane says it's pretty up there."

We walked for kilometres around the reservoir, talking and laughing, neither of us willing to broach the subject of how today had changed our relationship yet again. We sat beneath a tree holding hands as a fine mist closed in around us and eventually we lay on Barry's coat and made love.

A sprinkling of rain roused us from a lovers' slumber and we hurried back to the car. As the rain drizzled around us we sat in the privacy of the car's warm interior, secreted away from the world and its prying eyes.

"Didn't you see me coming across the car park?" I ventured.

"Yes darling. I watched you in the rear-view mirror – watched your every step."

"But why didn't you wave or come to meet me? Why did you just sit there?"

Barry took a breath and rubbed his hand over his face as if trying to find the words to explain.

"I watched you - hardly blinked for fear I'd miss one step. I tried not to move my head because I didn't want you to know I was watching. You looked like a tiny trapped bird. I wasn't sure if you were frightened or feeling guilty - maybe ashamed. I couldn't believe it. You'd come, against all the odds and it made me so happy."

"But if you thought I was scared why didn't you get out of the car and come to me?"

"I was worried you were coming to break it off between us. What I wanted to do was to fling out of the car and run to you, arms outstretched, shouting 'My love, my love'. I wanted to wrap you in my arms and hold you tightly to me, to smother you with kisses. But ..." Barry paused and looked away.

Taking his hands in mine, I forced him to look at me. "But what? Why didn't you come? It was hard for me."

He sighed. "... Because it had to be *your* decision. I forced myself to sit still and wait for you to come to me. If you'd decided you loved me it was better you came freely, take every step by yourself to cross the distance between us."

I kissed his hands and lay my cheek in his palms. Barry drove me to the car park and after a tearful farewell I walked back to the chalet. While walking I mused about what sets real love apart from other emotions. Perhaps real love is when your heart and your soul actually take over the decision making without you even being aware.

I'd never had sex outside and yet today we'd made love beneath a tree on a mountaintop, willingly, gently and beautifully. A previous taboo overturned without conscious decision on my part. I'd wanted Barry to touch me, wanted to feel his hands on me, to lose myself to him and be the cause of his moans and blissful shudderings. I smiled to myself and wondered if I was shocking. Later that night I lay awake, trying to make sense of all that had happened. As I fell asleep, my last thought was of Barry.

When I returned home my youngest son was stretched on the couch with gravel rash on his face and arms. Apparently he'd fallen off his bicycle on Saturday afternoon and as a result, Alec had kept him lying down watching television most of the weekend.

"We ordered pizza,' Alec said and I immediately felt the full weight of my guilt again.

On Monday morning a letter was in my locker when I arrived at work.

My beautiful Princess,
How lovely you were.
Be with me, kiss me, hold me, talk to me, make love to me ...
and love me. You are incredibly, astonishingly beautiful and I miss you every moment that you are not with me.
Thank you for coming.

Your Librarian XX

A week later a small parcel arrived at school for me. It contained a gift and a postcard of an aerial view of the alpine village. Barry's handwriting filled the back of the card.

My dearest Princess, I bought this postcard at the town near the alpine village.
I was going to post it to you as proof I was there, if you didn't come to meet me.
I'm sorry I doubted you. I miss you and I love you,

Your Librarian. XXX

The gift was a small rock mounted on a wooden plaque engraved with the name of the alpine reservoir and a date. Barry later explained he'd picked the rock up from under the tree where we'd made love that day on the mountain. He'd put it in his pocket to forever mark the memory, a tangible reminder of the day we'd first spoken aloud about our love for each other.

His simple gift was overwhelming for me. I loved him in enormous surges and in gentle waves; his words and his contented silences. I loved him passionately and painfully, so much that thinking about him could reduce me to tears.

First date of sorts

*I was made and meant to look for you and
wait for you and become yours forever*

ROBERT BROWNING

The local university contained a small art-house cinema and Barry suggested we go there one weekend to watch a matinee. I was terrified we'd be seen by someone we knew.

"But it's an art-house cinema darling. Nobody we know is likely to be interested in this movie. They're more likely to be at the big commercial movie-houses watching the latest blockbuster."

What Barry said made sense. Somewhat ashamed of myself, I realised even I wouldn't have known about the movie unless Barry had told me about it. And even though I'd attended the university as a mature-aged student, I'd never been to its cinema.

It seemed a wonderful opportunity to spend time with Barry and going to the movies, complete with its veil of darkness, would allow us to behave like a 'normal' couple.

Even so, I insisted we drive there separately and meet in the foyer. As I drove into the car park I scanned the parked cars to check there were none I recognised and that no-one I knew was locking car doors or walking across the car park.

Satisfied I was safe from detection I left my car and with my coat pulled tight around me and my head lowered, I hurried toward the cinema. I hadn't seen Barry's car anywhere and began once again to struggle with the idea this was some sort of cruel joke he was playing on me.

Perhaps he had no intention of coming. Perhaps he was just setting me up so he could laugh about me with the other teachers next week. *'Imagine her thinking I was serious about meeting her. As if I'd risk getting into a fight with a jealous husband. Really! Why would I bother? I hardly know her.'*

The foyer of the cinema was crowded with movie-buffs and university students. I hesitated outside the door, reluctant to move from the grey winter sky outside into the brightly lit room. Inside everyone and everything was so clearly defined. Outside I felt blurred, potentially faceless - under the radar. But inside I'd be easily recognised by anyone who knew me.

Biting my lip, I pulled up my coat collar and readjusted my scarf to cover part of my face. Then stretching slightly I scanned the sea of faces in the foyer.

Barry was tall; over 186 centimetres. He was standing beside a pillar, smiling, bending slightly forward to speak to someone in the crowd. Uncertain what to do, I stepped back from the doorway, beyond where the light spilt onto the ground. Had he brought someone else with him? Had he met someone he knew? Even worse, had he met someone we both knew? Perhaps I'd misunderstood the invitation. Perhaps he'd suggested the movie to lots of people and I'd misinterpreted, no - *wished*, he'd instead meant this to be a sort of first date.

Inside the foyer a small gong sounded to indicate the cinema doors were now open. People began queuing to show their tickets to the usher. Outside I shuffled across to peer between the advertising posters on the glass doors to watch Barry. Just like Hans Christian Anderson's *Little Match Girl* I stood in the cold watching the happy people inside.

The crowd thinned and I saw Barry was talking to two teachers we both knew. Teacher gossip had hinted this couple were having an illicit affair. Now here they were attending this out of the way art house cinema. The coincidence irritated me.

I watched as they nodded a goodbye to Barry and moved to join the queue. They walked close to each other but didn't hold hands. Perhaps they thought this served to prove they weren't having an affair. Instead they were just two friends going to see an obscure film at an obscure cinema on their day off, while their respective partners were elsewhere. Watching them, I realised how easy it is for outsiders to discern when two people are having a secret love affair.

Barry began looking expectantly around the people still lingering in the foyer finishing their drinks. He wandered a few steps back and forth and finally came towards the door of the cinema to look outside. Moving out from where I'd been hiding, I took a step into the light.

His face lit up. "There you are. I was worried you weren't coming. You'll never guess who's here."

"Yeah, I know. I saw them. I s'pose it's true then - about the affair?"

"Of course it's true. Didn't you believe it?" He shook his head in surprise. "You're such a funny mouse. You can be so clever and then sometimes you can be so naive." He reached out to take my arm and I jumped back as if stung.

"Don't take my arm. Don't touch me at all. What if they see us? I don't want them to know. I don't want anyone to know." The words had tumbled out without me realising how hurtful they sounded.

Barry sighed. "You're being ridiculous. They don't care, and of all the people who might see us, they're the least likely to say anything given their situation."

"I don't care. Don't touch me. You and I might just both be here at the same time by coincidence. Maybe we're not even aware the other one is here." I could hear myself trying to create a plausible story, an alibi; a believable lie. I felt frantic, on the edge of turning and running back to the car, of ending the situation, ending all of it - before it escaped and overwhelmed me.

"But we're just here to see a movie. There's no harm in that. I sometimes go to the opera with a neighbour because my wife doesn't like opera. It doesn't mean I'm having an affair with my neighbour."

"I don't know. Are you having an affair with your neighbour?" The cruel question was meant to shift the focus, give me time to think. Perhaps Barry would become cross with me and I could just leave and thereby avoid this current situation altogether. I knew he was telling the truth. He'd previously told me about going to the opera with various people because his wife didn't share his passion for the music.

But Barry didn't get cross. Instead he straightened slightly as if he recognised my ploy as an attempt to flee yet again. He leaned toward me and spoke softly, "Look, we've come to see the movie and we were going to have such a nice time, until you saw *A* and *B*. I've told you they won't even mention they were at the cinema, let alone that they saw us here. So why don't we just go in and watch the movie like we'd planned?"

Behind us there were only about a dozen people still waiting to be admitted to the cinema. I felt silly and disappointed. It had started as such a lovely idea but now it was all going wrong. I looked at the queue, looked at Barry, wished I'd never agreed to this, wished I could walk away. But at the same time knew I wanted to be here, wanted to be with Barry.

"It'll be dark in the cinema," he offered.

"Okay, I'll come in. But don't sit next to me. You go in now and sit down the front somewhere and I'll go in and sit in the middle. You turn right when you get inside the door and I'll turn left."

"God Miss Mouse – that's ridiculous!"

"I know and I'm sorry but I just can't ... it's the best I can do. We can still catch up afterwards and talk about the film. We can go for a drink or sit in the car and talk all about it. Please?" I looked up at Barry's eyes and watched him wrestle with my request.

"Okay, but it's stupid. Nobody cares if we sit together or not - nobody but you!" He shrugged and shook his head slightly, no doubt wondering why he tolerated my peculiar attitudes.

"You join the queue now and I'll come in after everyone else." I hesitated and touched his sleeve fleetingly. "I'm sorry to be such an idiot. You should leave me."

"I know," he said without enthusiasm and moved away to join the queue. Before disappearing through the door Barry looked back and smiled sadly at me. The lights were dimmed in the cinema and the trailers and advertising clips were showing on the screen.

Being the last person into the cinema it was a great relief to find a short row of seats just inside the door totally vacant - probably because of their poor location relative to the screen.

Quickly I sank into a seat and waited for my eyes to adjust to the dim lighting. I wondered where Barry was sitting, wondered where the other adulterous couple were sitting. I wriggled lower in my seat, deliberately not looking left or right, trying to convince myself if I couldn't see anyone, then perhaps no-one could see me.

The cinema darkened and the main movie started. It was a love story, full of beautiful golden sunsets and dark intimate moments. I was grateful for the darkness afforded by the intimate scenes and startled when the bright lighting of the sunsets exposed me to the cinema audience.

I hoped that because the script was so good everyone's eyes would remain focussed on the screen, making it unlikely I'd be seen. The realisation made me sad. Perhaps after all I could've been sitting beside Barry in the dark. We probably could have even held hands. No doubt he'd chosen the movie for the romance and beauty, something akin to what our relationship was becoming. But I'd ruined it - too scared, too worried about being found out.

I wondered if this would go on forever. I couldn't see a way out without hurting my family, hurting my children, in order to be with Barry.

Falling in love with someone other than the father of one's children was against everything I'd been raised to believe about families. A mother's first responsibility is to her children. Anything or anyone who hurt the children was the enemy. Yet in this situation it was me, the mother, who was in the wrong.

How could Barry be bothered with me? He said he could wait, said he just wanted all the free time I could spend with him and that would be enough until I was ready to take the next step, whatever it might be. Deep down I knew he hoped one day I'd be brave enough to leave my family to be with him.

Once, a few days after we'd discussed what might happen in the future, Barry had risen very early to nail a huge sign to a tree I always drove past on my way to work. In large capital letters his sign simply said:

Jump.
I'll catch you

I'd wept to read it. It seemed so easy. 'Jump;' such a small word for such an enormous task, one entailing an ocean of guilt, grief, dislocation and recrimination.

Would I survive such a jump? Would I even be the same person Barry loved, if I jumped? Perhaps it was the 'mouse' that attracted him. Perhaps in a way, he secretly admired my commitment to my children.

When the movie ended I was the first out of the cinema. In great haste I returned to my car to sit and wait for Barry to find me, as I knew he would. While waiting I read one of the novels he'd lent me. Nowadays there were always a few in my car.

My face was tilted down away from the car windows to reduce the likelihood of people recognising me as they passed by and to discourage conversation by negating eye-contact.

It seemed lately as if almost everything I said and did had to be thought through in great depth to ensure my relationship with Barry wasn't exposed. Sometimes the whole situation was so complicated, so exhausting. It was hard to make sense of it. Perhaps easier to just run, but ...

"Miss Mouse, Miss Mouse." Barry grinned at me through the passenger door and held up a brown paper bag he was carrying. "Come over to my car. It's over behind that tree." He pointed further along the parking area.

Once inside his car Barry pushed the bag toward me. "I bought you a cinema treat... even though you probably don't deserve one you ridiculous girl." At this he laughed to show he'd forgiven me, yet again. "Open it, open it."

It contained two chocolate-coated ice creams. Barry had bought them at the candy bar as he left the cinema. He knew they were a favourite of mine and yet I rarely bought them because of the cost. Ice creams are special treats for children, not their mothers.

I smiled, taken aback by Barry's capacity for listening and remembering things I'd spoken about and then use the information later to give me joy. He was such a romantic. I had no defence against the love he offered. We talked about the movie and crunched our way through the ice creams. Outside dusk began to settle across the trees and the car windows slowly fogged up with the heat of our conversation.

Musing on the memory of that wonderful day, I later wrote a poem to Barry.

THE KISS

Crunching icy-poles
one 'ridiculous' day

I lean across
and kiss you

Tongues dance seductively
hot envelops cold

Impassioned blood
melts the ice

Mouth lingers…
on mouth…

A shock
of give and take

Startled eyes open
we pull apart

Aroused we laugh
and look away

Bound evermore
by one spontaneous kiss

Don't say, don't say

*A woman who cuts her hair is
about to change her life*

Coco Chanel

In the early days of our relationship I thought Barry only liked me because of my innocence and naivety compared to other women he'd known. This was never more obvious then when the conversation drifted vaguely toward anything related to sex.

I'd learned about sex by watching a grainy and somewhat confusing movie at a 'mother and daughter' night held at the local Church Hall. My mother had told me we were going to have a special night together – that we were going out in the night to watch a movie. The boys and my dad were left with the full responsibility of doing the dishes after tea.

As I left the house in my coat and hat that night I'd poked a face at my brothers. They were washing my plates for a change. The night was already wonderful.

The lights went down in the Church Hall and a cartoon sketch tried, vainly in my case, to describe parts of my body I doubted even existed. A room full of ten-year old girls sat in stony silence beside their mothers watching this horror movie under cover of darkness. I began to wish I was home doing the dishes instead of here witnessing this appalling series of revelations.

Not a word was spoken between my mother and me throughout the screening. I remember feeling hot and embarrassed, too traumatised to even glance at her. Being born a girl seemed to condemn one at birth to being forever cursed with a lot of blood, secret agonies when swimming, and calendar checks before opting to wear a white dress.

As if this that wasn't hard enough to accept, it also seemed there was eventually to be a lot of poking and probing by unsightly males appendages hell-bent on going where they shouldn't be and certainly wouldn't fit. Mercifully the film ended and the lights came on.

"Do you have any questions?" my mother had asked me. With lowered eyes, I mumbled that I didn't. Before leaving the Church Hall she stood me in front of a trestle table that was groaning under the weight of seemingly pornographic books and brochures expanding on the messages in the film. I stood with traumatised girls and stared down at my plastic sandals wondering what my father would think about all this.

My mother insisted on buying me 'a little information book' and to my horror, began thumbing through the various publications to decide what would be suitable. Holding a few options in my line of vision she sought my opinion. "What about this one?"

"I don't need a book. I understood it." I looked neither left nor right and certainly not at the book she was holding. I thought a bag of jelly-beans or even a biscuit would have been nicer, given the disappointment of the film. I was already struggling with what lie I'd have to tell my brothers so they'd remain envious of my night out.

Finally my mother selected a booklet. On its bilious green cover was the photographed profile of an unhappy girl wearing a black school jumper. She was no doubt contemplating the life-long complications associated with being born a female.

Although I survived this 'baptism of fire' it helped to ensure I grew up to be a shy love-maker. I've never been a 'screamer' or a 'moaner' in the bedroom, nor have I ever asked for anything specific. In fact, my eternal plea after sex has always been 'Please don't say anything about it.'

This repeated after-sex request amused Barry. He thought women should say what they wanted and experiment. I grimaced when he showed me a lewd 'Karma Sutra' book he had in his library. "That's disgusting. Can't people just make love? Isn't it supposed to be gentle and soft? Does it have to be a gymnastics activity as well?"

Resigned to my shyness whenever sex was mentioned Barry would grin and mumble, "I know ... don't say, don't say."

A childhood spent in a houseful of boys with a mother whose childhood had been spent in another houseful of boys didn't foster 'girly-ness'. I had never really thought much about this, having gotten by as a teenager because my large breasts automatically attracted the opposite sex.

Soon after realising we were in love, I found myself standing naked in front of my bedroom mirror trying to see what Barry would see if I ever let him see me naked. It was during this appraisal I became worried about the quantity of pubic hair growing on my 'Venus mound' (a term I'd learned from Barry).

I looked at my pubic hair front on, then side on. 'Hmm – too bushy?'

I uncurled some of the springy mass to study the length of each hair. It was too long. I was too hairy - more ape than human. If left unchecked surely the hair might even attempt a siege higher up, perhaps growing on and on to cover my stomach. How had I let myself get to this state?

Having taken up early morning swimming, on a few occasions I'd scissored and dragged the razor around my inner thighs to eradicate 'strays' peeping out from the crotch of my swimming trunks. But standing there staring at my hairy womanhood it was obvious a more serious assault was needed.

I thought about shaving closer in to the 'main attraction.' While this was successful it was short-lived and within a day scratchy stubble heralded the arrival of a female version of the 'five-o'clock shadow'.

Shaving could be problematic, even embarrassing unless there was a definite timetable of when I needed to be at my 'smoothest'. I was already feeling guilty about this newfound friendship and the guilt could only increase if I found myself plotting about when to shave and when not to, relative to the likelihood of Barry and I sleeping together.

I settled for trimming back the undergrowth every time I shaved my armpits. This seemed a compromise that would be better than not shaving. It also included an element of chance in that I doubted I'd allow Barry to touch any bristly parts of me should the opportunity present. I left it to God. If Barry and I were 'swept away' on my shaving day, the chances we would make love were high. If passion arose on any day where bushiness or bristle was apparent, the chances were low.

This model worked at preventing us from having sex for quite some time. Then one hot day a girlfriend came to visit me. Wearing a loose-fitting singlet dress and sporting a tan, she looked stunning.

"Feel my legs," she demanded, holding up a honey-coloured limb. They were silky and hair-free and she raved about a brand of leg wax she'd recently discovered. "It's great. You only have to wax every few weeks," she cooed into my jealous ear.

"The more you wax, the less the hair grows back. You pull out roots and all, like weeds in the garden." It sounded wonderful and there was no denying she was hair-free and care-free.

Next visit to the shops I checked out the cost of her hair-removal treatment. It was very, very expensive. I couldn't justify spending that amount of money to make me hair-free for an illicit, intimate liaison that may never eventuate.

Weeks went by and I continued to shave, playing Russian roulette with God, my pubic hair, bristles, and Barry. God kept winning. A better woman would have been pleased.

I went to the supermarket and found a tube of generic hair removal cream. It was much cheaper than the wax treatment. I took it home and tried it on my legs. It didn't work very well and one tube wasn't even enough to do both legs completely so I was forced to wear slacks for awhile to conceal the hairless patches below my knees.

All this time, Barry and I continued to meet accidentally, sometimes deliberately, always secretly and most times briefly. It was agony and my love and frustration grew with every minute I spent with him. When not with him, I was thinking of him, phoning him, writing to him or reading his letters to me. While driving I was constantly scanning the road in the hope of seeing his car.

I went back to the toiletries aisle of the supermarket. This time I found a wax treatment rather than removal cream. It was a much cheaper brand than my friend's. I bought it and some days later locked myself in the bathroom.

My previous experience with the cream had taught me one box would be insufficient to do both legs. Not wanting to buy more boxes as a trial, I'd decided to apply the wax straight onto the 'target area'. Surely one box would be enough to do that area?

I decided trimming first would improve the success of the procedure so I snipped away a little. But it all seemed so appallingly intimate that I soon abandoned the trimming task, applied the strips and waited for the wax to set before I began ripping.

Now childbirth hurts with a huge, deep shuddering sort of pain. Waxing pubic hair hurts in thin piercing splinters. I've heard tell that root canal work on teeth feels like the dentist is dragging the end of the tooth off the jawbone. Waxing pubic hair then is akin to dragging each hair root from where it is surely attached to the wall of the uterus. Oh what pain!

With gritted teeth and sweating brow I continued to wax and rip, wax and rip. A myriad of small blood spots began to appear across my Venus mound, each one lamenting the loss of a single strand of curly hair. Large red angry welts rose up to ghost the outline from where each wax strip had been torn. Finally I ran out of wax. God is merciful!

For some days after it hurt to wear underwear. Accidentally brushing my Venus mound against anything caused me to flinch with pain, if not weep.

It was during the week of welts and wincing, that fate found me perched nervously on Barry's couch trying to convince myself and eventually Barry that this was *not* the day we should first see each other naked. I made all sorts of rational comments about the limited time available, the need to take the relationship slowly, and the benefits of getting to know each other really well. I talked on and on, all the while squeezing my legs together to remind me of my painful, plucked pubic area.

Barry appeared puzzled. He valiantly challenged every excuse I offered. "Can we at least just lie on top of the blankets on the bed? "No rude stuff - I promise. Just let me hold you and kiss you for awhile."

Scarlet with embarrassment I summoned up the courage to tell him outright. "I'm trying to tell you I absolutely don't want you to touch or look at my 'rude bits' tonight. I'm just not ready for that yet. You have to go more slowly."

A look of hurt flickered across his face.

I reached for my handbag. "Look," I said, "It's more complicated than you realise. I can't say it outright, but I've written you a letter to explain." I held out a note I'd written before arriving, in anticipation of finding myself in this predicament. "But you can't read the note until after I've gone."

At this Barry became angry. "That's not fair. You can't just say I'm not allowed to touch you and then give me a note and drive away. If you want to break up with me, say it to my face. I deserve that at least."

With a huge sigh I handed him the note. "I'm not breaking up with you. It's just something a bit embarrassing and I can't say it. You can have the note but only if you go into another room to read it. And you have to promise to *never, ever* mention its contents to me.

Barry took the note and strode off to the bedroom. I waited on the couch feeling stupid. All these months of trying so hard to appear sophisticated, clever, worldly in his eyes and yet here I was - a plucked chicken, red and swollen because girly stuff was both expensive and difficult to use.

Down the hallway I heard Barry laughing. "Oh darl-ing you are *so* ridiculous!" he called out to me. Re-entering the lounge room he caught me up in a big bear hug. "You're really quite insane. I thought you were leaving me. Now I find you've been waxing your *frondonagles*."

He threw his head back and laughed aloud. "What a funny girl you are. You're adorable! A plucked chicken eh? That's so funny. You have to show me now. C'mon it's only fair."

The tension was broken but I felt ashamed. "You promised not to talk about it so don't say, don't say!!"

"Yes, but that was before I knew what it was all about." He was still grinning. "C'mon. I need to see this. I've never had a girlfriend who waxed her 'rudey bits' for me. C'mon. You're so cute."

I eventually convinced him there was no way he was going to see anything tonight. Instead we sat together on the couch and laughed and talked for another hour before I had to leave.

Next time I visited Barry he presented me with a gift - a large scrapbook. Inside was pasted a collection of photos of Venus mounds he'd cut from men's magazines. The photos showed female pubic areas of every size and colour, some resplendent with long flowing hair, some with curly hair or short, bristly hair, and others completely waxed. There were even some style-cut into various symbols and shapes.

It was hideously rude! I was appalled and slammed the book shut.

Barry laughed. "Why don't we work out a style-cut for you?" he said, picking up the scrapbook and flicking through the pages.

I gave him a scathing look, said nothing.

"Oh well, when you're in a nursing home and I'm looking after you, I'll be free to shape those frondonagles into a little heart shape." he smiled and slipped the scrapbook into his bookcase.

"Hmph ... not if I kill you first," I muttered at his back.

Breaking up

Heart, are you great enough
For a love that never tires?

ALFRED TENNYSON

The thin veneer keeping our relationship hidden was shattered one day when a fellow teacher mentioned seeing Barry and me at the Art Gallery the previous weekend. The blood drained from my face as she spoke and my mind rushed back over the outing, searching for evidence of indiscretions that may have 'given away' our romantic involvement.

"Hmm – yeah, I've got an annual membership to the gallery. I go there a lot." I tried to sound casual, opting not to mention Barry in my reply.

"You must like art. I have to say it's not my thing." she said. "I went with a girlfriend because she wanted to see the Picasso exhibition and she promised if I went with her, we could see a movie afterwards." She shrugged indicating she considered it a fair trade-off.

"What was better, the exhibition or the movie?" I asked, hoping to steer the conversation into safer waters.

"Seriously? Have you seen Picasso's work?" she said. I gave a short chuckle and moved off down the corridor to end the discussion.

Lunchtime saw me remain in my classroom to avoid meeting the teacher again. I was terrified that within earshot of other teachers, she'd mention seeing Barry and me at the gallery.

After school Barry and I met in a park and I tried to explain my terror at finding we'd been seen together at the gallery. "It's too risky. We should never have started... I can't do it anymore; it's too hard. We have to stop meeting, stop everything. It's my fault and I'm sorry. But if you love me, please tell me to go." My heart was racing as I panted out my plea.

Sitting beside me on the park bench Barry shook his head and said nothing. His blue eyes, usually warm and friendly, were now grey and harsh.

"Please ..." I urged when he made no comment. "I love you desperately but I hate always lying to everyone - my family, my friends, people at work. It's too hard. It'll be better for everyone if we stop seeing each other. Don't wait beside the road for me anymore and we won't phone or write to each other. It's the best thing to do. You need someone with less baggage than me."

Turning away from Barry I watched some ducks on the nearby pond and wondered if they were paddling as frantically as me just to stay afloat. Why was it all so hard? Was Barry too intense, too possessive of my time? No, it was my fault; for wanting *everything* – the love and joy of being with Barry, as well as not failing my sons by leaving their father and disrupting their family-life. What a mess that would create. Would the boys come with me or stay with their dad - and what about my mum? It would all be my fault.

Barry spoke quietly and seriously. "I'd thought lately you were close to making some sort of decision. But I didn't say anything because I didn't want to push you. I wanted you to take the final step and jump – jump into my waiting arms. But now this - you've decided not to just retreat like all the other times, but to close the door on us completely?"

His voice sounded cold and hard and I felt him choosing his words carefully to ensure he said exactly what he felt in a calm, rational manner.

I couldn't think what to say, couldn't trust myself to speak. The thought of a future without Barry in my life was terrible, and I doubted I'd be strong enough to close the door he spoke about by myself. I wanted him to take that step, to end our relationship.

Seeing my distress Barry turned my face toward him and held my hands. "I'm still waiting at the foot of the precipice and I'll do everything possible to cushion your fall... I asked you once if a humble librarian could catch a princess. The answer is '*Yes, if she wants to be caught*'."

"The secret nature of our relationship doesn't worry me," he continued. "And I'm prepared to fit in around your family's needs and to wait for as long as it takes until we can be together permanently. I'm in love with you and therefore not put off by your supposedly complicated baggage." After a pause he added, "But at the same time I don't want to be a burden to you, if that's what you feel I've become."

I closed my eyes and wished he'd get angry and tell me to leave. But that was never going to happen. He was passive, knew I loved him and was just looking for an easy way out.

When I didn't speak, Barry made a decision. "If you're not happy to speak to me or see me again then that's what will happen. But only because that's what you want. It's your decision, not mine and I'll abide by that."

My heart ached on hearing his words. Stranded on the edge of uncertainty, I let the axe fall.

"Yes, that's what I want. It'll be best for everyone. I'm sorry; wish I was braver, stronger or whatever it takes to walk away from a marriage but I'm not. And I can't go on like this anymore either. So it's better if we just end it, not see each other again."

I brushed my lips across his cheek and walked away, feeling as though part of my body had been torn away.

Barry remained true to his word and didn't try to contact me. About a week after our 'break up' I lingered beside my home phone before picking up the receiver and listening – only the dial tone. I placed my finger on the first digit of Barry's home phone number, hoping he might somehow feel my anguish and sense me thinking about him. I waited a few moments before replacing the receiver in its cradle.

The following weekend I went away with some girlfriends to the beach. Under the pretence of buying some drinks while they sunbaked, I drove to a public phone booth. Inside the booth I told myself I was being selfish; that if I rang Barry he'd be angry and quite justified in hanging up on me.

Yet ignoring all my premonitions, I picked up the receiver, inserted some coins and wondered what to say when he answered. Perhaps he wouldn't be home, wouldn't answer. Perhaps I'd be saved the humiliation of him telling me off.

Dialling his number, I imagined the phone ringing in his kitchen. Even being momentarily linked by the phone line gave me joy and made me feel closer to him.

"Hello." Barry's voice was gruff and I thought about hanging up.

"Hello," Barry repeated, this time louder with more aggression.

"It's me."

"What do you want?" his words stung me like a slap.

I tried to think of the answer to his question, unsure what I wanted; other than not wanting him to hang up. I wished we could breathe and not say anything, just keep holding onto each other via the phone-line.

"Hello," he said again, perhaps irritated by my silence.

"I'm here....." My voice sounded thin and tiny.

Silence for a few seconds, then - "Where?" Still no gentleness in his voice.

My eyes skimmed the grimy glass of the phone booth. "I wondered..., I wondered..." I began to cry softly. No comment from Barry. "I wondered if you'd come back to me."

The words came from deep inside me without warning. I was glad it happened that way.

"I can't," he replied, his voice soft now, no doubt because he realised the impact of his two words.

I gulped for air. "Sorry. I shouldn't have phoned. Said I wouldn't. You're right. It's best this way. I'm sorry."

Barry's voice cut in over my apology. "I can't come back because I didn't leave. I'm still here. You left me - remember?"

I clenched the phone tighter. "It was a mistake... I can't do it. I miss you too much... I need you." I was crying and laughing all at once.

"Where are you?" His voice was now intimate, almost a whisper.

"I'm with some girls at the beach-house for the weekend. We can't meet." Even as I spoke I realised nothing had changed – we were still hiding.

Overlooking this, Barry instead said eagerly "Can you phone me tomorrow morning, 'bout 8 am? I have to go out at ten to help set-up the hall for the school bush dance."

"8 am? How can I get away from the girls so early?"

"Make an excuse. Say you're going to buy milk or a newspaper. Just work out something and call me from the phone booth at 8 am. I'll be waiting." At this he paused before saying, "I'm always waiting for you."

Now Barry was helping to create the lies for me. Everything was a tangled web.

At 7.45 am the next day a lone cyclist pedalled down a deserted road to the shop opposite the beach. A sign on the shop door advised it would open at 8.30 am. I leaned my bicycle against the outdoor seat.

The sky was dense with ocean clouds and the sea wind was chill. The grimy phone-booth offered some protection and I reasoned we'd have about half an hour to talk before the shop-keeper arrived. I was pleased the opening time of the shop would furnish me with a ready-made excuse for my delayed return to the beach-house.

Opening the phone-booth door I was met with a joyful burst of orange and yellow lighting up its interior. Sticky-taped to the inside glass panels were a dozen long-stemmed calendulas, each floral head faced toward the door for maximum impact.

I hesitated, overawed. Surely he hadn't? But would he have? I looked up and down the street – no-one, no cars. I looked back at the flower-filled phone-booth. It would be about a six hour round trip from the cottage to the phone booth. Surely he hadn't? But then maybe he had?

In less than half an hour the shopkeeper would arrive and see this amazing display. Quickly I began detaching the flowers and assembling them into a much more explainable 'bunch.' Having succeeded in this before the shopkeeper arrived, my feeling of frenzy calmed.

I phoned Barry's number.

"Hello, who's that?" He'd answered instantly and I listened hard trying to detect a hint of mischief in his voice.

"It's me ... of course. Did you come down here last night?"

"Why would I do that?" It sounded like he was grinning.

"I don't know. Why *would* you do that?"

"You're a funny little thing. Imagine thinking I'd drive all the way down there and then drive all the way back again. What would be the point?"

"Flowers perhaps?"

"Flowers? Do you want me to bring you some flowers?"

"I think you already did, didn't you?"

"I'm not sure. What colour are they?" I laughed with joy because he still loved me and would go to any lengths to prove it.

Unfortunately even though we were so very careful, Barry and I were sighted together a few times in the early years of our relationship. Each time my immediate reaction was to beg him to end the affair. It was by now obvious to me I would never walk away voluntarily, I loved him too much.

Each time I took fright at our relationship being exposed, Barry would calm me down. "Darling, don't ask me to tell you to go. I know at the moment this life is far from perfect, but to be completely apart would be unbearable. I can't even conceive of a life without you. I love you."

He was beautiful. Everything about him was neat and orderly, from his well-trimmed beard and filed fingernails to his crisp cotton shirts, woollen jumpers and dark denim jeans. In my mind he personified safety and common sense and intelligence and dignity. I wished I could be with him always, wished we could just disappear together without the world noticing. But it was impossible!

One morning when I arrived at school, I was called to take a phone-call in the staffroom. It was Barry. He'd made the call himself without enlisting the other male who always rang on his behalf.

"Hello, this is a surprise," I said turning my back on the one other teacher in the room.

"I can't believe it! When I got to school a guy was waiting outside the office for me. He served divorce papers on me. I can't believe she'd do that." He sounded more agitated than I'd ever known him.

Taken aback by his distress I floundered for something to say.

"Well you haven't lived together or been a couple for years, so I suppose she wants to sort it out. You probably need to meet with her and discuss what you both want." I felt crushed to think Barry was distressed at the thought of divorcing his wife. Perhaps he stilled loved her after all.

"What?" he snapped, a hint of confusion in his voice.

"You should meet her. Sort it out. After all, you've been married almost ten years." I was glad Barry couldn't see the slump of my shoulders or hear the breaking of my heart as I spoke.

"Don't be ridiculous! I'm not angry about the divorce. I'm angry she had the papers served on me at school. It was embarrassing. We could have handled it all privately. There was no need for this. I've no intention of contesting the divorce." Barry quietened down as he spoke. He'd phoned me to talk through the outrage he felt at having his private life displayed in front of his colleagues.

"Yeah, that's awful. She should have spoken to you beforehand. What happens now?"

"There'll be a court hearing. Apparently she doesn't want a property settlement. We'll both just keep our own assets and I'm not the father of her kids and haven't lived with them for years so there's no child support issue." By now the aggression had gone out of Barry's voice. The effect of his initial embarrassment had waned.

"Uh-huh," I nodded, knowing nothing about the divorce process. "So does that all make you happy?"

"Yeah. It'll be good to get it over with. I should've started the ball rolling myself years ago; just didn't get round to it. But this'll be good."

"Okay, well just stay calm. The other teachers will understand. By the end of today it'll be old news, so don't worry too much. Fill out whatever forms you have to and get them lodged. You'll be fine. I'll meet you after school tonight. We'd better hang-up now, it's nearly bell time.... Don't worry anymore okay?"

At the other end of the phone I heard Barry sigh. It was the sound a distressed child makes when their mother has soothed their hurt.

"Yeah okay. Thanks for listening. I love you. See you tonight."

Some weeks later the new Principal at my school called me into her office to ask if there was any truth to the rumour about Barry and me being romantically involved.

"No," I lied. "Who told you that?"

"Apparently one of the parents saw the two of you driving around Preston last Monday when in fact, you'd phoned in to say you were taking the day off because of illness."

It was mortifying to be having this conversation with the Principal as if I was a naughty student. But thankfully the reality was that on the day in question I'd taken Heath to the doctor and then nursed him all day at home through a bad cold.

"Well they were wrong. I was home looking after my son and have a doctor's certificate to prove it. I was nowhere near Preston. Perhaps the parent should've checked their facts before telling you what they thought they saw. And anyway, what business is it of theirs what I do when not at school?" True to the adage 'offense is the best defence' I had come out fighting. But as I spoke my fists clenched and my breath shortened.

The Principal shuffled some papers on her desk and gave a small cough. "You're quite right. They should've checked the facts first." She looked at me with slightly narrowed eyes. "It would be awkward here if there was any truth to the rumour, given that Barry's wife works here." It was a tactful warning.

"Ex-wife," I corrected.

"Yes, of course. Well there's no more to discuss then. I'm sorry a mistake was made." She moved a file onto the desk in front of her.

"A very unfortunate mistake," I said and left her office.

When Barry and I next met, I cried and tried to convince him to give me up. Once again he refused and once again I was glad. On my way to work the following day, the asphalt on the last bend of the road was covered in chalked hearts. Scrawled inside each heart, in large letters was:

BJ
L
SG

I smiled, but at the same time hoped for rain to wash away the evidence.

LOVE (2)

First weekend together

Time is very slow for those who wait.
Very fast for those who are scared.

WILLIAM SHAKESPEARE

Barry wanted us to go away for a weekend. "I want us to be together for hours and hours without having to watch the clock all the time. Just imagine - we could talk and walk, go out for a meal and just be together."

Until now our relationship comprised a collection of stolen 'moments' some as short as ten minutes when we met on the side of the road. Sometimes we'd go to a movie and sit holding hands in the darkness of the theatre or we'd wander around art galleries or botanical gardens or go for walks. Like ghosts, our time together was hidden in the dark corners, in the shadows of life.

I'd abandoned my regular Friday night 'happy hours' with work colleagues and instead went to visit Barry at Waldene. We'd eat pita bread dipped in hummus and talk for awhile before making love between the blue sheets of his king-sized bed while the forest looked on through the windows.

Then I'd shower before hurrying away to make dinner for my family. The drive home was always a tumultuous emotional mix of adulterous guilt and inexpressible love and joy at having found such a person as Barry.

One Saturday morning when I came out from my weekly supermarket shopping a torn envelope under my car's windscreen wiper bore a hastily scribbled plea –

Please find time to be with me.
Even a minute
Whenever you can

Nervously I scanned the car park but could see no sign of Barry. It wasn't his local shopping centre but knowing my weekend shopping routine he must have made the trip especially, must have walked the car park looking for my car. But he wouldn't have known whether I was going to be alone or with one of my sons or my mother. He'd taken a terrible risk.

It made me uneasy knowing Barry had ventured into this part of my world and been here at my car as I pushed a trolley around buying food for my family. The two worlds should never brush up against each other.

Yet while my family's demands caused my days to rush by, for Barry, alone in the forest, the days spent waiting to see me must seem like an eternity. Sometimes I tried to imagine what our arrangement must be like for him. Although he loved me, he was absolutely powerless to change our situation. My children were young, my husband was unwell and my recently widowed mother needed frequent consoling and support. I felt pulled in every way, barely able to cope even before falling in love with Barry. There seemed no way through.

Finally I engineered an excuse to be away from my family for a weekend and Barry rented a small cabin for us in the Grampians. Terrified of being found out, I insisted on parking at the airport rather than leaving my car at Waldene. Driving to the airport where Barry was to meet me, I began having second thoughts and wondered if the whole weekend might be some sort of elaborate set-up.

After all, how well did I really know Barry? Perhaps he wanted to end our relationship in a way that would pay me back for not putting him ahead of my family's needs? Maybe he wouldn't even arrive at the agreed parking place to get me?

Once before as a teenager I'd been stood up and even now still felt the hurt. No doubt there'd be shame and embarrassment if Barry stood me up and later our paths crossed again. Would he tell the other teachers and would they laugh at me behind my back?

My head was full of uncomfortable thoughts but in spite of the possibility of any of them coming true, I kept driving, willing to risk everything just to be with Barry for this short, sweet escape. It was a testament to the impact Barry had made on my life.

At the airport Barry was standing on the footpath outside the parking area. I pulled over and wound down my window and we greeted each other nervously.

"I thought you wouldn't come," he said, studying my face intently.

I scoffed. Imagine that! Barry had been experiencing the same anguish as me. Yet he too, had still driven to the airport. What a peculiar pair we made.

"Ditto," I said and we grinned at each other like children sharing a joke.

"You drive in and park, then walk back to here. I'll bring my car around. I'm parked up the road."

My stomach clenched– we were actually going to go through with it. Driving into the car park a new thought settled in my mind. What if Barry now drove off? Once again I felt the weight of my guilt and my shame. I'd have to deal with the 'joke' if it was finally played out.

Fearing the worst I walked back to the gate with faint steps. Barry was there and his eyes shone as he folded me into his chest.

We were in love and about to run away together. I buried my face in his jumper and his arms tightened around me to create our own secret world.

"I'm so glad you came. I've wanted this for so long," he said, kissing the top of my head. It was wonderful and terrifying - wonderful to love him so very much, yet terrifying because the potential consequences of that love were too enormous to even contemplate.

I would eventually learn to compartmentalize my life. When I was with Barry I'd shut out the part of my life where I felt powerless and of little importance. During our times together, I'd try hard to love Barry freely and let him love me in return.

We drove for four hours to get to our weekend hideaway. It was a luxury to have so much time to talk to each other. Our conversation rambled up and down the hills and valleys of our life-experiences, our likes and dislikes, and all the funny and sad thoughts and memories we wanted to share with each other.

We stopped at a bakery for morning tea and Barry watched my joyful agony as I deliberated about what cake to buy. Normally my finances didn't stretch beyond buying my sons an occasional treat, yet here I was being asked to choose something for myself.

Barry preferred scones to cakes and never ate hot pies, preferring the taste of them when they were almost cold. It was delightful to be learning these little idiosyncrasies about each other. As we drove we sang, made up poems and challenged each other to a range of car-spotting and memory games. We felt young and carefree.

When we finally arrived at our destination we'd lost our initial nervousness. Barry pulled up at the reception office with a flourish. I looked from the office door back to Barry expectantly.

"You go in," I said hunching down in the passenger's seat.

Leaning back, his arm stretched over the steering wheel, Barry stared at me, obviously aware that for some reason the magic had suddenly evaporated.

"What's up?" His brows wrinkled in puzzlement.

"I can't go in … they might ask our names. Sometimes you have to sign things and give your home address. I can't go in." Suddenly feeling small and pathetic, a bubble had burst for me. In my haste to be with Barry for the weekend I hadn't thought through this part of the adventure.

"That's silly," Barry laughed. "They don't care what your name is. They just care that we pay."

I huddled against the door. "I can't go in. They'll know we're not married. I'm sorry. I just can't go in." My eyes smarted with tears and I couldn't look at Barry. I felt ashamed, so stupid, such a fool.

He watched me for awhile then shook his head slightly and gave a small shrug. "Listen my darling sweetheart …" It was the first time he'd ever called me that. I realised we'd imperceptibly moved to a different level. The word had been spoken easily, as if he'd always addressed me as 'sweetheart.' Perhaps secretly he had, as he sat alone in the silent times thinking about me, waiting and plotting to see or speak to me.

Darling sweetheart - it demanded my attention. Slowly I looked up into his face, saw the determination in his eyes, watched his mouth as he spoke.

"… We've come away to be together. We've come far away from anywhere where people might know us. We've come away so we can walk down the street holding hands and sit across from each other in a restaurant and talk and laugh as if we're a couple - like all the other couples. If you're still too frightened to do that even here, then we may as well go back now."

He sat quietly, waiting for me to make a decision. He may have been fighting back his own disappointment, frustration, even anger

– but he just sat, waiting for me to speak. Maybe he was resigned to the futility of our relationship.

I felt frantic. Minutes passed.

"I'll do all the talking if it helps," he suggested.

"Will I have to sign anything?" I asked, instantly conscious of how infantile my question sounded.

"They only ask the owner of the credit card to sign, and that's me."

Barry suddenly grinned.

"You know if I pay it means it's a date, don't you?"

I couldn't help but laugh. This was a reference to an earlier conversation about the code of ethics I'd applied as a teenager. I'd told Barry that, 'As long as a girl pays her own way she's free to leave whenever she chooses. The minute she lets the man pay, there's an expectation that the man's entitled to something in return.'

Apart from a four-year age difference, Barry and I came from widely different backgrounds in terms of socio-economics, etiquette and religion. I frequently shocked him when I spoke about growing up 'on my side of the tracks.'

"A date eh?" I smiled, making a decision. "Well I'll try, as long as you do all the talking and writing."

Barry leant across and planted a quick kiss on my cheek. We got out of the car and walked towards the office, me taking care not to walk close enough for us to hold hands. I was acting the role of 'long-term wife' and I mumbled something about the fresh air and the scenery in the hopes my voice would carry to the manager.

Access to the office was barred by a fat, sprawling dog snoozing on the doormat in the afternoon sun. Even at the best of times I'm frightened of dogs, but given my anxious state and my concentration on role-playing a wife not remotely interested in having sex – the appearance of the dog seriously impacted my performance.

I froze, waiting for Barry to banish the beast. Instead he laughed. "You're the only person I've ever met who's so frightened of animals. It's a Labrador - a guide dog," he offered by way of enlightenment. All I could see was a dog – teeth, slobbering saliva, wet nose and probably dreaming unimaginable, horrid, carnivorous dreams.

Barry bent down and rubbed the dog's head and back. He spoke in that sickening, crooning voice dog-people use when talking to dogs. "You're a good girl aren't you? Yes you are. And you're having a sleep in the sun aren't you? Good girl."

A glance in my direction confirmed I was not going to be persuaded the dog presented no danger. Thankfully the door to the office opened and the manager appeared.

"Sorry about Leila," he said beaming down at the living doormat. "Come on girl get up." He nudged the dog's rump with his shoe and it staggered to its feet and loped away around the corner of the building.

"Sue's not good with dogs," Barry said. I flushed and the two men smiled at me indulgently.

"Oh Leila wouldn't hurt you. She's twelve years old; spends most of her time asleep these days."

The manager stepped back and ushered us into the office. I patted Barry's arm and said gaily, "I'll just wait in the car love, okay?"

"Sure darling," Barry grinned back at me, my first out-loud use of the endearment nick-name '*love*' not lost on him. He stepped up into the office leaving me to scurry back to the car.

It was a relief when Barry and the manager re-emerged with Barry carrying a key to our cabin and a sheaf of brochures advertising local attractions.

"There you go," he said hopping into the driver's seat.

"It wasn't that bad after all, was it my little mouse? Perhaps from now on I'll call you my Darling Little Miss Mouse."

It was the off-peak holiday season and we were the only tenants at the resort. Our cabin was located in a secluded spot far removed from the manager's residence, its back wall flanked by a huge hill.

Barry turned the key and pushed open the cabin's door. "Shall I carry you over the threshold?" he asked.

I blushed. He meant it to be funny, but his words filled me with guilt. I laughed nervously and remained standing confused and upset outside the door. Here was yet another line to be crossed; an opportunity to stop before things went further.

I looked down at the door step, considered my feet, waited for them to move and wondered if they'd instead turn and walk back to the car. I knew Barry wouldn't be angry if my feet chose to do that. He'd be sad and disappointed but he was a gentleman and would accept the decision.

Seeing my hesitation Barry seemed to hold his breath for a moment. "Are you okay?" I wondered if he'd read my mind. Was he trying to keep the fear from his voice?

I thought about what I'd be doing if I hadn't come away. I could see myself cooking and washing and cleaning back at home. I'd be scurrying around smoothing everyone's ego and keeping a low profile so as to keep the peace. Back '*there*' I felt noticed for my omissions more than for my presence. It was difficult for me to see myself through Barry's eyes. He didn't see the part of me that was all about housework or mothering. He talked about some person he saw hiding beneath those roles, about loving me for 'me'.

I lifted my head and looked into his tortured eyes. His whole being seemed concentrated on me and he stood waiting for me to make a decision. Across his face I saw all the love he offered, all the yearning of his heart. Something inside me gave way.

"I'm just a bit nervous. Sorry. I'll be all right." I stepped into the cabin.

Barry straightened and flexed the tension from his shoulders. He followed in behind me and gently closed the door. The world and everyone else now existed beyond the door and Barry and I were alone, here together on the other side. We took a few hesitant steps – two explorers in a strange new world.

The cabin was new and fully self-contained. The front door opened into a cosy lounge room containing a two-seater couch, coffee table, television and video machine. A cheery kitchen-dining area opened off the lounge.

We peered shyly into a sunny bedroom, neither of us saying anything as we stared wide-eyed at the soft white doona covering the double-bed. My throat felt dry and I tried not to think. Glass doors on the far side of the bed provided access to a small timber patio offering spectacular views across virgin bushland.

Stepping back into the lounge-room Barry opened another door further along the wall. It was a small second bedroom. He laughed nervously. "It's a two-bedroom cabin - one for you and one for me."

His eyes swept across my face seeking my reaction to his attempt at a joke. I smiled, not trusting myself to answer, but somehow grateful there was still a possibility I wouldn't do the wrong thing. Just what I meant by the 'wrong thing' I wasn't prepared to consider for the moment. It was just enough to be here with Barry for even a few hours, pretending we were a couple.

Besides, anything could happen before nightfall. We might quarrel or be talked-out or become bored with each other. We could even have packed up and left by then. Better to just live in this glorious moment and block out what might happen next.

Barry carried in the food he'd bought for the weekend and

loaded the refrigerator. I brought in our bags and nervously placed them beside each other on the double bed, conscious of making some sort of statement by their placement. Thankfully Barry made no comment.

'It's no big deal,' I told myself. 'Even now, my case can be moved to the other room if I change my mind. Just because two bags are beside each other on the one bed doesn't mean anything. I could've put them together unintentionally.' I went on trying not to think about the weekend ahead of us; tried to just be happy to be here with Barry, to be loved and in love. No need to think beyond this. Time enough for fear, uncertainty and recriminations later.

We sat at the dining table and pored over the brochures the manager had given Barry. We worked out where to go for dinner then freshened up and walked into the town.

A stroll along the main street brought us to a low dark green wooden building pushed in beside a huge overhanging tree. The top half of the wall facing the street comprised small, square-paned windows which glowed warm and friendly from the orange candles burning atop each table inside.

"It looks magical," I enthused as Barry opened the door. "It's like a scene from a Charles Dickens novel. It feels like snow might fall at any time, or a village clock might begin to chime."

Inside I was delighted to find that in place of table cloths, the tables were covered with large sheets of plain white paper. A jar on each table held a collection of coloured pencils and a sign encouraged patrons to draw or write on their 'tablecloth'.

"Let's write something?" I said pulling the pencils towards me.

Barry shook his head. "I want to talk, not write. Besides, it's just a novel hook for distracting kids long enough so their parents can eat their meal in peace." He reached for the menu, seeming to dismiss the whole idea.

I was disappointed. "But we might never come here again. I'm going to write something; something auspicious!"

He looked at me with a twinkle in his eye. "You're a funny little thing. You can be so grown-up and then suddenly you're like a butterfly, like a little girl. He shook his head and opened the menu.

"Do whatever makes you happy," he said and pretended to study the menu while all the time stealing glimpses of me over its edge.

"I'm going to write a poem."

"Hmph. You can't just come into a restaurant and write a poem. Poems take time."

"You're kidding aren't you?" I said mischievously. "I can write a poem about anything and in record time too. Go on, give me a topic and I'll prove it."

Barry leaned forward, "Think you're pretty clever don't you?"

I nodded. "Yep"

"Okay. Write me a poem about socks." He laughed as I grimaced at his suggested topic.

"Hmm. I'd hoped for something more romantic. But hey, if 'socks' is the topic, then socks it'll be." I held my head in my hands and thought for awhile, conscious of the playful light in Barry's eyes.

In red pencil I wrote the word 'SOCKS' on the paper between us. Then using a different colour for every line, in order to buy thinking time during the pencil change-over, I wrote some rhyming couplets, reading aloud and matching sounds as I went. I made a few scribblings and back-tracked and soon Barry began offering suggestions to help me complete each line. We laughed as we worked and tried to outdo each other with witty suggestions. The waiter stayed away until the poem was finished.

SOCKS

Socks are gloves made for feet

To keep them warm and snugly neat

Socks come in rainbow colours

Pink and blue and all the others

Some are long and some are short

Knitted by mums or perhaps store-bought

Some socks are for bed and some are for sport

Some aren't washed as often as they ought.

Clowns wear socks and princesses too

Toed-socks are special, just like you!

We signed the poem and Barry drew a border of small socks around it.

"There you are," I said proudly. "... Told you I could write a poem about anything."

"That's not much of a poem," Barry sniggered. "Shakespeare didn't write like that."

"Hah – more's the pity." It was fun. We were like children playing a game. All my previous worries were momentarily banished. We were just having innocent fun; a relief after the nervous strain of the day.

"Can we tear our poem off the tablecloth?" I asked Barry when we were leaving the restaurant. He snorted.

"It wasn't that great a poem. Shakespeare writes better. Let's just leave it for others to enjoy when they sit there."

I smiled in acquiescence, but at the same time was hurt he didn't want to keep the poem as a memento of our time together. I wondered what he wanted from me if not to create and collect tiny memories such as these. A feeling of shame swept over me as I contemplated the answer to my question. What made me think it would be anything other than sex?

We wandered back along the darkened street, my pace slowing at the prospect of what might happen next. We walked close together, our arms and hands brushing against each other until Barry took my hand in his. I felt self-conscious and awkward and tried hard to relax my fingers across the firmness of his broad palm.

All around us the night held its breath. I wished we could walk on through the night and into the day, could walk on and on, never arriving anywhere; wished we could just practice holding hands in public until it felt natural. Perhaps we could learn to walk and hold hands and talk and laugh, all at the same time.

How good it would be to walk without thinking or worrying – without guilt or shame. I wished we could walk back to yesterday or on to tomorrow. Coming away with Barry and holding hands in public were giant steps for me. On this first trip perhaps we could just learn to walk at ease with each other. It would be enough.

The second bedroom at the cabin provided me with a 'get-out' clause. I pondered how Barry would react if I said I didn't want to do anything more intimate this trip. Would he become angry? He was a man after all. He'd feel cheated. Would he plead with me? Would he pack the car immediately and force us to go back then and there? Would it be the end of everything we'd had until now?

Would all the softness and tenderness and longing be ripped out and thrown away?

I shivered slightly. Barry readjusted his hold on my hand and smiled at me.

"What's up Miss Mouse?" he murmured, as if reading my inner thoughts. "My tiny Miss Mouse..." Barry lifted our clasped hands and gently kissed my fingertips. We walked on in silence, our clasped hands swinging back and forth, a reflection of my emotions. A creeping sadness stole over me as the night sky blanketed us with words unspoken.

Barry walked large and strong beside me, his face turned away. He stared up at the stars and the trees above, peered into shop windows and feigned interest in darkened gardens beyond picket fences. He didn't look at me. Time passed, marked only by the crunching of the gravel beneath our feet. Through the gloom, the cottage came into view on the path ahead.

"Almost home darling - I bet you'll be glad to get inside out of the darkness eh?" Barry gave me a small uncertain smile and dropped my hand to fumble for the keys.

"Hmm yes it's dark now. Must be after 8 pm I s'pose." I floundered for something to say that wouldn't expose my tangled emotions. I didn't want us to have a fight but to just go slowly and let the night sort itself out without us having to make any decisions.

The silence between us was deafening as Barry opened the cottage door.

Night fall

> *With the first dream that comes*
> *with the first sleep I run, I run,*
> *I am gathered to thy heart*
>
> ALICE MEYNELL

"Hey, I brought a movie for us to watch," Barry said suddenly as he stepped into the cottage. "I think you'll like it. It's short and has no dialogue. It's about a small quartet, and more particularly, a cellist who falls in love." At this last, his voice softened a little. He looked at me as if seeking my soul's response.

I wasn't really into classical music but was grateful his suggestion had broken the silence, and watching a movie would stretch out the time between now and later. *Later* - what on earth will happen later?' I pushed the thought from my mind.

"That sounds great," I said. "But what are the odds on you being able to work the DVD player?"

"You cheeky possum," Barry laughed, and some of the tension drained from the room.

While Barry busied himself with the technology, I kicked off my shoes and nestled onto the couch. He had once chided me for always sitting in the middle of a couch, leaving him no option but to sit close to me. Mindful of this, I deliberately snuggled into one end and folded my legs up beside me. It was my subtle attempt to slow the pace and put some distance between us. I didn't want to be held responsible for any outcome not of my own choosing.

Barry turned off the light and the room took on the ghostly grey of the television screen. He looked at me in the far recesses of the couch and hesitated before sitting on the floor in front of me, his long legs stretched out towards the television. Pushing the 'Play' button on the DVD's handset, he leaned back against the couch, his shoulder brushing against my folded legs. It was an unspoken statement and I was left to interpret its meaning.

The movie was totally silent except for its music. A string quartet had been asked to perform for the beautiful daughter of a wealthy lord. Carrying their instruments, the musicians walked across golden fields and down countless autumnal tree-lined lanes to a grand country manor. On their arrival the cellist was swept away by the daughter's beauty and his performance was filled with his stolen glances, demure smiles and passionate yearnings.

A short time into the film Barry reached over his shoulder and began stroking the bare toes of my right foot. Uncertain what to do, I froze and watched his hand as it cradled each toe before sliding softly onto the next one. No-one had ever touched my feet in a sensual way. I found it difficult to relax, difficult to watch the film. My eyes were mesmerized, fixed on Barry's hand seducing my foot.

I hated the tiny bud of my little toe. It bent slightly as if trying to hide behind the next toe. I wondered if Barry would be repulsed by it, so held my breath as his fingers arrived at my shy toe. His face remained fixed on the television and unfazed, his hand continued its slow seduction, as if operating independent of him.

Studying his profile, it was difficult to glean what he was thinking. Feeling out of my depth, I dared not move or speak, instead I studied my feet again. They were too big; tiny feet were supposed to be a sign of beauty. My high instep looked almost regal in high heels but the length of my feet meant they could never be called 'delicate.' Now I wished I'd rubbed cream into them so they'd be soft and scented.

'God Almighty,' I thought, '... as if dieting and grooming, clothing choices and checking for bad breathe, and trying to be witty and clever weren't challenging enough. Now apparently feet mattered too.'

It was exhausting. What were feet anyway? Just things at the end of your legs - like the stand on the bottom of a vase, an engineering feature to ensure balance. Surely they weren't something else to be added to the list of 'what matters between lovers'. Yet there was Barry, stroking my foot and it seemed incredibly intimate.

Hardly breathing for worrying about what Barry might be thinking about my feet, I sat frozen - a trapped bird, caught in the hunter's hand. On the television the cellist continued to pour bitter-sweet music from his aching heart.

Barry turned to look at me. "Do you like the movie?" His hand temporarily stilled, but stretched out possessively across all my five toes.

"It's beautiful – the scenery and the music. Amazing that so much can be said without any dialogue." We'd both spoken as if oblivious of Barry's hand on my foot.

He nodded and turned back to the television, at the same time moving along the floor to be closer to me. Without saying anything, he straightened my leg slightly and rested my ankle on his shoulder so that my foot sat near his ear. His caresses now included the high arch of my instep and my heel.

Unable to relax and suspended somewhere between distress and awe, I was horrified to feel other parts of my body rouse, a rising tide beginning somewhere deep inside me.

On the television, the quartet finished their performance and the daughter simply nodded approvingly before leaving the room and breaking the cellist's heart. Beneath a dying sun the musicians trudged away through rose-hued fields as waves of soulful music heralded the end of the film.

Barry's lips brushed my foot.

He didn't look away from the television or say anything. It was as if he'd placed the kiss unconsciously, like a mother might kiss the head of a baby she is holding – innocently, protectively, for no purpose or motive other than a spontaneous feeling of love.

I looked at Barry's outline against the light from the television. He was at once familiar and beautiful. His broad forehead and intricately carved ear-lobes gave him an academic air.

I'd often wondered if he'd grown his thick moustache and clipped beard to further that impression. A few restless hairs marked a trail down towards his throat and his Adam's apple. Barry's Adam's apple suggested great strength and virility. 'Virility' I thought, and felt myself shrink with shame.

"Are you okay?" Barry turned to look at me, no doubt having felt my body's slight tremor.

I nodded, uncertain what to say. He placed my foot back beside me on the couch and turned around fully, to kneel in front of me. He covered both my feet with his hands and looked into my face.

"Listen – we don't have to do anything. Okay? I just wanted us to be together for a weekend. It doesn't matter if nothing happens. I just want to be with you." He fell silent - watched me.

A rush of emotions raged through my heart and my head. I loved him greatly and was being silly. My behaviour was taking away all the joy. It was as though *I* was the one fixated on sex. Most of this special day I'd spent analysing and worrying, weighing-up and speculating. All because for some inexplicable reason, I'd decided there was extra guilt involved if we ran away for a stolen weekend and had sex as well.

I was being so immature, so ridiculous. Here was Barry so open and honest – so forgiving and loving, and I was so ... so pathetic! It was amazing he still loved me and was willing to put up with my antics. He'd be better off without me. My eyes filled with tears and I buried my face in my hands.

Barry leant forward and kissed my fingers gently. "Don't cry. It's alright. You worry too much." He reached over and turned the television off and the room fell into darkness. I heard him breathing as I struggled to think what to say or do.

"Why don't we go and sit out on the deck? I'll get you a glass of wine and we can look at the stars. They'll be wonderful this far from the city." He leapt to his feet and went into the kitchen and switched on the light. I heard the wine being poured and slowly got up from the couch and wandered out to stand beside him.

"Here you are Miss Mouse; wine for m'lady." His voice was light and cheerful. He was making every effort to help me begin afresh, to recognise the sincerity of his words. He handed me the glass and kissed my cheek. Then taking my other hand he led me through the bedroom and out onto the deck. A flood of stars stretched across the inky sky.

We sat on wooden deck chairs, a small table between us. "Now that's a night-sky," said Barry, leaning back to stare up at the sight. The air was balmy and from the forest came the scratching and skittering of possums and other nocturnal wanderers.

I nodded. "The air's so fresh it almost hurts to breathe." I sipped my wine and felt everything returning to normal again. The table between us gave me space, calmed me.

The sky seemed to stretch on forever, its wide expanse highlighting our relative insignificance. I gazed blankly out at the forest, tasted the air and felt the evening breeze around me. We sat in companionable silence for a few minutes.

"Sometimes ... I get frightened that if you get to know me, you won't like me," I said suddenly, without looking at Barry. I hadn't realised what I was going to say. Until I heard myself speak the thoughts had only existed ill-formed and hazy, in some secret part of my inner self.

"Why wouldn't I like you?" Barry's voice was gentle beside me. He continued to stare up at the sky.

I hesitated before speaking honestly, quietly into the darkness. "I'm frightened of not being able to keep up with you – with your wit, your knowledge. You know so much and I feel so inadequate beside you. I'm frightened of failing in your eyes, of not understanding what you talk about. Then you'll see the dullard I really am, instead of the person you imagine me to be. I'm frightened if you see the real me, you'll leave me."

My voice wavered and I lowered my head. "That would be awful. I don't want you to go. I've got nothing to offer you and yet I don't want you to go." Feeling small and frightened, I realised I'd said too much and now couldn't take it back.

Barry snorted softly. "You're frightened *you* won't be able to keep up with *me*? He turned in his chair to look directly at me.

"My darling girl, I'm terrified *I'll* lose *you* if I'm too slow to keep pace with you. When you tell me about your childhood and describe the world through your eyes, I wonder we even grew up on the same planet. Then I worry that maybe I don't know anything about life except what I've read in books. I'm always terrified you'll find me lacking. You once told me in that self-deprecating way you have, that you're 'bog-Irish' by descent. But I think you're the funniest, cleverest, girl I've ever met. You laugh all the time and you make me see the ridiculous in everything and everyone, including myself. I love being around you."

He turned his chair toward me, took my wine glass and placed it on the table before holding my hands. His face reflected the ghostly white of the moonlight.

"Darling, I know lots of women who know about politics and art and music. They talk long and seriously with me and ask me for my opinions and suggestions about different things. It's all very flattering. There was even a woman once who used to keep a notebook of clever things that I said to her."

I scoffed, astonished at this last comment.

"Yeah, well that's a whole other story." Barry glanced down at our interlocked hands to hide his embarrassment. "The thing is that I know lots of intelligent, knowledgeable women and I can see you fit the same bill, but you've got something extra."

"Big boobs I suppose or a fat bum." It was my vain attempt to lighten the conversation and hide my embarrassment. Barry ignored my attempt at humour.

"... You're like a child and a woman wrapped into one person. You're clever and yet so innocent. You're whimsical and joyful and passionate. You make me cry and you make me laugh. You're a heroine and a villain, and being with you is like running as fast as I can. I want to go on quests for you and bring you surprises; want to throw my arms around you, lift you and twirl you around like a princess. I want to carry you off and be strong and funny and clever for you. I want to follow you around and protect you. I feel on edge all the time I'm with you."

He'd spoken rapidly, almost frantically and now he paused. Then without looking up, "I can't even really tell you how it is for me. There aren't words to describe it. I love you - and that's the best I can do." He said it simply, almost sadly, before sinking back in his chair and staring off into the night. The forest noises washed over us as we pondered each other's words.

I broke the silence. "It must be tiny."

"What?" Barry asked.

"The book of witty things you'd said - the one that lady kept ... must've been a tiny book." I giggled and took a sip of wine.

Barry chuckled. "You little witch."

I stood up. "It's late – time for bed. I'm going to have a shower."

I squeezed Barry's arm and kissed the top of his head. "It was a wonderful day." He remained seated and although he nodded slightly, didn't look at me. Perhaps he was frightened I'd see the unspoken question in his eyes. Stepping through the glass doors I pulled the drapes across behind me.

While showering, I thought back over the conversation we'd just had. How amazing we were both nervous of not living up to each other's expectations. And Barry had made such a long and beautiful speech to try to explain how much he loved me. I imagined him sitting alone on the dark deck, his ears straining to discern if the shower was still running. Would he be trying to decide if I'd expected him to follow me into the bathroom and join me in the shower? Perhaps he'd be wondering if I'd come to him warm and damp and naked, my skin mauve in the moonlight.

But no, even if he wanted to come after me, I was sure he'd force himself to remain on the deck until I'd decided what would happen next. Barry would be true to his word. Nothing would happen unless I initiated it.

I hopped out of the shower and for a moment stared out through the bathroom window. The wind had risen and where earlier each tree had stood calm and independent, they now tossed and swayed into each other, branches and leaves flaying. They reminded me of lovers thrashing and tangled together in a storm of passion.

I turned out the lights and closed the bathroom door before padding softly into the bedroom. Hardly daring to breathe I lifted the covers and slipped silently between the sheets. I lay on my back, eyes shut, perfectly still with my arms pressed down along my sides.

A few minutes later the door from the deck slid open and Barry's head appeared through the drapes. "Knock knock. Is anybody here?" he whispered.

"No. I don't think so."

"Hmm. Well, I'll have a shower then."

"Good plan."

When Barry returned from the bathroom he stood uncertainly at the foot of the bed for a moment. "Who's been sleeping in my bed?" he finally asked.

"Nobody."

"Perhaps I should check."

No answer.

The covers lifted slowly and I felt Barry's hand slide along my right hip, brush across my stomach before gently cupping my breast.

Quickly, as though burnt, he withdrew his hand and the blankets fell back onto me. "Oh my God! There's a sheila in my bed!" He sounded like a delighted teenager. "What will I do? Call the housemaid, call the manager, call the police perhaps?"

Holding my breath, I remained silent.

A few minutes passed then I felt the bed sag as Barry hopped in. We both lay quite still.

"It's me," I finally whispered to the ceiling, my eyes still shut.

"I know." Barry murmured without moving.

"I'm hiding."

"Good hiding place." I felt him smile. "I won't tell anyone where you are."

I opened my eyes and slowly stretched across to hold his hand.

Later that week a small computer- generated poster arrived for me in the mail. The background comprised rows of large plump hearts, and the page was bordered all around by a chain of smaller hearts. Emblazoned across the poster in capital letters in a font worthy of a palace missive was written:

*THE TRUTH IS
THAT I JUST
CAN'T STAND THE
IDEA OF LIVING
WITHOUT YOU.
YOU ARE AS
NECESSARY AS
AIR, FOOD AND
WATER.*

Your Librarian xx

LOVE (3)

Offerings

Perhaps the greatest gift you can give another person is to believe in them.

ANON

It had been a long day of teaching before dashing home to cook dinner for the family, then out the door again to get to the university lecture theatre by 6 pm. I was studying for my Masters Degree and had to attend the fortnightly three-hour night lectures.

The majority of the thirty or so students in the lecture were immigrants and the lecture usually dragged along at the pace of the student with the least grasp of the English language. It was both exhausting and frustrating to attend such a session after working all day. Although a waste of my time, other than for the purpose of having my name marked off the roll, attending ten evening lectures in one semester would save me having to do the subject via a twelve-month correspondence course.

Tonight as usual, I sat in the back row, ignored the classroom noise and read the recommended text attempting to make sense of the key concepts by myself. Finally the clock showed 9 pm and the lecturer bade us good night.

It was scary walking across the campus in the dark with the bushes and trees rustling and swaying menacingly against the night sky. Hurrying through the almost deserted car park, I opened my car door, slid into the driver's seat and quickly locked all the doors. It took a few minutes to organise my books and bags on the back seat.

Suddenly opposite me, a car flashed its headlights on my windscreen. The lights flashed again and I froze in terror - a rabbit trapped in their glow. Peering through the darkness to my great relief I realised it was Barry's car.

He hopped out and strode across to me. When I unlocked the passenger door he flung himself into my car, bringing with him the comforting smells of Waldene and the forest.

"What're you doing here?" I was both amazed and delighted.

"Reading." Barry laughed, obviously amused by his own wit. He wrinkled his forehead in mock puzzlement. "Trouble is - it got so dark I couldn't see the print on the page, so was forced to listen to the radio instead." His boyish grin made it hard not to love him.

"You liar! You came here to see me."

"Did so!" he chided, turning the usual schoolboy denial of *'Did not!'* on its head.

I laughed. "But you didn't know when my lecture was s'posed to finish. How long have you been sitting here?"

"Hmm..." Barry put his head on one side and stared out through the windscreen. "I left work at four, went to see a movie, bought a hamburger – probably got here about seven."

"That's crazy. Did you want to see the movie or were you just filling in time before coming here?"

Turning fully to face me Barry replied. "I wanted to see you. It doesn't matter if I went to a movie or whether I stayed back at work or whether I just sat in a park somewhere. I wanted to be here when you came out. I wanted to see you."

He said it softly, so honestly. I clasped his hands and kissed his fingers. "I love you," I murmured.

With all humour removed, Barry leaned across and whispered in my ear. "I know."

The following week he promised not come to meet me after my lecture.

"It's a silly waste of your time. The lecture finishes so late most times we could only sit together for half an hour in the car park before it'd be time for me to go home. But poor you! Not only do you have to fill in hours after work before seeing me a few minutes, but you then have to drive three quarters of an hour dodging kangaroos on dark, country roads to get back to Waldene."

Barry disagreed. "But darling I don't mind waiting as long as there's a chance to see you, even if it's just for half an hour." I insisted and eventually he conceded on condition I phoned him to confirm I'd made it home safely. "You don't have to speak to me. Just let the phone ring a few times then hang up. I'll know it's you and then I'll be able to sleep without worrying."

"You worry too much. I'll be fine." But I agreed to ring as a trade-off for him promising not to wait for me after night class anymore.

The next week scurrying to my car after the lecture I felt a bit sad knowing Barry wouldn't be there waiting. My eyes scanned the car park thinking he might have broken his promise. But there was no sign of his car. Selfishly for a moment, I regretted dissuading him.

Hopping into my car and turning on the engine, the glow from the dashboard revealed something caught on my windscreen. I leaned forward to discern what it was – leaves trapped under the wipers or perhaps an advertising flyer? University students were forever leaving pamphlets under windscreen wipers championing some obscure cause like '*Save the Gecko,*' '*Demand free lunches in the Student Union,* '*Animals are People too.*'

I opened the door and stretched around to dislodge the item. It was a small plastic bag containing three little dolls. They each wore a pale tartan dress and sported long plaits tied with little tartan bows. A handwritten card accompanied the dolls.

I'm missing you cutie.
Love from a secret admirer. XX

A defiant offering left by someone told to stay away, yet I couldn't help but smile.

Later the same year, I transferred to the head office of the Education Department and was given the responsibility of developing and delivering a state-wide training program for mathematics teachers. Given the large amount of state government funding attached to the initiative, I researched long and hard throughout the days and into many nights in order to justify the department's belief in my abilities.

After many months involving much feedback and revision, the program was finally ready to be trialled on a group of sixty teachers. My boss booked me into a motel attached to the conference venue to stay the night before the training. This would enable me to gather my thoughts, check the catering and prepare the training room.

In all my years as a teacher I'd never been treated to such luxury. Usually the most teachers in the public system could expect was the allocation of lower bunk on the school camp, and even that came in return for the 24/7 care of a swarm of excited students. I was sick with nerves in the lead up to the training and Barry tried hard to calm me.

"You'll be great. Don't worry. You've done all the research - you know the content, you wrote it after all. Besides, it's all been checked and re-checked and it's been 'okayed' by the bosses."

"Yeah, but we both know the bosses probably taught 'Home Eco' or Year One kids. They probably don't have a clue about maths and wouldn't know if the content was correct or not. If it 'falls over' it'll be my head that rolls."

"You're being ridiculous. Anyway the teachers coming to the training will just be rapt to be away from school for two days. Throw in the catering aspect and they won't care what you talk about." Barry shrugged.

I knew what he said was probably true. When I was a classroom teacher selected to attend some training, my enjoyment had been split fairly equally between the prospect of time out of class with a catered lunch and the actual content of the training.

The weekend before the roll-out of the trial I was on edge and Barry suggested we go for a walk. "Talk me through the two days," he said as we set out. I gave him an overview and tried to describe various activities I'd included and their purpose. He nodded and asked questions to keep me focussed on the key ideas. It was surprising how well I remembered the content and the flow of activities.

"You'll be great," Barry said when we'd finished talking. "You just need to relax. You know your stuff. The teachers will love you."

"I just know I'll feel sick at the start - probably vomit. I vomited in my old job with the Department of Social Security when they made me run a management course. I was so nervous." I flinched at the memory.

"Seriously?" Barry stopped abruptly on the path, "You actually vomited?"

"Yes. I keep telling you how nervous I get."

"What happened?"

"Well, I didn't actually vomit in front of the trainees. I did it in the toilet before the training. They didn't know. When the training started, I gradually calmed down but it was a horrible way to begin. After the session I was always so exhausted."

Barry hugged me. "Poor Miss Mouse. You'll be fine - just relax."

I checked into the motel mid afternoon. The receptionist looked through her records. "Yes we have you here for two nights and the training will take place in the Bellevue Room. We've set up tables for 60. Is that correct?"

"Yes," I said somewhat sadly, having hoped a mess-up in the arrangements would've seen the whole thing postponed for another time.

The receptionist passed me the key. "Room 15; straight down the corridor and turn right." With her hands together in prayer formation she gestured toward the corridor behind me, then bent them to the right as if her instructions were challenging. "Fifteen is on the left." Her hands parted, the left one veering across to depict where I would find the left.

"Thank you," I said wishing she was in my audience tomorrow. Given she felt the need to demonstrate left and right to me I felt sure I would have enthralled her with my knowledge of complex mathematical concepts like fractions.

She glanced down at the check-in register and added, "By the way, it says here there was a delivery for you today. It's been put in your room."

"Probably from my boss," I said proudly. "There's a lot riding on this program and we're all a bit nervous about how it'll go."

"Mmm," she replied without interest. "So room 15. Breakfast is in the dining room from 7 am. Enjoy your stay." She smiled and dismissed me by turning away to sit at the computer behind the reception counter.

Room 15 was decorated in a plush pale green that was both calming and pretty. At first glance there was no card or flower bouquet on the little table or the bed. I thought my boss might have sent some form of 'Good Luck' wish. I opened the wardrobe, deciding that perhaps the 'delivery' was instead an overlooked extra box of training material. The wardrobes were empty.

Maybe the delivery had been made to the Bellevue Room rather than my room? Lifting my suitcase onto the bed I decided to use the bathroom before going in search of the Bellevue Room and the missing delivery.

Standing in the shower cubicle was a black plastic bucket containing a bottle of expensive champagne. Tied around its neck by a yellow ribbon was a small gift card. The Education Department frowned on using government money for alcohol so this was an unexpected surprise. My boss must have paid for the champagne herself. Imagine that! She went up in my estimation immediately.

I opened the card - Barry's handwriting.

The bucket is for you to vomit in before the training.
The champagne is for you to celebrate after the training. I know you will be great. I wish I could be there to hold your hair back when you vomit.
I love you.
Your librarian xx"

A lonely cottage

*The simple lack of (him) is more to
me than others' presence*

EDWARD THOMAS

When the Christmas holidays came, Barry had booked to go overseas for almost the entire six-weeks. He'd reasoned because he had no children and wasn't religious the festivities didn't mean anything to him. "Besides," he said, "Christmas holidays are the longest break in the education year so it's worth going overseas, given the cost of flying from Australia to anywhere in Europe."

I dreaded the thought of us being apart for six weeks. Barry intended roaming alone around Europe's Balkan states. He pre-booked rooms in several different hotels where he would be travelling and gave me phone numbers, dates and specific times to ring him while he was overseas.

Throughout the six weeks I called concierges on the other side of the world from public phone booths. The concierges only sometimes understood English and it was often a battle to make them understand I wanted to be connected to 'Barry Johnston's room'.

Sometimes it took as long to make the connection as the time we got to speak to each other before my phone credits expired. It was frustrating but the moment Barry's faraway "Hello' came down the phone- line I forgave everyone.

During Barry's absence the weather in Victoria promised recording-breaking heat for sustained periods. He'd asked me if I would visit Waldene in his absence and water his vegetable garden and orchard and record the rain-gauge data in his record book.

On my first visit I arrived at the cottage early morning. The temperature was already in the high thirties as I unlocked the front door and stepped into the silence. I felt like Goldilocks tip-toeing from room to room. Each internal door was closed and locked, even though the key remained in the lock.

Barry used to lock each door and remove the keys before going on holidays. But a few times thieves had broken in and smashed through the doors, leaving him to rebuild and re-install every one. The experience had taught him to insure his contents adequately, take reasonable precautions to deter theft during his absence but leave the keys in the locked, internal doors.

Leaving the keys in the locked doors was his attempt to annoy any thieves. They might take his goods but he would at least frustrate the process, because he assumed they would have to wrangle with the keys in the locks rather than break down the doors. The cottage was still robbed on a regular basis, but Barry's private victory was he never had to rebuild the doors again.

Today the locked doors seemed cruel and hard – daring me, warning me not to pry or go further because no-one was here and the house was alone.

Normally I was free to dart from room to room, to search out the curious, hunt for strategically placed surprises, locate a special book, lie on a bed and stare out at the forest or clamour upstairs to gaze down into the valley at sunset. But today I was forced to pause, consider, hesitate, then slowly - like an interloper, turn the key and press down on the handle to gain entry.

Today the house watched me. The pine walls were familiar yet different; usually enfolding and comforting, now they hinted at some greater thing lurking, mystical, above and beyond the building itself. Barry's absence weighed heavily on the house – it was devoid of its heart and soul.

I was hungry and wondered if it was a reflex action caused by being at Waldene. These rooms usually greeted me with warm aromas from the wood-fired stove and specially chosen edible delicacies. This house was where shards of ice often winked at me from a glass of champagne.

But not today - today the house was cold and the small table was cleared of all bowls and glasses. I opened the oven door and peered into the neatly swept, empty mouth. The cavity beside the oven revealed a collection of twisted newspaper and kindling set ready for the next fire. It too, awaited Barry's return.

Rummaging in the cupboard for something to eat all I could find was Barry's jar of 'possum biscuits.' This was a sad collection of broken and out-dated biscuits he bought cheaply to feed a small family of possums that nightly climbed down a tree beside the cottage to wait patiently for him outside the sliding door. The small, shy animals now trusted him enough to reach out and take the food he offered them by hand. Each year they brought their offspring to show him; frightened, wide-eyed balls of fluff staring at his outline silhouetted in the doorway against the glow of lights from inside the cottage.

Unscrewing the lid of the 'possum biscuits,' I took out a limp gingernut and nibbled at one edge. If he could see me now he'd be sorry he wasn't here, I thought. He'd realise I'm lonely when he's gone - go through my days waiting to be with him. He'd be sorry he went away and left me.

Moving to the couch I studied its surface in detail, seeking an indent on the armrest where Barry's head might lie when he stretched out to read ... nothing.

Perhaps there might be a scuff mark where he rested his shoes on the other arm rest... still nothing. Almost shyly I sat on the end of the couch where Barry always sat. The memory of him calling me a teaser for sitting in the middle of the couch made me chuckle. The sound startled the silent house.

I considered the distance from the end of the couch to its middle. Leaning back I stretched my arm along the top of the couch to see how far my fingertips could reach without moving my torso. Barry was taller; his reach would be longer than mine. I wriggled toward the centre of the couch to compensate for the difference in our potential reach.

I stared at my hand lying along the couch. So this was where his hand had been – waiting, hesitating. Had he curled his fingers - willed them to reach out and touch my hair as I sat beside him all those years ago? Had he needed to reach across a little in order to make contact? Had the sun streaming in through the window encouraged him? How long had he waited? Perhaps the action had taken him unawares – swept along with the moment, had he touched the aberrant curl at the nape of my neck without realising?

Rousing from my thoughts, I ran my hand along the leather of the couch – caressed it, perhaps thanking it for being an accomplice in an act that had changed my life forever. The windows looked away, down towards the valley, devoid of opinion.

But I'd promised to water the garden, check the rain gauge and record any rainfall. Outside I examined the gauge, puzzling all the while about why he thought this endless recording necessary. Was it just a hobby? Perhaps he thought the weather bureau would one day ask him for the information. Perhaps he amused himself by predicting future rainfall based on his historical data. I couldn't understand his fascination for it. In my mind it either rained or it didn't – wet or dry, drought or flood but most often something in between, season after season, year after year.

The 'rainfall ledger' was kept on its own small shelf beside the fireplace. Opening it, I entered the information. Barry had recorded the rainfall in the ledger twice a month for many years. The carefully ruled book and its data was a source of pride to him. The orderly pages showed dates and corresponding rainfalls with great precision in neat, tidy rows.

The sight of his firm, perfectly formed handwriting made me ridiculously happy. His pen-stroke was assured just like him. My handwriting looked awkward and infantile on the page beside his.

Once he'd laughingly described my handwriting as 'chicken-scratchings - small and darting and furtive.' I'd felt ashamed. Too late Barry realised his words had hurt me.

The next day he had sent me a card on which he'd written: *'Write to me, write to me, only write to me. I love to see the hop and skip of your letters upon the page'* suggesting he perhaps liked my childish handwriting after all.

I ran my fingertips across his handwriting in the rainfall ledger – turned the page and felt the indents made by his pen stroke on the underside of the paper. A thought drifted into my mind and I quickly drew a little cluster of hearts around my entry in his perfect rainfall record. Almost instantly I grimaced. Flicking back through the pages – row upon row, perfectly ruled, perfectly completed, page after page, year after year. And now a tiny cluster of love hearts, a blot on an otherwise perfect page forever.

What would Barry say when he saw them? Would it matter to him they'd been done spontaneously after seeing his handwriting, because I was missing him, because his handwriting had momentarily bridged the world and brought him back to me?

Closing the ledger I pushed it back onto its shelf. It was done - a love letter of sorts. It couldn't be undone.

I wandered down the hallway to the master bedroom. The shades were fully drawn on the Eastern windows and the full-length windows on the South wall glared out openly at the forest, daring it to overrun the cottage in Barry's absence. The king-sized bed took up most of the room. Barry had built it decades ago. He'd carved a small heart in the centre of its wooden headboard.

Removing my shoes I stood in the centre of the lambs wool floor rug at the foot of the bed. My toes wriggled, luxuriating in the soft touch of the fleece. On the wall above the bed was the large framed print of the Athenian woman dressed in layers of gossamer green. Her beautiful eyes looked out, patient and serene, somehow innocent, yet simultaneously full of the secret knowledge of womanhood.

We exchanged glances, the woman and I, reassuring each other if you love them enough, the men will return, just as Ulysses had eventually returned to his Penelope. In the wake of battles and loss and unimaginable horrors, he had returned. Sure and steady he'd never forgotten his love and he had returned.

I lay down on my side of the bed, arms by my sides, stiff and rigid. Without the extra weight of the Barry's body on the other side of the bed, the mattress didn't oblige by sloping just enough to roll me towards the centre. Beyond the windows the whispering eucalypt swayed and pushed each other around in their attempt to see me lying alone on the bed.

Struggling with an overwhelming feeling of loneliness I remained perfectly still for a few minutes, before slowly rolling across to Barry's side of the bed. With my head on his pillow I closed my eyes and tried to visualise him, tried to imagine him right at this moment somewhere overseas, tried to think myself into his thoughts, tried to send him a message.

Long ago I'd copied a poem from a book and given it to Barry. The words of the poem offered hope that two people could always be together regardless of the physical distance between them. When we were apart and missing each other Barry sometimes murmured fragments of the poem to me:

> 'As I cannot now touch your face,
> Nor take you by the hand,
> I send my soul through time and space
> To greet you: you will understand'

Could my soul travel through time and space to walk beside him? If not my soul, then perhaps just a faint sense of the memory of me - of us together. Just enough to make him stop whatever he was doing and think of me – think of me back here, think of me thinking of him. Barry had told me that each night at 6 pm he would face towards the East and think of me on the other side of the world. He hoped I'd feel him near and know he loved me.

I opened my eyes to look at the clock beside the bed. It showed 12.45 pm. But I didn't know exactly where Barry was, didn't know what time it was there. Curling into the foetal position I tried to think of 'nothing,' to just float like a leaf from nowhere to nowhere. Thoughts of Barry scratched at the fringes of the 'nothing' and gained access to my thoughts once again.

With a sudden movement I rolled off the bed to stand, hands on hips, and glare at the clock. It ticked slowly on, choosing to ignore me completely. Going to the antique chest of drawers, I pulled the top drawer open. The aging timber complained at my rough handling and I bent to savour the smell emanating from the drawer. The soap Barry always used to wash his clothes left a strong, clean, carbolic smell on everything it touched.

The drawer was full of neatly folded singlets and underpants. All the same brand, colour and size. I lifted out a folded singlet and held the soft cotton cloth against my cheek and an enormous sadness swept over me. Standing there holding his singlet in the silent house I felt pathetic. But I missed him, wished I could just stand here and do nothing - think nothing. Like the Athenian woman, I wanted to just remain here, motionless, lifeless - until he came back to me.

Holding the singlet by its shoulders I let it unfold, raised my arms to an estimate of Barry's height and tried to imagine him standing before me wearing the singlet. Disappointed, I let my arms drop. It was impossible to imagine of him standing here in his underwear. There was no memory in my head of such a bold experience. It was a nonsense - unimaginable.

The singlet hung limp and dejected in my hands. I remembered a day – a day when the dance of the sun on my car's windscreen, the rush of air through the open car window and the heady scent of the surrounding eucalyptus forest had filled me with excitement. Around the many twists and turns of the country road Barry and I had each driven, one car behind the other, upwards towards the cottage. I'd felt young and carefree, as though on a circus ride, as I'd followed his car up the road.

Then ahead of me, Barry's driver-side window had opened and at the next bend I'd caught a glimpse of him grinning back at me. His right arm had appeared out through the window clutching his shirt which he proceeded to flap as if shooing a flock of birds away. Then he'd drawn his arm back inside as his car disappeared from view around another bend in the road.

Hugging the bend I'd followed until Barry's car came into view again. Now he was waving his singlet out the window. Somewhat shocked, I'd realised he was undressing as he drove. It made me laugh being both delightful and horrifying. He was making love to me already – here; as we drove up the winding road to the cottage. Never before had anyone been that frantic to be with me. Yet here he was waving his clothing like a flag of surrender.

I loved him for that - for that and for all the small but precious actions and words he did without hesitation or embarrassment. Each one telling me he loved me.

Shaking myself back to the present I looked again at the singlet in my hands. Was this the one he'd waved at me? The Athenian woman watched. She seemed to be trying to suggest something from her place on the wall.

Placing the singlet on the edge of the bed, I pulled off my t-shirt and bra before shimmying into the singlet. It hung mid-way down my thighs and its low neckline and large armholes left much of my breasts exposed.

Somewhat guiltily I padded across to stand in front of the full-length mirror fixed to the door of the antique wardrobe. Turning this way and that I examined my reflection, pleased to be inside Barry's clothing.

"Well, what do you think?" I asked the all-knowing Athenian. "Hmm – yes I know. It's a bit big." I gathered a handful of the large singlet behind my back to reduce its overall size. My breasts disappeared in behind the tightened material leaving just a seductive outline of the two large orbs and their erect nipples evident in the mirror.

"He'd love to see that. I'll tell him about it one day." I said to the mirror. Barry would be delighted to hear what I'd gotten up to in his absence and be sorry to have missed seeing it. He'd probably beg for a re-enactment.

The singlet fell back into place when I released the material gathered behind my back and my breasts were once more visible at the large armholes. I turned sideways to see if my '*broft*' was exposed.

'*Broft*' – it was a made-up word. Barry had once asked me to set him a quest. He wanted to prove I was a princess and he was my willing servant. I'd asked him to bring me a 'word'- a special word of my own, a secret word only we would know.

Weeks later when I'd forgotten the conversation, Barry had given me a tiny jewellery box. Inside on a small piece of paper was written the single word '*Broft*.' It was his gift; a word he'd created especially to describe the cool, alabaster section of skin that marked the place where the underside of my breast met the skin of my torso. He'd said it was the sweetest, softest, most secret part of my body - always cool and almost translucent for never having been exposed to the sun.

Broft was a noun we'd decided. A noun that became a verb when, lying beside me in bed Barry had trailed his fingers across the area, stroked the underside of my breast, and declared himself to be 'brofting.' The word was beautiful and I thought it was a most wonderful gift.

My broft was not visible at the armholes of the singlet. I was reluctant to remove the singlet and return it to the drawer.

Then grinning mischievously at my reflection I put on my shoes and went out to water the garden. Hardly anyone ever visited Waldene, so I felt fairly confident no one would see me in my peculiar state of undress. The sun's rays bounced off my shoulders and tried to reach the pale skin at the side of my breasts.

I turned on the tap and water gushed from the hose sending rainbow sprays all around. I felt deliriously happy - felt I was creating a memory for Barry, a gift to be shared on his return. I'd tell him about the heat and the sun and about my breasts jiggling freely as I wandered around. Spraying the water high up on an angle caused a fine sheen of water to fall back on me. I would tell him about frolicking in the garden in his wet singlet.

It would titillate him; maybe punish him a little by suggesting a most wonderful scene he'd missed, because he'd gone away from me. I sprayed water up into the air again and allowed my hair to become damp enough for small rivulets of water to run down between my breasts.

The image was now complete. Surely I must seem like a forest nymph in a sun shower. Barry's eyes would light up at my descriptions and he would smile and muse about the scene for months to come.

I watered the garden, turned off the tap and wound up the hose. The illusion was over and just as a cloud sliding across the sun will change the sky, so did my happiness disappear. It was time to get dressed again, time to go back to my family. There was nothing more to do here until Barry returned.

Take your partner

> *... I would ride with you upon the wind and dance with you upon the mountains like a flame.*
>
> WB Yeats

When Barry returned from overseas we inadvertently went to our first dance together. Although raised in a very religious household Barry had abandoned religion completely at the age of sixteen.

"I studied history and politics at secondary school and Uni and finally realised the Church had a lot to answer for. So I decided I couldn't be a part of it anymore," he'd told me.

Moved by the thought of Barry as a youth, making such a monumental decision; one that ever after would put him at odds with the rest of his family, I made no comment, merely listened and bled for his mother. His courage and resolution showed the seeds of the adult he would become.

Barry introduced me to opera and classical music. He taught me about tenors and sopranos and Wagner and Mozart. I became mesmerised by the singing and the romance of the performances and the power of music and dance to evoke the full range of human emotions.

The church he'd attended as a child frowned upon dancing, declaring it a form of lechery. Barry often joked about the church's stance saying. "I'm telling you, they disapproved of sex because it might lead to dancing." Yet so deeply instilled was the church's edict that even now, as an adult Barry didn't dance and had never asked me to dance. But he loved to watch people dancing.

When we'd go to the opera, he'd talk not only about the music but about the swirl of the women's skirts and the beauty of a fragile female hand on a man's shoulder. I could tell he was captivated by the romance of a man's arm protective and possessive around the waist of a woman as they danced.

Standing beside him when we went to parties I could feel him watching the dancers - feel a longing in him; feel him wishing he could join in. But he'd been too long in the church. He'd been able to abandon their preaching on all things but this. Dancing for Barry would be forever somehow sinful. It was a hurdle he seemed unable to leap, for all his outward rejection of the church.

In contrast my family were not religious. We laughed easily, sang unashamedly and danced enthusiastically. My mother had won trophies for dancing when she was a teenager. It was to our house my friends flocked to perfect dance moves in front of mirrored wardrobe doors to the accompaniment of loud music from a record player. I loved to dance.

Pandering to Barry's love of music and my love of picnics, I suggested we go to a twilight jazz session at the zoo. The brochure explained patrons would be allowed to wander the zoo for an hour after closing time before picnicking on the lawn to hear live music and dance.

It was amusing to hear Barry's response. "Should be interesting to walk around the zoo and watch the animals settling down for the night; quite unique in fact, especially with the day-time crowd gone."

"Great," I said, thinking about the magic of live music under the stars and a picnic basket laden with treats. "I'll book tickets." We went, each seeking our own version of happiness.

"I don't understand why most people are just heading straight to the picnic area. Aren't they interested in seeing the animals?"

Barry asked when people jostled us aside as we passed through the entry turn-stiles.

"S'pose they want to get a good picnic spot," I hinted.

"But there'll be room for everyone and in an hour it'll be too dark to see the animals."

"Hmm," was all I could offer by way of response.

Accompanied by a very small handful of other people, we walked around the animal enclosures. I carried the rug and Barry carried the picnic basket.

The animals' evening behaviour fascinated Barry, while to me the animals seemed like they'd done a hard day at the office and now just wanted to be fed and disappear into cages at the rear of their enclosure - there to lie down, scratch and sleep.

Over on the picnic lawn the music began to play. We hurried across the zoo to squeeze onto one of the small spaces of grass remaining in the picnic area. Barry spread the rug and we sat down. He poured me a glass of champagne and handed me a plastic plate bearing two chicken drumsticks.

The music flowed over the crowd and slowly couples began to abandon their rugs and move down to the temporary dance floor in front of the bandstand. Watching the dancers I shimmied slightly. Barry pretended not to notice.

"I brought pate," he offered.

My eyes were fixed on the musicians and the dancers at the far end of the lawn. Out of the corner of my eye I watched Barry watching me. He checked the wine bottle - only one glass gone.

I smiled in the direction of the music. It was wonderful. I moved my shoulders and swayed to the beat, conscious of Barry gnawing away on his chicken drumstick beside me. Humming quietly to myself, I turned my senses away from him and towards the music. Sitting there under the first stars of the warm evening sky and listening to the velvety tones of the band was peaceful yet uplifting.

Barry leant across and tapped my arm. "Do you want some pate?"

Somewhat startled, I turned to look at him. "Huh? ... No thanks." Almost instantly my eyes slipped away, back to the bandstand.

"It's a bit like the Pied Piper," Barry mumbled. "I wonder if it's possible to hypnotise a whole crowd just with the prospect of dancing." He paused as if expecting a response. When none was forthcoming he continued, this time obviously talking to himself. "Bit like 'Conga lines' I suppose. People get dragged into them like they're in some sort of trance."

The musicians stopped for a break. My gaze returned to Barry, the spell momentarily broken. I ate the pate and thanked him for the wine. Barry refilled my glass and I giggled, the joy from the music spilling from my eyes and throat. We nibbled on the picnic and watched the crowd seated around us. Overhead the sky slowly darkened and more stars came out to celebrate the evening.

"I wish we could dance," I murmured, straightening a corner of the rug.

"You know I don't dance."

"I could dance by myself. I don't really need a partner for this sort of music. You could just wait here and I could go down near the bandstand and mix in with the mob and dance. It's such wonderful music."

A look of sadness flickered across Barry's face and I sensed him struggling with his inner demons.

"Sorry, but I don't even know the first thing about dancing. Anyway, I'd be more likely to be a ballroom dancer, not ...a ..." He struggled for the word. "...a shimmier..." We both giggled. The word sounded hilarious when spoken by Barry. "It'd be humiliating enough to try to ballroom dance, but how would I go shimmying at the zoo? It's impossible!"

But I could see he felt sorry for me. He was probably angry to find the church still had control over this part of his life at least.

Barry looked at me then down to where the people had been dancing. "I'll come down to the dance floor with you." My head jerked up at this statement. I could see he was somewhat aghast at his words. Startled, he clarified himself. "But I'm not dancing. I'll just stand there and you can dance with me. We'll just pretend I'm your dancing partner. We'll stand at the edge of the dance floor."

It was obvious Barry was appalled at this turn of events. I imagine his innards must have been doing somersaults. But clapping my hands with delight I leaned across and kissed him, hoping to quiet his terror somewhat. At that moment the music started again.

"I love you so much" I said and leapt to my feet.

Holding hands we moved through the crowd. I led, shimmying and laughing back over my shoulder at Barry as we went. Down near the band Barry stood in the shadows at the very edge of the dance area. He stood, body erect, arms hanging loosely, awkwardly, by his sides. Facing him, I began to swing my hips and torso suggestively.

Barry rolled his eyes as if appalled, but he couldn't stop the smile spreading across his face. He loved seeing me so happy. Encouraged, I stepped closer to him and brushed my breasts against his chest playfully. Barry flushed but continued to smile, caught up in the occasion.

"Behave yourself," he murmured, probably with no expectation I would.

Stepping back, I raised my hands above my head and gyrated a few times, shoulders shimmying and hands clapping. I was transported – the music seemed to have flown into my blood and now I *was* the music.

Barry watched me with delight but still refused to join in. Instead, he folded his arms across his chest and glanced up and away from me, skimmed the dancing crowd and tried not to be drawn into the spell.

I could almost see him recognising the 'evil' the church had spoken about. It must have been titillating to watch all the bodies writhing to the rhythmic backdrop. The dancers were laughing and happy as if the music had coursed through their veins like a drug, making them something 'other', something fluid and free-flowing.

Leaning forward I held Barry's face between my hands and kissed his lips, at the same time feeling his hips against my hips, my breasts against his folded arms. I moved slowly, seductively and Barry's manhood suddenly became aroused. Embarrassed, he shuffled back slightly to calm himself.

Sniggering I danced around him, deliberately sliding my breasts and hips against him as I moved. I loved him, loved his inner struggle not to move with the music, loved that my dancing aroused him. I felt delightfully wicked.

Sliding around to face him again, I reached for his hands, hoping to entice him to unfold his arms and dance with me. But Barry's arms remained locked. He stared hard into my face then rolled his eyes upward to reassert that he did not dance.

"You should be arrested!" he grunted with a smile. The music ended and the musicians put away their instruments for the evening. I could feel Barry relax now the music had formally ended.

Months later in a casual conversation, Barry mentioned he sometimes wished he could dance. The mammoth statement shocked us both.

"But I can teach you. It's just about swaying in time to the music. You can sway."

Barry shook his head. "No - I wish I could dance *properly*; a dance where I'd get to hold you, like a waltz, or something. Where I could twirl you around, like they do in ballroom dancing?"

At this he stopped, straightened up and looked away. "But I can't dance. I just don't think it'd ever be a possibility. It's just a 'wish'. It's not important."

I felt sorry for him, but knew his ego wouldn't allow him to do anything that would make him look foolish. Yet I also knew learning to dance usually began clumsily and people did look a bit foolish in the beginning.

"But I could teach you an informal sort of waltz. Not a stiff-backed ballroom dance, but a softer, easier style – the one most people do. It's easy. It's a bit like sex really."

At this Barry groaned quietly.

"You just have to hold each other, put your rude bits together, and get your legs and feet in a line – one male leg, one female leg, one male leg and one female leg. Then you walk forward and I walk backward, and I go wherever you direct me. It's pretty easy. I could teach you. It'd take no time to learn."

He was reluctant, not convinced, not prepared to run the risk of failure. I sensed him not wanting to appear ridiculous in front of me. But I persisted. It was such a little wish, one he could easily achieve with my help. Eventually Barry agreed to have one attempt during a lunch hour.

We met at the end of the dusty country road half way between both our schools. Beneath a canopy of eucalypt with no music other than the drone of summer blowflies and bees, we began. The legs, the rude bits, the arms and backs and shoulders – locked together in a dancer's embrace, we slowly began to shuffle around.

I could tell Barry felt awkward and nothing like the gliding cavaliers he admired so much in the dance scenes of operas and films. But I loved the feel of his arms around me, loved the fact we were slow dancing in the middle of nowhere with an audience of birds and trees. The sun on my head and shoulders and the feel of Barry pressed against me was wonderful. The half hour passed quickly.

"It's useless! I'm no good at it," Barry declared when it was time to leave.

"You did well. It's only the first time and we're already moving around without inflicting pain on each other." I laughed, attempting to cheer him.

"No, it's no good. I can't do it. It doesn't look like waltzing."

"But no-one does real waltzing except ballroom dancers. Most people just shuffle around like we did. If you want to do ballroom waltzing we'll have to go for proper lessons. What would be the point? We're never going to enter a ballroom dancing competition."

"No I don't want to go for lessons. I don't even know when we'd ever waltz anyway. It was just a thought, just a stupid whim. I don't even need to know how to dance."

He was closing down so no good pushing the subject any further. Obviously he considered it a threat to his self-image and he didn't want him to lose face in front of me. I loved him as the strong and confident person he was and whether he could dance or not was of no consequence to our relationship.

Some years after our 'country lane waltz,' Barry and I were invited to his cousin's wedding. We sat at a table with his elderly aunt and uncle and the table talk explored politics and history. Not having much to contribute to the conversation I watched the other guests instead. At one point, Barry reached under the table and squeezed my hand. Looking up I recognised his silent apology for the conversation. I smiled to reassure him everything was alright.

Down at the front of the marquis, a static crackle signalled the disc jockey was about to begin the evening's music. "Testing, testing... one, two, three. Is anybody out there?" Behind me I could hear Barry discussing the latest federal government debacle with his uncle. Their voices had hushed, but the deep timbre of Barry's voice was easy to distinguish.

Having decided the sound system was correctly adjusted the disc jockey called for silence and made a well-rehearsed speech about the formality of a wedding and the need for a bridal waltz to mark the occasion. I turned my chair slightly away from the table to see the dancers better. The music flowed and the dance floor became crowded. Barry brought me another glass of champagne and as he bent to give me the glass he murmured "Are you having a good time?"

"Mmm... it's wonderful." I squeezed his arm gently and pulling him down toward me whispered in his ear, "I love you."

Barry stood up. He looked relieved but cast a glance towards the disc jockey and the dance floor. "I'm sorry I don't dance," he mumbled.

"I know. It doesn't matter. Just listening to the music is wonderful." I took a sip from the glass and looked away towards the dancers to absolve him from further guilt. Barry sat down and returned to the table conversation with his uncle.

As the evening wore on the wedding guests began to circulate around the tables and other relations came to speak to Barry's uncle. Barry stretched out his arm and ran his fingers across the back of my neck. Startled, I shuddered. "You gave me a fright. Is everything okay?" Between the music, the family conversations and laughter inside the marquee it was difficult to hear.

He hesitated then tilted his head ever so slightly. "I love you," he mouthed, like a schoolboy whispering to a friend across a classroom.

"I know," I mouthed back.

With a nod of his head Barry gestured toward the dance floor, "Wanna dance?"

"Really?" I said aloud, eyebrows raised and eyes wide open.

Barry stood up and taking my hands, gently pulled me to my feet.

"Only if we dance at the side of the dance floor – there's a spot over there near the entrance to the marquee. See it?" he pointed to a tiny space secreted between an amplifier and a wall. Technically the space was not really part of the dance floor but I was willing to overlook this, given the tremendous effort Barry was making on my behalf.

"It's dark there," he continued, "... no-one will notice us. But don't do any funny stuff. Don't rub against me or anything. Just the shuffling stuff we did in the road that day. And just one dance, okay?"

I was amazed, overjoyed. I felt the palm of his hand dampening as he led me through the crowd and into the tiny shadowed space - our own private dance floor. I could hardly imagine his fear.

"Now remember," he nuzzled my neck and mumbled into my ear, "Keep those breasts off me."

Throwing back my head I gave a loud, joyful laugh and pulled Barry closer to me as he took his first public dance step. Above us I felt the angels weep.

STEPPING OUT

Bushwalking preparations

> *... But I would walk 500 miles*
> *And I would walk 500 more*
> *Just to be the man who walks a thousand miles*
> *To fall down at your door*
>
> THE PROCLAIMERS

Barry was an ardent bushwalker. Listening to his enthusiastic descriptions about his bushwalking experiences made me want to have a go at it myself. Of course it was a slight drawback I'd never walked anywhere other than around the local shopping malls, but I was confident that with a bit of training, we'd be able to do a bush walk together.

I imagined myself wandering alongside Barry far from other people. The sun would shine down on us as we ambled along well-worn, meandering forest tracks. We'd share secrets and occasionally perch atop fallen logs to munch on energy bars and stare up into the trees. Barry would point out important plants along the way and I'd learn all about bushwalking.

Then at day's end we'd dine in a country hotel to celebrate the walk before falling exhausted between the crisp white sheets of a quaint bed and breakfast establishment. It sounded like a superb day. I wondered why I hadn't taken up bushwalking before this.

After contacting some local walking groups I received brochures and descriptions of walks each club had planned for the months ahead. They ranged from half-day walks to week-long camping treks. Based on my limited experience it seemed sensible to begin with some half day walks and build up to a full day walk. Maybe this would even lead to an overnight walk depending on how I got along with the group and what extra effort would be required to camp out.

Given the sporting focus of Alec and my boys on Sundays, it wouldn't be difficult for me to go with the walking group for a few hours one Sunday a month. If I coped with the half day walks and liked the other walkers, later I'd work out how to get away for a full day walk and perhaps an overnight trek.

"Look at these photos." Barry and I were sitting together after school and I held the brochures up for him to see. "This one's called 'Razorback Ridge' in the Cathedral Ranges, and this one's Lederderg Gorge – fantastic! There are shorter walks too – Heidelberg to Eltham along the river, a rail Trail to Warburton. Must be walks taking place all over Victoria every Sunday."

Barry sat in unenthusiastic silence watching me read through the brochures excitedly. But his silence gradually drained my joy.

"What's wrong?" I said stuffing the brochures back into their envelopes and stacking them into a pile on my lap. "I thought you'd be happy to know I was thinking about trying bushwalking."

He sighed. "I am happy. But I don't understand why you want to join a walking club. I could take you walking. We could just go ourselves. We don't need to be with a group of strangers."

"But I can't go bushwalking with just you. Can't you join the bushwalking club with me and we can still be together? Being part of a club means I'd get regular newsletters and be able to go on long walks once a month. If I go with you I'd have to lie about what I was doing." Once again the same fundamental problem surfaced in our relationship. "I can't go bushwalking with just you. That's ridiculous!" I repeated for emphasis.

Barry nodded, but said nothing. We changed the subject and my bushwalking experience seemed to have ended before it began.

A few days later an envelope was delivered to my home from the *Waldene Bush Walking Club*. One page described the supposed history of the 'club' while another page provided the proposed walking agenda for the coming semester.

"What a lot of homework! Is there an annual subscription or a 'per walk' fee if I join your walking club?" I asked Barry the next time we met.

He laughed. "For a Princess there is no fee. You just need to nominate which walk you'd like to do and when. And by the way, all walks and all dates are flexible for Your Highness." He grinned and we spent the next half hour discussing the walks he'd researched. This time we were both excited.

When I finally agreed which bushwalk I'd go on with him, Barry presented me with a specially bought pink clipboard with a pink pencil attached.

"You record the distance you walk each day," he explained, pointing to a column on a carefully ruled page attached to the clipboard. "I've listed some suggested weekly targets. You start out with a few kilometres per week and then gradually increase the number of kilometres walked each day. In a few months you'll be ready for a genuinely challenging bush walk." Barry seemed delighted with his plans for me.

'Kilometres' was a plural. That made me slightly uneasy. I knew it was about one kilometre from my house to the nearest train station and I hated that walk when forced to catch the train to the city for meetings.

'Suggested targets' implied a specific number that would be considered sufficient or insufficient. I stared at the pink clipboard, played with the pencil, wondered how flexible Barry would be about his 'targets'. Perhaps bushwalking was a terrible mistake. I wondered about the strength of my underarm deodorant.

"It'll be hard to calculate the distance I walk each day when training." My voice sounded thin and whiny.

"We'll start doing some walks on Sundays and I'll estimate the distances. I can also map out some shorter routes around Greensborough and write down the kilometres by my car's speedometer. Then if you walk those routes you'll know exactly how far you've done." Barry was trying to be helpful, thought I wanted a solution. He hadn't sensed my sudden lack of enthusiasm for the whole idea.

But it was too late to back out so I began.

Sometimes Barry walked with me and I was happy, other times I walked alone and was cross. I recorded my data on the pink clipboard and Barry drew smiley faces when my weekly targets were met and was disappointed when they weren't.

He taught me the term *personal best* and we celebrated when I managed a personal best for a day or a week. Annoyingly Barry began referring to this as my '*PB*,' as if I was some sort of professional athlete.

When we walked together, Barry encouraged me and gave me tips. "Try to take slightly longer strides to cover more distance with less effort. Always push yourself to take just a few more steps before quitting for the day. Even 100 steps extra each day makes a big difference over a long trek."

Trudging along behind him I'd nod absently and try to resist the urge to ask if we'd walked enough for today.

When I struggled walking up hills Barry would call down from ahead where he stood waiting for me to catch up. "Look down at your feet rather than up at the hill ahead and when the going gets tough set yourself a minimum number of steps you'll take before stopping to rest."

He gradually became very irritating. "I have set a minimum number of steps," I once yelled back at him as he waited above for me. "It's five!"

At this Barry had 'tissed' and turned away to resume walking. He walked with a slow, steady gait regardless of the terrain. I watched as he strode around a bend and disappeared from view without looking back. Cursing him under my breath, I started walking again and on reaching the bend found him sitting in the shade waiting for me. "Who's a tired girl then?" he asked as I sank down alongside.

"Sorry. It's just so steep and I'm so tired."

"I know. But it's not fair to get angry at me."

We sat for a few minutes and drank from our water-bottles. "Well, Miss Muffet ..." Barry ginned and patted the top of my head, "time to get going again."

Once when we were walking I suggested we should skip for awhile. "Skipping covers more ground in less time. I love to skip – great big high skips along flat paths; it's almost like flying. Can you skip?" I asked.

"Men don't skip," Barry responded solemnly.

But I wondered fleetingly why my suggestion was rejected outright, whereas we acted on his suggestions almost without question. Concealing my pique, I laughed aloud.

"Don't or can't?" Clapping my hands I somehow felt the victor in the conversation. Barry ignored me and we plodded on.

The day arrived when Barry announced I was now finally ready to attempt a full-day walk in the hills around Marysville. The plan was for us to stay at a motel in the township on the Friday night, set off early Saturday morning, trek all day, then return to the motel in the evening, exhausted and victorious.

The dates were almost confirmed when I commented casually about how good it was that the 'park people' built toilets along the walking circuit for tourists and bushwalkers.

A frown spread across Barry's forehead. "What?" he asked somewhat absently, glancing up from the book he was reading.

"The toilets – it's a good idea ... for tourism."

"Toilets?" Barry closed his book and turned to face me.

Something was amiss; I was showing my ignorance in some way. I quickly changed my statement to save face. "Oh I know they won't be flush toilets - probably those long-drop toilets like at the Sunbury Pop festival."

I gave a short scoff, hoping to mask my revulsion. How well I remembered those toilets at the pop festivals of my teenager years. I'd visited them sparingly, preferring to go without food or drink rather than be forced into the horror contained within their hessian walls.

"Dar-ling." It was what Barry said when I confounded him.

"Hmm? Try to stay calm, I warned myself.

"Darling - there are no toilets." The statement hung in the air above my head like a guillotine; a guillotine that beheads dreams of sunshine and strolls and shared secrets and successes.

"But 25 kilometres is a long way. I don't think I can go that long without going to the loo." It was a small whimpered statement, fully exposing my naivety.

"It'll be okay. I'll carry a shovel."

"What good's a shovel?" My words came without forethought.

Barry tilted his head slightly, a smile playing at the edges of his mouth. He waited for me to think it through, watched as a look of realisation spread slowly across my face.

"You must be joking! There's no way I can 'go' in the forest. That's disgusting! Are you telling me people dig a hole in the ground and wee in it? Do they fill the hole in or do they just leave little ponds everywhere? My God, that's revolting. And what if they want to do more than wee?"

Barry began to laugh. He laughed until he cried. When he calmed he explained in more detail. "You funny girl – you only use the shovel if you want to do more than wee." He smothered another chuckle.

Standing in front of him, hands on my hips, I was angry for being so ignorant. I was ashamed not to have previously thought about this feature of bushwalking. I'd been raised in the concrete suburbs and my limited experience of the outdoors was restricted to weekends bunking in relations country homes or living in caravan parks and navigating the ablutions block. Never in my life had I been asked to forego access to a toilet completely.

"I won't be able to do it. I just can't. I'm sorry."

The smile slipped from Barry's face. I tried to imagine what he was thinking. He'd be disappointed in me that was certain; for giving up without even trying. I felt stupid and pathetic, but surely 'no toilets' was asking too much of me. It would be too awful ... but I didn't want to fail him.

I thought about the pink clipboard and its matching pencil. Barry already thought I was something of a 'princess,' but he'd also thought with his encouragement I could do a bushwalk. He believed in me more than I believed in myself.

I might be able to do the walk – but this humiliating bit of it was too much to ask. I wanted to yell "*I am not an animal!*" a catch-cry remembered from some old movie. It was all too disgusting. What was wrong with people? How could they see this as acceptable behaviour? No I couldn't do it.

"We could go for a picnic out in the forest and you could have a practice," Barry suggested.

"It won't work. I just know. There's no way I'll be able to. It's revolting." I wanted Barry to rescue me from the conversation.

"Not even a wee? You don't even need to dig a hole for that." Barry looked out the window leaving the question for me to consider.

"But I don't know how. Do I take my jeans off? What if I wee on my shoes? It's okay for you guys, but girls can't aim you know."

"My Little Miss Muffet," Barry soothed. "You'll do fine. We'll just go for a practice and you'll see it's really nothing." He stood up and put his arms around me and ashamed, I hid my face against his chest. It seemed an enormous thing to ask of me but for him, I could at least try.

A few weeks later we drove to a forest on the suburban fringe. I felt awkward and was not looking forward to the task ahead. I usually wore jeans but today I'd opted for stretch track pants. There was some solace in knowing I'd at least be able to quickly pull them up if interrupted in my attempt to urinate in the bush. Even so, the thought depressed me.

"What are you thinking?" Barry asked conscious of my unnatural silence in the passenger seat.

"I'm thinking if my pants are down around my ankles and I squat to wee, the chances are very high that I'll wee right onto my pants; seems to defeat the purpose really. May as well just leave my pants on and wee down my leg." I continued to stare out at the scenery, before giving a snort of derision.

"What?" Barry asked.

"Someone once told me boys wee when they wear wetsuits. They reckon it provides a lovely warm sensation against the cold of the ocean. It's disgusting! Never borrow someone's wetsuit, that's my advice. What the hell was God thinking when he invented wee anyway?" I turned to face Barry as if expecting an answer.

"You're ridiculous."

"Hmm ... probably." I looked away again.

"Look darling, you'll be fine. Just kind of pull your pants out of the way when you crouch. It's not hard. You'll be fine."

A few hours later when we were walking along a stony path deep in woodland I stopped suddenly and dropped hold of Barry's hand.

"What's up?" he asked frantically scanning the path ahead for signs of danger.

"It's time ... I have to go!"

"You'll be great," he said enthusiastically. "Just remember to keep your pants out of the way. Go in there behind that bush." He gestured to a large native shrub beside the path. "I'll wait here."

I looked from Barry to the shrub and back again. "Are you kidding? You'll be able to see me from here. I'll need to go much further off the path."

"Don't be silly. Who cares if I can see you? Anyway, I won't look. I'll face away."

"No way! I don't trust you not to peek. I have to go much further in and you have to walk a bit further along the path and promise not to peek. And you have to keep watch and call out if you see someone coming."

Barry nodded his head in despair. "You're crazy. You're making a big thing out of nothing."

"Well then I can't go. I'll just have to hold on until we get back to town." Stomping off along the path my eyes stung with tears. With each step I silently chastised myself for having no experience at this bush stuff. Barry was probably fed up with me. I walked on, reluctant to stop and look back.

Suddenly behind me I heard him singing loudly:

"A frog went walking on a summer's day

Uhum, uhum,

A frog went walking on a summer's day

He met Miss Mousie on the way

Uhum, uhum,

He said Miss Mousie will you marry me?

Uhum, uhum,
He said Miss Mousie will you marry me?

We'll live together in the apple tree

Uhum,

Uhum, uhum, uhum."

I swung around to see Barry skipping in great leaps along the path. Coming level with me he stopped, a huge grin on his face.

"I thought you couldn't skip."

"I said men don't skip, not that they can't." He laughed - a playful puppy waiting to see what impact his antics had on its owner. I loved his grinning face. I loved that he'd come after me, had sought me through the childhood act of skipping.

Taking a deep breath I looked off into the bush. "Okay, I'll give it one more try. But can I please go a bit further off the path?"

"Go as far as you need, but not so far you get lost coming back." Barry bent and brushed a kiss on the top of my head. "Come on Miss Mouse, let's try again."

We wandered a bit further down the track hand in hand. "Did you just propose to me?" I asked, not looking at him.

"It's a song darling. Don't get carried away. Besides, how can I propose to you? You're still married."

"Hmm... well it sounded like a proposal."

Barry grinned and squeezed my hand.

We came to a place where the scrub was quite thick on either side of the path. "What about here?" Barry asked.

"Maybe." I no longer felt like urinating. The trauma of the last ten minutes had removed the urge completely.

"Well you go in there and when you're far enough in, yell out to me and I'll go further along the track. I promise not to peek and I'll let you know if someone's coming. You'll be okay. We haven't passed anyone on the track since we started."

Despite his instructions I remained beside him, mulling something over.

"What?" he asked, frustration in his voice.

"I haven't got any toilet paper. I didn't think to bring any." I looked into the bushes beside the path, exhaled exhaustedly and avoiding eye contact, waited for him to solve the problem.

"Darling you just use leaves. You don't need toilet paper. Just grab some large leaves off the nearest bush and use them. It's easy and they just become leaf litter."

My eyes slowly tracked a path up to his face. "Of course I use leaves. Why would I think any different?" My voice was full of sarcasm. "I'm to wee in the forest, keep my pants out of the way and mop up with leaves. It's a nightmare!" With that, I turned on her heel and pushed into the tangled scrub.

Now deep off the path I searched for a suitable tree. It needed to be wide and bushy, a thick shrub taller and much broader than me - a tree that would hide me from view completely either standing or crouching. I picked my way through the scrub now and then turning back to make sure I wasn't visible to Barry. I could no longer see him, but every so often he called out 'Coo-ee' to reassure me he was still there.

"Coo - *wee*" I mumbled to myself, sniggering at the pun.

Finally I found a suitable bush. "My *lavor-tree*" - I grinned, pleased at my wit.

Pulling my track pants down and out of the way as best I could, I crouched down only to spring up again thinking '*snake-bite!*' A stiff blade of native grass had stabbed my naked behind. I shuffled across to crouch again and wait.

Around me the forest rustled quietly in the hot afternoon sun and insects droned amidst the leaves. A slight breeze caressed my naked rump and ruffled the edge of my t-shirt. I thought about what I'd do if a wombat or wallaby came crashing through the bush. Looking around nervously I began to hum to alert any animals to my presence and I wondered if my bare behind should have been sunscreen protected. It had never before been so openly exposed.

"Coo-ee" Barry called from somewhere.

I considered the appalling sight I was currently presenting to any would-be Peeping Tom – the pure white orb of my backside slowly reddening in the noonday sun. I stood and pulled my pants up. This was a waste of time. My body was never going to allow me to wee outdoors. Years of toilet training and suburban manners and etiquette could not be undone by the mere act of crouching in the forest and hoping.

Barry wouldn't be pleased but it wasn't my fault. Some people can do some things and others can't. He'd just have to accept that this was something beyond my skill-set. No matter, I'd just 'hold on' or maybe if my bladder got to bursting point, a miracle would happen and I'd wee in the bush - but not here, not now. I trudged back through the trees to find Barry.

"Coo-ee," I called nearing the path. Barry came striding to meet me.

"Hooray, here comes Miss Mouse," he shouted, clapping in mock applause. "How did ya go?"

Folding my arms, I coughed slightly and hesitated, realising my explanation was perhaps not going to be well received.

"I couldn't go - can't do it." Having blurted the words out, I grimaced and stood humiliated, frightened to look at Barry. The bush now seemed unusually quiet, making me wish a marauding wombat would suddenly appear.

"That's ridiculous!" Barry's voice was firm and a little angry. "Go back in there and don't come out until you have. You're just being ridiculous."

His over-use of the word 'ridiculous' indicated he'd run out of patience. I gulped, knowing there was nothing I could say to appease him because he was right of course. Shrugging I looked down at my boots.

"Go on. I mean it." His voice had softened slightly but it was obvious he wasn't going to change his mind.

I stepped back into the forest, mumbling curses and worked my way back to my *lavor-tree* to assume the crouching position once again. Should have lied, I berated myself. He'd have been none the wiser. But lying wouldn't solve the problem, just delay it. I waited. No 'Coo-ees' this time; could've been alone in the forest. I tried to focus on the task at hand.

Come on, I chided myself. It can't be that hard. Close your eyes and pretend you're on a toilet somewhere... nothing.

You know he means it. We could be walking along hand in hand. We could be celebrating. Come on - doesn't have to be a full wee - just something, just a trickle. Come on, you can do it."

Finally both appalled and delighted I hurried back to show Barry that one of my Blundstone boots was now wet - proof of my success. Barry caught me in a bear hug.

"You're amazing," he said and I felt deliriously happy.

Over the hills and far away

Does the road wind up-hill all the way?
Yes to the very end. Will the day's journey take the
whole day? From morn to night my friend

CHRISTINA ROSETTI

Some weeks later Barry and I finally stayed overnight at the tiny village of Marysville huddled in the foothills of the Great Dividing Range. Our plan was to walk 25 kilometres in one day. All our training had been aimed at this adventure.

At 6 am Barry woke me. After breakfast he put everything we were to take onto the bed then carefully and methodically apportioned the items between our two packs, making sure my pack was much lighter than his.

"Do I get to carry the food?" I asked.

"No way," Barry laughed. "How do you think I'm going to make sure you finish the walk? I need bribes – especially for you my little *food-hawk*. You can carry the water."

"Seems a bit unkind," I said playfully. "What if I'm starving and you're miles ahead of me on the track?"

"Exactly!" Barry had obviously been thinking through the logistics of this walk for a long time. "Oh – and by the way, I brought a map for you." He fossicked in his pockets and pulled out an A4 piece of paper. He sat on the bed and gestured for me to sit beside him.

"I've marked our route so you can see where we're going. If you get lost just follow the line I've drawn."

"Don't lose me! If I get lost it'll be your fault. Don't walk too far ahead of me." I was terrified at the thought of becoming lost in the forested hills. My sense of direction was bad enough in the suburbs where I had some hope of stumbling on a remembered landmark. I'd have no hope in a forest.

Barry looked at me in surprise. "But darling it's not hard to follow the map. Besides, there are signposts along the way."

"I don't care. Promise you won't lose me!" I begged.

Somewhat taken aback by the earnestness of my plea, he folded the map and put it into my backpack before turning to me. "I promise not to lose you. But I've changed my mind. If you do somehow get lost I want you to just sit under the nearest tree and wait for me to come back. Will you promise me that? Don't wander off the path. Just sit down and wait and I'll come back and find you."

Wrapping my arms around him I lay my face against his chest. "Promise," I murmured.

"Good girl," he said and hugged me.

The main street was deserted as we sauntered down to the entry point for the numerous bush tracks winding through the hills. There'd been a light frost overnight and here and there, smoke from kitchen chimneys rose straight up in the damp morning air. The dense blue-green eucalyptus forest rolling endlessly over the hills surrounding the town seemed ominous now we were to begin the walk. Perhaps this was to be a battle between the forest and me.

The end of the main street heralded the edge of town where the asphalt gave way to the crushed stone of the walking tracks. I was very excited and for a moment felt something of what Sir Edmond Hilary must have felt when he'd finished his training and mapping and packing and finally the day had arrived to 'set off' and conquer Everest.

I wanted to call out, to sing, to somehow mark the moment. I turned to look at Barry. He was watching me in amusement, his whole face smiling.

"So my little bush-walker, what's up?"

"I'm so excited. Hope I can make it. Thanks … for putting up with me."

"My pleasure pretty one." We held hands and walked through the gate and onto the track. Barry looked at his watch. "It's 8 am. I expect we'll get back by about 3 pm. Are you ready?" I nodded and we set off.

Initially the path was wide and meandered through native gums and ferny grottos. We crossed back and forth over bubbling creeks by walking on little split logs or leaping between well-positioned rocks. We talked and laughed as we strode along. The further we walked, the louder became the thunder of the nearby rivers and waterfalls, swollen with winter rain and melting snows.

The lush undergrowth shaded the track and kept us cold. The track narrowed and became uneven, forcing us to walk in single file. Barry went ahead and held branches aside for me. As the morning wore on the sun forced its way through the trees and the temperature increased. While Barry walked along undaunted, I trudged silently behind him, the distance between us widening with every minute.

Eventually Barry stopped under a tree to wait for me to catch up. I tried not to pant from lack of oxygen as I approached him, tried to regulate my breathing for the last twenty metres between us so he wouldn't notice I was already struggling.

I crumpled down next to him. He looked rested and cool. "Are you hot?" he asked nodding towards my chest. Looking down I saw most of the front of my once fresh t-shirt was now damp with perspiration. All that is, apart from a small circle around each nipple. The pull of my back-pack had caused my breasts to thrust sky-ward, thereby protecting my nipples from any gravitational run-off.

"You look nice darling. Mm, mm," Barry said, staring with merriment at the two dry circles.

I groaned and yanked off my backpack. The back of my t-shirt having been trapped between my body and the synthetic pack, was soaking with perspiration. The mountain air blowing over the exposed wet cloth was cooling - a science fact verified. It was small compensation. I gulped some water from my flask before pressing it against my forehead hoping the metal would cool my face. "How far have we walked?" I asked.

"Give me the map and I'll show you." Barry looked at his watch then up at the sun as if checking its accuracy using some old scouting trick. "We've been walking about two hours."

"So we've still got about five hours to go?" It didn't seem fair. "But we'll be stopping for snacks and lunch a few times won't we? So it's not really another five hours of walking is it?" I sounded like a pathetic child.

Beside me Barry said nothing, instead studied the map in greater detail. *'Hopefully looking for shortcuts,* 'I thought to myself sadly.

He took a pen from his pack and made a cross on the map. "We're about here,' he said handing the map back to me. It was just as well he'd made the cross small, otherwise it would have blended into the word '*Start*' that was printed on the map.

"But we haven't even walked anywhere if you're right. Surely we're further along than that?"

"Don't worry darling. There's plenty of time. We'll make it. You're just getting into you're stride … and anyway, the first part was a bit steep. It'll be easier going when the track drops down into the valley again. We'll stop for morning tea in another hour, okay?"

He was using his 'kind' voice and I sensed he was feeling a bit disappointed in me. No doubt he'd planned on us making faster progress.

"Have you had enough rest?" he asked, at the same time getting to his feet. I hadn't, but slowly dragged myself back up to stand beside him.

We began again. This time I held the map in my hand and kept looking for markers along the track to prove we were further along than Barry had estimated. Funny thing about maps - they don't effectively show 'uphills' to the novice map reader. Over and over I read and re-read the walk distance in kilometres, but it seemed most of the distances quoted were actually straight up and therefore took much longer than anticipated.

Barry strode away with me bringing up the rear. He was wearing shorts and for awhile admiring his calves proved a wonderful distraction for me. Full, round and powerful, Barry's calves gave the impression of plump, ripe fruit. Each muscle was clearly defined with every step he took.

Although Barry's torso had a reasonable amount of hair, his legs were almost hair-free. I'd once read that cyclists shave their legs to reduce wind resistance and potentially increase their speed. Long ago Barry had belonged to an amateur cycling club but I couldn't imagine him shaving his legs. He'd be too wary of the woes that befell Samson as a result of shaving. The thought made me chuckle.

"Wait!" I called out suddenly.

Barry turned quickly and hurried back to me. "What?" concern for me evident in his voice.

"You're gorgeous. I just wanted to tell you that."

He looked taken aback, then embarrassed. "Darling is this a ploy to stop walking?"

I ran my hands down his arms and took his hands in mine. His hands were large and firm making mine look child-like in comparison. I kissed one of his palms then the other and cupped my face in them. "You are so beautiful."

"You funny girl … is something wrong?" Barry tightened his hands around my face and kissed my cheek.

"I was watching your calves. They're almost mischievous. They make me think of a naughty little boy who's just come in from climbing trees or jumping fences and chasing balls. The mother in me has this overwhelming need to smack them."

"You're being silly" Barry laughed but I sensed he was a rather pleased I approved of his calves. Probably in cycling the strength of one's calves brings some degree of status.

"What can I say? You've got the most gorgeous, *smackable* calves any mother ever saw and today they make me very much in love with you. In fact they're sending me crazy." I dropped his hands and stepped back.

Barry shook his head. "Well you're not going to smack them and we need to keep walking. Maybe you should walk in front and I can look at you for a while."

About twenty minutes after I'd taken the lead our pace had increased incredibly. I was very self-conscious with Barry walking behind me. He was always only a step or two behind and never dropped back. I'd increased my pace to accommodate the length of his step compared to mine. It was exhausting.

Hoping to create the impression I was coping with the challenge, I tried to walk more upright and to breathe quietly, rather than take the occasional bent-over, gasping breaths that had been my practice when walking behind him. The track began to wind up yet another hill and I knew I wouldn't be able to keep up the pace much longer. Just when it seemed I'd have to suffer the humiliation of begging for time-out, from behind me came words of salvation.

"You've got the cutest little bottom. It's a bit runty from all this walking but it's still adorable. I think I'll call you *runty-bum* - my little *runty-bum*." Barry laughed as always, at his invention of yet another nick-name for me.

Screeching to a halt I spun around to face him, my hands simultaneously reaching behind to cover my backside. Unbeknown to me my long tee-shirt had concertinaed up behind my backpack leaving my rear end in full view.

"Honestly! How can I be a serious bushwalker if you're walking behind ogling me? And you walk too close behind anyway. You should leave more space between us. Time you walked in front again!" It was difficult to sound overly angry when his words had both flattered and rescued me for a few moments at least.

Barry smiled enigmatically. "Let's sit down and have a drink ... and because you're such a good bushwalker you can even have a muesli bar," he offered by way of an apology."

When we resumed walking Barry took the lead. Hours later deep in the forest, the walking track ran beside a small pond. We sat at the water's edge with the hills rising in folds all around us and the clouds forming and re-forming above us.

"How far do you reckon it is from here to that log?" Barry asked gesturing to a tree wedged upright out in the water.

"Hmm, about thirty metres. Why?"

Barry stood up and searched around for a stone. "What will you give me if I can hit the log with this stone?"

I laughed. "I haven't got anything. You've got all the food. I'm just carrying the water."

"Will you let me take a photo of you without squirming and ruining it like you usually do?"

"Maybe."

Barry threw the stone. *Clunk*. It found its mark then bounced off into the water.

"You owe me a photo."

"Wait a minute. I said 'maybe.' Besides you didn't say what would happen if you missed. I don't think that was a real bet."

Barry searched for more stones. "We should start walking again," I suggested, getting up.

"Come on - one good photo of you if I hit it. And if I miss, I promise not to try to photograph you for one whole month. That's a fair bet."

"Hmph."

"I'll take that as a yes," Barry said and threw another stone.

'*Clunk*' – another hit.

"Okay. That's definite then - one photo owing."

I shook my head.

"All right - if I can get four hits in row, you owe me four minutes of photography.

"You're kidding yourself. You can't get four hits in a row."

"It's a bet darling. I've already won the right to one photo. Now I'll even risk that photo as well. Four hits for four minutes. All or nothing; what do you say?"

"I say you're full of yourself. You can't get four in a row."

"Take it or leave it," he challenged.

"Go on then, smarty-pants."

Clunk, clunk, clunk, clunk.

"That's unbelievable. You were joking though weren't you?" I ventured, hoping he'd be kind. In answer to my question Barry bent down and picked up three more stones.

"No, no more. You're a cheat. I hate having my photo taken. You know that. Can this just be a joke? Say it isn't for real."

"I'll give you another chance," Barry said. "I'll let you off the hook if I don't hit the log with these next three stones. But if I hit the log every time then I get the right to at least one naked photo or four minutes of photography."

"No way! No more betting." I pulled on my back pack and bolted down the path. Behind me I heard a soft '*clunk, clunk, clunk.*'

Four hours into the walk I sagged against a fallen log and watched Barry's white canvas sun-hat bob among the trees far ahead of me on the track. Every so often he *Coo –weed*. He sounded chirpy and gay; probably thinking his call would encourage me. There were so many responses I'd liked to have made if I only had the energy to shout or even enough saliva left to croak out a sound.

Eventually I staggered up yet another incline and found Barry sitting on a large flat rock beside the path waiting for me. "Finally!" he said and rolled his eyes toward the sky. I was in no mood for humour and remained standing.

Barry shuffled across to make room for me on the rock beside him. "Come and sit down. I want to talk to you." Although fed up with the whole bush walking experience, the offer to sit for awhile was too good to refuse. Slumping down beside him I eased the pack off my sweat-soaked back.

"I haven't spoken to you for ages," I managed to say, hoping to make him feel guilty for setting the bar too high for me. "Are we nearly there?"

"No - not quite." For the first time in our relationship I noticed Barry looked quite cruel from some angles.

"But you said it'd only take five hours. It must be almost five hours now. Don't tell me you lied to me?" My anger rose.

"Darling," he said, putting his hand on my perspiring knee, "that's because you're plodding. You're supposed to be bush walking.

But you're just lifting your feet and putting them down without really striding out. You're making hardly any progress at all."

"Plodding!" the word snapped out. I was a bit fed up with people who *strode out* and who estimated time by looking at the sun, and of unreliable maps and endless walking tips and muesli bars masquerading as food.

"Have another drink of water and this lemon fruit bar," Barry said, pulling two bars from his pack. He ripped open an orange fruit bar and chomped down, staring along the path ahead.

"I'd have preferred the orange bar. I don't like lemon," I complained, hoping to hurt him."

"Sorry," Barry said and kept chewing.

When we resumed walking it was in stony silence. I tried to 'stride out' and Barry walked on ahead, stopping every so often to glance back and make sure I was still following.

Eventually the path descended for the last time and became a flat stretch alongside the road leading back to the township. At the sight of the road my sprits lifted. We were going to make it; 25 kilometres in one day. It was amazing!

"Hey you!" I yelled up the path. Barry turned.

"What now?" His tone suggested he thought I was still angry.

"I'm just popping into the bushes for a wee. Okay?"

"Righto," Barry grinned.

A few minutes later a friendly "Coo-ee" heralded the end of our disagreement.

Although we completed the 25 kilometre walk that day it took over seven and a half hours rather than the five Barry had anticipated. I knew it was my fault and that he'd been very tolerant of me. It was therefore almost fair when half an hour after arriving back in the town my rear end and lower back developed large red welts - an allergic reaction to a plant I'd brushed against when urinating in the bushes.

Barry and I laughed for hours as we waited for his anti-histamine tablets to work their magic.

The coat

Clothes maketh the man.

SHAKESPEARE

One afternoon when I arrived at Waldene Barry said he wanted to show me something he'd received in the mail. "Look at this," he said, passing me a photo of Sylvia, the wife of one of his friends. It had been taken by a professional photographer to put on the website of the nudist retreat the couple owned. Leaning along a fallen tree trunk in the Australian bush, Sylvia was absolutely naked except for a pair of heavy Blundstone boots. She looked glamorously slim and perfectly at ease with her nakedness. The sun through the trees peppered her skin with light giving her an elfin appearance; a fragile being resting in the forest.

"It's nice," I said, trying not to sound jealous. "Same Blundstone's as mine. But it's a bit creepy isn't it - using a naked photo of your wife to advertise your business?" I handed the photo back to Barry and stepped past him into the lounge hoping to signify the end of the conversation.

Barry sniggered, nodded and looked at the photo once more before dropping it into a drawer in the sideboard and pushing the drawer shut.

"You owe me a naked photo or four minutes of photography time. Remember the bet you lost when I threw the stones at the log?"

"I didn't bet. You're kidding yourself. I said '*maybe.*' I never agreed to the bet.

Barry mused aloud. "It's a pity. You'd be gorgeous to photograph naked. What about if you just let me take one naked photo of you? You'll be able to look back on it when you're old - see how beautiful you were."

"Forget it! I hate having my photo taken and being naked would be a billion times worse. Besides you could never get it developed. The shop people would all get to see it and that'd be awful."

"I'd be proud. '*That's my girl,*' I'd say to them when I collected it. The blokes'd think I was a lucky man."

"Yeah and the ladies at the shop would think you were a pervert. Don't say about it anymore. It's not going to happen, so forget it."

"That's a shame," Barry said and our conversation moved onto other topics.

I thought about Sylvia's photo for days after. I hated Barry's friend for organising the photo to be taken and even for publishing it on his webpage. But most of all I hated him sending a copy to Barry. I wished I'd never seen it or even heard about it.

All my physical flaws came back to taunt me. I was not, nor had I ever been slim and I wasn't an out-doorsy sort of girl. Trees were full of creeping, sliding, stinging, biting things. They were not something to drape your naked body along. Besides, I thought, who lets people take naked photos of them except models for men's magazines? Did Sylvia realise the photo would be circulated? But mostly I wondered if the photo was still in Barry's sideboard drawer.

I hated that photo! It was disgusting, rude – cheap! I wished Barry hadn't shown it to me. It was awful knowing what Sylvia looked like naked. How could we ever sit across from her over lunch again, now we'd seen her naked?

Weeks later, still struggling with the whole thing I thought about stealing the photo from the sideboard and destroying it. If Barry noticed its absence it would prove something to me. Although I wasn't prepared to speculate what that might be.

My family had gone to a night football game leaving me at home alone. I took my woollen 'yard-duty' coat from the wardrobe. It was a thick, heavy coat that reached half-way down my calves, making it the ideal uniform for patrolling schoolyards on freezing winter days. Slipping out of all my clothes, I pulled on the coat and buttoned it all the way up to the v-neckline.

Wrestling my inner '*stupid*' voice, I pulled my Blundstone boots onto my bare feet, wincing a little as the leather dragged across my skin. Fleetingly I wondered if Sylvia had actually worn tiny socks for her photo-shoot to prevent any potential foot blisters. But the thought was transitory, soon to be replaced by the words '*naked except for her boots.*' The phrase kept reverberating through my brain. It sounded courageous and exciting – bohemian even.

Without looking at myself in the mirror, I hopped into my car and drove away, headed for Whittlesea. As I drove I tried to sing along with the radio to silence any further comment from my '*stupid*' voice and dispel my inner fear of being pulled over by the police. Although wearing a coat, my naked skin at the v-neckline when I glanced in the car's visor mirror seemed to scream, "Fully Naked!" I slowed to five kilometres under the speed limit and was totally alert to all the road regulations.

As I drove down Waldene's steep driveway, a skill I'd mastered over the years, my headlights reflected off the cottage windows. Barry threw open the front door and strode out aggressively ready to challenge whoever was coming onto his property so late at night. I parked and stepped out of the car.

"Darling," he said in surprise, recognising the car in the darkness. He came towards me. "Is everything alright?"

"Yes," I replied firmly, in fact so firmly my tone stopped him in his tracks. We stood a few metres apart, our faces ghostly in the moon-washed forest. Unbuttoning my coat I let it fall to the ground around my boots. Now my arms hung awkwardly by my sides. I tried to imagine myself an Amazon Warrior, naked and fearless. But in reality I felt somewhat silly.

"I'm better than Sylvia." My voice was loud, defiant. Then far less like a warrior ... "Aren't I?" my hands moving to cover my breasts and pubic area.

Barry looked me slowly up and down, a small smile playing on his lips. I looked away into the darkness.

He stepped forward and picked up my coat. Draping it across my shoulders, he pulled me in against his chest and kissed the top of my head. "You are the most gorgeous Miss Gorgeousity in all the world."

I put my arms around him and my '*stupid*' voice died away.

"I love you so much," Barry said, hugging me tightly with a soft chuckle.

We clung to each other silent and happy for a few minutes, while all around us the forest settled for the night and the moon continued its journey across the sky.

"Can I take your photo?" Barry murmured.

"Hah – as if!" I scoffed.

Saddle Up

> *When you reach the end of your rope*
> *tie a knot in it and hang on.*
>
> FRANKLIN D. ROOSEVELT

Within months of our 25 kilometre day-walk Barry floated the idea of us doing a longer trek involving two nights of camping out.

"But would we have to carry a tent?" My only experience of tents was when my husband and I had taken our young sons on a 10-day camping trip to Uluru. Our ugly brown tent had been a huge two-bedroom structure requiring more scaffolding than Sydney Harbor Bridge.

"A tent, sleeping bags, sleeping mats and a stove – maybe water depending where we go. But probably best to go where there's water – at least for this first trek." Barry spoke enthusiastically, almost to himself, as he contemplated the prospect of our trek.

Erring on the side of diplomacy I didn't ask him for clarification about what he meant by this 'first' trek. Instead I asked, "How much does a tent weigh?" - remembering my exhaustion after the day-walk when all we'd carried in our packs was lunch, snacks, water and sunscreen.

"I've got a tent but it's old and heavy. The new ones are really light-weight. We could buy a three-man one. I'll carry the tent in my pack and you can carry the poles in yours."

"But my backpack's small. Poles won't fit. And you said we'd need sleeping bags as well. There's no way all that'll fit in my backpack."

Barry shook his head. "You won't be carrying your daypack. I'll carry a large trekking pack I bought in Morocco and you can use my old canvas trekking pack. It's much larger than your daypack but we can pack it so it's not too heavy for you to carry."

If I hadn't experienced all the pre-walk training required for our earlier walk and the struggle of actually walking the 25 kilometres in one day, I could easily have been carried away by the romance of a camping trek with Barry.

Really? - my inner voice queried. How many kilometres will this trek be? And will it wind relentlessly uphill most of the way? Besides what will we eat out there in the wild? I shuddered in memory of bush toileting requirements. And of course there'd be no showers. *Seriously?* - my inner voice asked.

But after a few gruelling months of training I found myself standing beside Barry in late autumn staring up at a mountain range that towered above us. The bush-walking guide books described this walk as 'hard' even during spring and summer.

"Please tell me that's not snow on the top?" I asked, narrowing my eyes in the hope of revealing a different possibility. A cold wind whipped my hair across my face.

"Could be," said Barry. "... it's the end of autumn after all. But we'll only be camped on the very top for the first night. The second night we'll be lower down on the other side. Besides there's a hut at the top with a fireplace if the weather gets too bad for a tent."

"Oh good, 'cause I'd hate for my hair to get wet." Barry turned to look at me, no doubt recognising the sarcasm in my voice. My neck gave a faint arthritic crick as a warning not to stare up at the mountain top for too long. I lowered my gaze to study the gaiters Barry had insisted I wear to keep snow out of my boots.

The forecast was for a clear and sunny day. Barry had packed both backpacks. Mine was a relic Barry had resurrected from his attic. It had all the constraints of my mother's corset. After much wrestling and grunting I was 'saddled' in true pack-horse style.

Are arms meant to rotate that far back? I felt my shoulder sockets complain. The pack seemed the perfect device for correcting posture or perhaps for treating scoliosis. The pull of its straps forced my shoulders back and straightened my spine in order to position the weight evenly across my hips. I tried not to notice my double D-sized breasts sticking out like compass directives pointing us ever onward.

"My God - this thing weighs a ton! I'll be lucky to make it from here to the start of the trail," I wailed as I staggered around looking for somewhere to sit in the car park at the start of the trek.

"Don't sit down," Barry shouted. "It'll be too hard to get back up and we're leaving in a minute. But don't worry, you'll feel like a moon-walker when you take the pack off at the end of the day" he smiled at me encouragingly. "It's a great sensation. Just wait and see."

"That's what they said about child-birth," I mumbled.

Once Barry was saddled into his backpack we set off. In a very short time the bush had lost all its supposed 'magic' for me. The sound of gurgling water in a myriad of nearby streams and creeks put me in mind of tears as I trudged along in the knowledge this trip had been a terrible mistake.

My t-shirt, once fresh and crisp, began to dampen with perspiration. I glanced down at my chest in despair as the damp, dark stain spread across my entire front except once again, for the two circles around my upturned nipples. Groaning, I hunched further forward hoping a drooped stance would hide my shame or at least cause the perspiration to run down and fill in the two dry patches.

Mercifully about three hours into the trek Barry called back to say we'd take a short break beside the next bridge. This required more grunting and wrestling to dislodge the backpack from my sweat-soaked body.

"Walk around. It's like moon-walking. It's a weird sensation. You'll love it. Go on - walk around a bit," Barry said excitedly. I was too hot, too tired, too over it all, but I could see he'd been looking forward to this moment, so I took a few steps.

Hold your arms out. Can you feel it?" He was very enthusiastic - more so than me. To indulge him I lifted my arms and took a few more steps. He was right. Barry's description of 'moon-walking' was absolutely correct. Released from the weight of the pack my body felt weightless, like I was walking on air.

"Must be what a horse feels like when the rider and saddle come off. Or what a donkey feels at day's end after lugging supplies all day. It's amazing." I giggled. "But now I'm dying to lie down for a minute. Okay?" I flopped on the ground, flat on my back, arms stretched out at my sides – a bushwalking crucifix.

"Are we almost there?" I asked the sky above.

"No, not quite," came Barry's reply.

Trying to provide me with a benchmark he said, "We'll be near the summit when the trees become shrub height – a result of the snow and the wind at the top stunting their growth." I swivelled my eyes to look at him. His face wasn't as scarlet as mine and his polo shirt was dry except for small areas under his armpits. For the second time in our relationship I noticed he had quite a sinister leer from some angles.

Staring up at the trees I thought they were so tall someone could quite easily build a three bedroom house from a single tree and still have wood left over for furniture. A trickle of sweat ran down along my cheekbone and I considered how irritating it is when some people seem to know everything about forests and tree heights and wind and snow.

We recommenced walking. "Into the valley of death trekked the brave 300 year old…," I quoted to lighten my mood. But we weren't in a valley. Instead we were walking up, up, ever up yet again! My mood didn't lighten. I wondered if I was losing the plot – dehydration, exhaustion perhaps.

I tried another quote. 'Look up and live.' The company maintaining the power lines used that slogan in their public safety message. Hardly sensible in this instance, given I was by now bent double with the weight of my pack and could only muster the energy to lift my feet, not my eyes as well.

I opted for murmuring the chant I'd taught my children long ago to help get them through their visits to the dentist. "It'll all be over soon. It'll all be over soon. It'll all be over soon.' The chant made me feel a little better. Perhaps I was hallucinating.

Glancing around I yelled at Barry's back ahead of me on the track, "These bloody trees aren't getting any shorter."

"Shut up and keep walking," Barry's response floated back to me.

An eternity passed. My legs were sweating, my head was sweating, my back was sweating. Even my backside was starting to feel damp. We stopped for lunch and Barry gave me one of his 'pep-talks for plodders.' As he spoke the sky began to darken and a rush of cool air blew across the back of my damp t-shirt causing me to shiver involuntarily.

"We'll have to get a move on if we want to be at the top and pitch the tent before nightfall," he said, looking up to examine the clouds. "There could even be rain later and if that happens, I'd prefer to be in the tent rather than outside trying to pitch it."

"I'm going as fast as I can, but the pack's so heavy and it's such a long way." Having made this attempt at apologising I stood up and lifted my pack so Barry could strap me into it again. "Maybe you should go on ahead and start pitching the tent. If I just follow the path I'll catch up, as long as there's only one path and you pitch the tent near it." It was a sensible suggestion but even as I spoke, my innards shrank with fear at the thought of trudging alone on the mountain in the dark.

"No, you'd be too scared," Barry replied as though reading my thoughts. But somehow hearing him say the words made me feel ashamed.

"Don't be silly. I'll be fine. It can't be that much further surely."

Barry looked toward the path ahead, glanced up at the sky again and checked his watch. "You promise you'll stay on the path? Even if you get too scared or it gets too dark or starts raining. Even if you can't walk any more, promise me you'll stay on the path? Just sit down and I'll come back for you as soon as I've pitched the tent and offloaded my gear. Promise?"

I nodded, holding back the appal I felt at his acceptance of my suggestion. "Promise," was all I could manage.

"You're such a brave mouse. No wonder I love you. Here's a torch just in case." With that Barry kissed the top of my head and strode off.

The moment he disappeared from my view the forest seemed darker and more foreboding. The gnarled, stunted trees with their tortured branches and spiked florets waited on either side of the path, daring me to come closer. Picking up my pace I hurried along after Barry, my breath now coming fast and loud. Above me the night sky was slowly closing in. My hands and the end of my nose were cold even though my chest was hot and heaving. "Damn mountain," I snarled, the sound of my voice in the silence serving to increase my feeling of panic.

I walked for about twenty minutes when a movement up ahead caught the corner of my eye. "Coo-ee," I yelled, immediately wishing I hadn't. What if it wasn't Barry? What an idiot I was!

"Coo-ee Miss Mouse. You made it. Good girl!" I straightened up, hitched my pack a little higher on my back and took a deep breath. Taking longer, more confident strides I moved on to where Barry had almost finished setting up the tent.

The compact blue structure stood on a level patch of ground nestled inside a small circle of shrubby mountain growth. "The shrubs should protect us from the wind to a degree and the overhang of the tress will hopefully reduce the amount of snow and rain that might fall on the tent overnight." Barry explained, standing up with a look of satisfaction. "Come and I'll show you the hut, just in case we need to go there during the night."

He led me further along the path to a rough-hewn wooden hut about three metres square. Pushing open its heavy wooden door Barry pointed out its hard-packed dirt floor, two very rough wooden bunks devoid of mattresses or coverings bolted onto the walls and an ugly stone fireplace containing a metal grate.

Propped up against a wall stud beside the fireplace was an aged notebook with a pencil attached to it by a string. I lifted the book down and thumbed through its pages. It was full of messages from hikers who had been to the hut. Some had written words of gratitude for finding the hut in inclement weather, others had written humorous ditties and some had written words of welcome to those coming after them.

I read some of the entries aloud. They made me smile. "Seems weird, way up here on the top of a mountain on a cold, dark night that people can be so kind and friendly to strangers they'll never meet. I love that." I grinned at Barry. "It was worth the whole day's walk just to see the hut and the words in this book. Funny eh? Sort of like a pilgrimage."

Back at the tent Barry allocated me the job of unrolling our sleeping mats and sleeping bags and setting them up inside the tent while he cooked dinner. I was fascinated by the tiny fuel stove he pulled from his backpack. A metal billycan, a packet of frieze dried macaroni-cheese and a few cups of water and very soon the smell of food cooking wafted through the air.

Inside the tent I took off my boots and zipped our sleeping bags together before slipping the double bed sheet lining inside. Kneeling at the tent door, I stuck my head outside. Inside the tent was already noticeably warmer than outside. "All done in here. Will I come out or are we going to eat in the tent?"

"I'll bring the food in. It's too cold out here now. You turn on the torch and just rest; won't be long. Do you want a coffee after dinner?

This was an unexpected surprise. "Did you bring coffee?" Given Barry didn't drink coffee this was a very generous gesture.

"Anything for m'lady." He bowed low to the ground in my direction.

We slept warm and snug all night until I was awakened by the sound of voices.

"Darling," I whispered, nudging Barry awake. "There's someone outside."

Barry sprang up and dragged on some clothing before thrusting himself aggressively out of the tent. I huddled down in the sleeping bag and tried to dress without making any noise.

"Hello," Barry called walking in the direction of the voices. Whoever was there had gone past our tent towards the hut. I couldn't make out what was being said but heard murmuring followed by short bursts of friendly laughter. Once dressed, I slipped out of the tent and went in search of Barry.

He was standing with two male trekkers and they were all staring out towards the mountain ranges rolling away below us. Barry was pointing out different locations across the vista. I hadn't noticed the beauty of the view when arriving in the gloom the previous night.

Stretched out before us was wave upon wave of dense greenery, of treetops in the valleys and matted shrubs in the high country. Here and there in the clear morning sun, patches of snow sparkled in strips across leaves. The air was so cold it almost hurt to breathe and the white of the snow laying on the ground in the campsite was blinding. There were no houses, no traffic to be heard, only this glimpse of Eden at the top of the mountain.

The talking stopped and the three men looked across at me. "Hello," I said giving a small wave and moving to join them.

"You must be Barry's trusty companion," one of the men said making me think he was a Quaker or from some sort of weird religious group.

"Pardon?"

"…Thought you were a dog; pretty funny." At this he gave a short laugh and looked at Barry, who grinned widely in response. My forehead wrinkled in confusion.

"Pardon?" This time I directed my question at Barry.

He rolled his eyes slightly and said softly, "Don't worry. I'll explain later." He was obviously uncomfortable with whatever the explanation was, so I nodded and fell silent.

"Anyway," said Barry, "…time to make breakfast otherwise we'll never get to our next campsite. Good luck and I hope your day goes well." The three men shook hands and Barry and I watched as the trekkers set out across the snow.

"They're walking along the mountain spur to get to a hut about thirty kilometres away. Glad it's them and not me." Barry said, as we turned to go back to our tent.

"What did he mean when he said he thought I was a dog?" I stopped walking, ready for an argument.

"Darling it was a joke."

"I'm not laughing."

"Well," he said, looking guilty and reaching out to hold my hand, "...when you go on an overnight walk in a national park there's usually a log-book. Did you notice me writing in a book at the start of the trail?"

I nodded.

"Well you're supposed to write the names of everyone in your group in there, as well as the date and place you began the trail and the date and place you expect to come out. That way if there's a fire or something, the rangers will know who to come looking for and where."

"But what's with the dog thing?"

Sighing Barry continued. "Well you'd never let me write your name in the logbook along with my name would you?" He looked directly into my eyes.

"No of course not. I don't want people to know we're here together."

"I knew that. But I wanted the rangers to know I wasn't alone – in case something happened. So I in the log-book I wrote *Barry Johnston and Sue his trusty companion*. It was all I could think to do. It didn't matter because normally you wouldn't have found out. It's just bad luck those guys read it and thought you were my dog; even worse luck they met up with us."

I giggled. "Oh my God - that's precious! You're so adorably funny." I planted a kiss on his cheek.

Although we were to walk further today than yesterday, the walking was easier as most of it was downhill. Barry promised there was a 'shower-of-sorts' at the next campsite and I walked faster and happier in anticipation. We arrived at the campsite just on dark and set up the tent. While I organised the sleeping bags, Barry went off to test out the shower. I turned on a battery-operated lamp and sat on a log to await his return.

There was almost no wind and we were the only tent in the campsite. The stars hung large and brilliant in the sky making me wish I could sit and gaze at them forever. When Barry returned he described some of the quirky features of the 'shower-of-sorts.' I set off with a torch to find it, leaving Barry to light a fire.

The isolated shower had no doubt been built of timber felled from the surrounding forest. It was a roofless structure and once inside with the door closed, I stared up into the square of sky above me. The treetops were ink black silhouettes against the star-lit sky and all around birds rustled and called to each other as they settled among the branches.

The torchlight picked out my small pile of clothing at the far edge of the concrete floor. I placed the torch on the floor with its light shining towards the rough timber door of the tiny cubicle rather than towards my naked body. Although dim, the light was sufficient for me to find the one tap on the wall, while at the same time its glow beneath the door would alert others that the shower was occupied.

The grimy tap was warm to the touch, still holding some of the heat from the day. Steeling myself against the anticipated cold water, I turned the tap slowly to the right and looked up expectantly at the battered showerhead.

Somewhere behind the wall a noise announced the imminent arrival of a trickle of tepid water from the corrugated iron tank servicing the shower. While pleased the water was not freezing, I smiled to myself, remembering Barry enticement of a 'shower-of-sorts' to keep my spirits up as we'd trekked the last ten kilometres today.

I washed hurriedly and turned the water off. Standing there, naked in the semi- darkness, I wondered if I should towel myself dry or just shake and brush the water off to avoid having to carry a wet towel tomorrow. Deciding to forego the towel, I scraped the water from my limbs with my hands before jiggling around the cubicle to shake off any excess droplets.

Laughing at my antics, I imagined myself a member of an indigenous dance troupe, or perhaps a Zulu, taking small jumps in the air as I'd seen tribesmen do in Zulu Warrior movies.

Suddenly a voice spoke from beyond the side wall. "What are you doing?"

Terrified, I made a grab for the towel and threw my clothes over the torch. The cubicle fell into darkness. I held my breath and stood perfectly still. My ears strained, listening for unwanted noises.

Outside the night pressed down on the small wooden structure standing alone in the middle of nowhere. I lifted my head slowly to stare up at the sky, conscious at any moment someone might appear over the edge of the walls. My heart beat loudly in my chest.

"I told you there was a knothole in the side wall and you should plug it with a sock or something, just in case someone else came to use the shower." It was Barry's voice. I exhaled loudly.

"You frightened me!" I bent down to find the torch and shone it in the direction of his voice. Sure enough, there was a small hole in the wall about waist height. An eye was pressed to the hole. "How long have you been there?" I demanded.

"About five minutes. You didn't think I'd let you be out here showering all by yourself with a hole in the wall and no roof on the shower. Anybody could have come along. And I knew you wouldn't plug the hole. You never do what you're told do you?" Barry scolded before adding, "Good dancing though - loved the jumping. Mm - nice rude bits."

A Door Closes

The end of a marriage

It had been twelve years since I'd first met Barry in the school library. Since then my sons had finished their primary and secondary schooling, my mother had come to live with us, and although Alec and I kept up appearances our marriage had disintegrated. When my youngest son began work my role as a home-maker was over.

Oscar Wilde once said there comes a time 'when one must choose between living one's own life, fully, entirely and completely or dragging out some false, shallow existence that the world in its hypocrisy demands.'

Throughout those twelve years Barry and I had moved from being friends to becoming lovers. In spite of all the constraints on us, we were still in love with each other. Now was the time we should begin our life together. But I couldn't work out how to end my marriage. Barry and I had endless discussions about this. He drew me a flow chart to explain all the options, the possible consequences of each and how I might manage these.

I was frantic. Would the house be sold? Where would that leave my teenage sons and my mother? What would the breakup of the family do to Alec given his ongoing battle with depression as a result of his health? What words could I say to end our 26 year marriage?

The situation resolved itself however when I came home one Sunday afternoon from visiting Melbourne's Art Gallery. I'd travelled by train and met Barry there. My family rarely asked for details of my outings, their weekend usually full of different sporting activities as participants or viewers. My mother bowled and the boys and Alec were lovers of football.

When I arrived home, Alec was sitting at the end of the kitchen table, his head hanging down, arms resting on his thighs. He raised his head as I came in and I stopped, sensing something was wrong. Turning his face to look at me he said so sadly, "I can't go on like this."

So it had finally come out. I felt myself shrink. "Okay," I said. "I'll move out." I turned on my heel and left the room.

With hindsight I have no idea what he meant by his statement. But I've never wanted him to explain further, because if he was referring to my relationship with Barry, then I'd wonder how long he'd known and why he'd ignored it. If he was referring to something about his health or his day, then I'm left wondering why he didn't question my response. Either way I prefer not to think beyond what was said.

We are still friends, but to this day Alec and I have never discussed his statement any further.

Alec was a good father and our sons loved him. He took them enthusiastically to athletics clubs, swimming lessons and football clinics. Marriage and children were for him the culmination of his life ambition. Our marriage died because we grew apart and no longer shared the same interests or aspirations.

I reasoned the fairest thing was for me to leave the house. Alec accepted my suggestion without argument. Guilt-ridden because I'd caused the end our marriage I didn't want Alec to suffer by having his whole life turned upside down. The boys could decide if they wanted to come with me or not. For the time being I would move into a place of my own and introduce Barry to the family slowly.

Gathering all my courage I told my mother I was going to live somewhere else and invited her to come with me. She gave me a lecture on '... the girls these days' and a speech about marriage being forever.

She ended our discussion by snapping, "No, I'm not coming with you. I'll stay here and look after the boys. Besides it's just a whim on your part. You'll come back, so it's not worth my trouble to pack up and leave." My mother's tone of voice dismissed me as though I was an errant child.

I left the room, not telling her I'd been in love with another man for many years and had done everything I could to ensure my family hadn't been hurt by that love. Nor did I explain that after all this time Barry and I were now entitled to be together.

The following week I moved into a small house in the next suburb. "I can't come straight to Waldene," I explained to Barry. "The boys would never understand if they knew we'd been having an affair all this time. They just need some time to come to grips with the separation. At least now we won't need to sneak around anymore. We'll even be able to go on holidays as a couple. I know it's not perfect but it's going to get better and eventually we'll be together in the same house."

Barry acquiesced and when I moved into the house he arrived with bags of groceries, flowers and champagne. We cooked dinner and afterwards for the first time in our relationship we were free to map out a list of the things we'd do and places we'd go together. Our shared future was at last within grasp.

Each year thereafter we travelled to faraway places – Barry studying the history and architecture while I observed the people. We wrote travel diaries and later entertained each other by reading our very different accounts of what we'd seen. We bought season tickets to the theatre and opera. We visited art galleries, had picnics and went for long walks.

I was promoted to a job in the Head Office of the Education Department where I could indulge my passion for writing –

articles, submissions, training packages and letters. Barry was a sounding board for my ideas, helped me with research and edited my writing.

Newly motivated, Barry wrote and published a book about his time in East Timor as a United Nations Observer for the People's Popular Consultation (part of the independence vote process). He also began writing the history of the Draft Resistor's Union, although his progress was slow because he was meticulous about every word he wrote and every fact he included.

In the property settlement from my marriage, my share of the asset pool equated to the family home. I moved back to Greensborough just as my mother had predicted, although she hadn't foreseen my marriage ending and Alec moving out. Heath was already living elsewhere and Blake though at home was working full-time and had his own life.

Given its isolated location and the work required to maintain the 17 acres of forest Barry and I decided it would be impractical for us to live at Waldene in the long-term. Our plan was to eventually sell Waldene and live at Greensborough so Barry began renovating the Greensborough house.

Within months of my return to the family home, my mother was diagnosed with an aggressive breast cancer and for the last six-months of her life I became her full-time carer. I'd always imagined how well Barry and my mother would get on; both so well-read, intelligent and principled. I knew mum would be impressed by Barry's politics and involvement in the anti-conscription movement.

But my mother was now 85 years old. She was so unwell when she finally met Barry, the cancer and the chemotherapy having severely weakened her. My cameo memory of the two of them is my mother sitting in the sunshine on the deck, a feeble shrunken old lady under a rug, and Barry striding past her with a six-foot pine post over his shoulder.

"Hello Mrs Porter," he'd called cheerfully.

"Hello," she'd mumbled, rousing from her slumbers to give a little wave; unsure where she was, or who had called to her.

In September 2008, following my mother's death, Barry and I walked the Kokoda Track in Papua New Guinea, we cruised the Pacific Ocean and made plans to visit Peru the following year. Our life together had begun.

The last chapter

On the 7th February 2009 the temperatures in Melbourne were forecast to exceed 45 degrees Celsius. Morning radio was already describing an outbreak of fire in the tinder dry pastures at Kilmore East, forty kilometres from Waldene and sixty kilometres from Greensborough.

I was booked to deliver some training in Flemington, close to the city all day. I kissed a sleepy-eyed Barry goodbye at the breakfast table in Greensborough.

"I'll phone you when I finish work and we can decide about the Country Music Festival," I said picking up my bag to leave. The previous year I'd dragged him to the Whittlesea Country Music Festival. We'd had such fun watching the passing parade of 'cowboys' and 'cowgirls' with hats, boots and in some cases even spurs, we'd discussed attending the next year's festival. The opening concert was scheduled for that night.

"It's hardly opera is it?" Barry complained. "It's probably been cancelled 'cause of the heat. That'd be tragic, wouldn't it?" he said, rolling his eyes in amusement. "Anyway I'm going to finish a few jobs here then I'll go up to Waldene to check everything's okay - just in case ash from the Kilmore fires blows that way. Phone me at Waldene."

"Okay. Be careful darling..." I said and left him sitting at the table.

While I delivered my training the most devastating fires in Australia's history swept across the state of Victoria. The Black Saturday bushfires destroyed 450 000 hectares of land and took 173 lives. I lost Barry and Waldene in the fires.

I was in shock for many months. Those months were filled with police interviews, coroner's inquests, a royal commission, and a sea of counsellors, psychologists, charity workers, bureaucrats, volunteers, and solicitors.

A government requirement saw 'clean-up teams' arrive at the property to drag and scrape the fire-ravaged site clean. As if losing Barry and the cottage wasn't enough, I was left alone on a lunar landscape watched by the naked forest of dead, black tree trunks.

It took me a long time to find a way forward again after the fires. There were so many new building regulations and so much reluctance by everyone when I said I needed to rebuild. But it was the one goal I could focus on and slowly, one step at a time, I worked my way through all the 'nay-sayers' and all the rules, and all the paperwork and I had a tiny cottage, a mini-Waldene built on the site. In so doing I found myself again and I grew.

Now I share my time between Waldene and Greensborough. I write, I read, I think. I listen to the birds and nurture the plants, and I remember that once I was a princess and a librarian loved me very much.

> *Waiting is a sign of true love and patience.*
> *Anyone can say I love you, but not everyone*
> *can wait and prove it's true.*
>
> Anon

Acknowledgements

While the love story between Barry and I remained secret for many years, writing this memoir to describe those years was done with the help and encouragement of many individuals and groups. The members of my writing groups:

- *Word Weavers writing group Whittlesea*
- *University of the Third Age creative writing group Eltham*
- *Carpe Diem Writers, Society of Women Writers Victoria*
- *Odyssey Memoir writers Watsonia*
- *The Camino De Santiago Walk & Write group Spain 2018*

The individuals who edited and gave feedback on different parts of the manuscript:

- *Lee McGill*
- *Judy Vizzari*
- *Kayleen Pankowski*
- *Judy Godsil*
- *Lea Trafford*
- *Peter Sullivan*
- *Patricia Arts*

There are others to thank I'm sure but I hope they will forgive me if their names are not listed here. It is difficult to include everyone who helped over the five years it took to write Waldene – Love in the Shadows. I would like to thank each and every one of you for not judging me, for your empathy, honest feedback, suggestions and efforts on my behalf and for understanding how very important it was for me to tell this story.

Sue Gunningham. 2020

www.ingramcontent.com/pod-product-compliance
Lightning Source LLC
Chambersburg PA
CBHW020856020526
44107CB00076B/1869